Measuring Operational and Reputational Risk

For other titles in the Wiley Finance series
please see www.wiley.com/finance

Measuring Operational and Reputational Risk

A Practitioner's Approach

Aldo Soprano

Bert Crielaard

Fabio Piacenza

Daniele Ruspantini

WILEY

A John Wiley and Sons, Ltd., Publication

Telephone (+44) 1243 779777

Email (for orders and customer service enquiries): cs-books@wiley.co.uk
Visit our Home Page on www.wiley.com

Other Wiley Editorial Offices

John Wiley & Sons Inc., 111 River Street, Hoboken, NJ 07030, USA

Jossey-Bass, 989 Market Street, San Francisco, CA 94103-1741, USA

Wiley-VCH Verlag GmbH, Boschstr. 12, D-69469 Weinheim, Germany

John Wiley & Sons Australia Ltd, 42 McDougall Street, Milton, Queensland 4064, Australia

John Wiley & Sons (Asia) Pte Ltd, 2 Clementi Loop #02-01, Jin Xing Distripark, Singapore 129809

John Wiley & Sons Canada Ltd, 6045 Freemont Blvd, Mississauga, ONT, L5R 4J3, Canada

Wiley also publishes its books in a variety of electronic formats. Some content that appears in print may not be available in electronic books.

Library of Congress Cataloging-in-Publication Data

Measuring operational and reputational risk : a practitioners approach / Aldo Soprano.
p. cm.
Includes bibliographical references and index.
ISBN 978-0-470-51770-3 (cloth)
1. Risk management. 2. Risk assessment. 3. Operational risk. 4. Corporate image.
I. Soprano, Aldo.
HD61.M428 2008
658.15′5072–dc22

2008047074

British Library Cataloguing in Publication Data

A catalogue record for this book is available from the British Library

ISBN 978-0-470-51770-3 (HB)

Typeset in 11/13pt Times by Aptara Inc., New Delhi, India
Printed and bound in Great Britain by TJ International Ltd, Padstow, Cornwall, UK

To my grandfather Filippo for his special advice and for all the Sundays listening football on the radio together . . .

To Stefy, for her patience and wisdom

To my wife Erika and our parents

In everlasting memory of Matteo Pavan

Contents

Foreword

I believe Managing Operational and Reputational Risk has a major strength that clearly distinguishes it from most books currently available on the same subject: the combination of a rigorous, scientific and empirically based approach to risk measurement with the expertise and insider view of senior risk managers of a major and diversified financial conglomerate such as Unicredit Group.

This significant strength can be detected in every single chapter of the book, where the authors carefully combine a solid, analytical and theory based approach with the hindsight of their direct, real life experience as risk managers in one of the largest European banking groups, which has always been on the frontier of the risk management and capital management practice. This combination offers the reader a useful insight – not only on methodological issues, but also on empirical and organizational aspects related to risk management – that is rarely found in similar books.

I found the chapter dedicated to insurance policies and risk transfer as one with a significant value added – rich of detailed information and analysis – where the authors clearly offer and insider view on the potential benefits and methodological problems of this kind of risk management policy that, despite the increase in efficiency and risk coverage, is still relatively unexplored by the banking industry.

Finally, I found the chapter dedicated to reputational risk as probably the most valuable, relevant and original contribution of this book. Indeed, while a number of textbooks on operational risk have been produced in the recent years, reputational risk has received much less attention from the risk management industry and academic community and yet its relevance and potential dangers have been clearly highlighted during the recent international financial crisis. The chapter on reputational risk is also enriched, just as the other sections of this book, by a number of real life case studies that offer the reader a useful grasp both on the relevance of this type of risk and on the way the approaches presented in the book can be applied.

To conclude, I believe that this work by Aldo Soprano, Bert Crielaard, Fabio Piacenza and Daniele Ruspantini represents a compulsory tool for risk managers, regulators and academics doing research in the area or operational and reputational risk.

Andrea Sironi
Università Bocconi

Preface

In global financial markets and adamant media attention, managing operational and reputational risk is becoming increasingly critical for international companies: the impact on clients and results will be felt not only in the short term but will affect growth sustainability in the long run. Increasingly, a financial institution's reputation, seen as clients', counterparties', and regulators' perception of a company's trustworthiness, is strictly linked to its risk management capacity. Relevant reputational and operational events will affect market value and likely undermine results, limiting margins and hindering growth: companies nowadays have fathomed that developing and improving operational and reputational risk control is a key success factor.

Assessing and monitoring bank's reputational risk exposure will improve underwriting, strengthening credit management and relations with clients, investors, and governments. Likewise, a structured operational risk control will deeper understanding of processes and provide, in turn, analytical cost drivers, higher efficiency, and service quality, leading to lower losses and costs. Monitoring operational risk also improves problem solving: regularly controlling risk indicators operational losses, and, customers' claims, will get critical issue identification and fixing.

Reputational and operational risk management will result in a broader monitoring exercise, weighting revenues on the actual costs incurred. Additionally, there will be benefit in terms of client relationships, improving company's market perception: it will enhance customer retention, new acquisition power. Management is today aware of the corporate social and environmental responsibilities; amongst the drivers of a company's reputational risk management policy.

The company's management must evaluate of the capital impact of both operational and reputational risks: risk-adjusted performance measurement is needed for timely and correct decision taking, and commonly used indicators such as EVA and RARORAC ought to include operational and reputational risk components for accurate return analysis and investment decisions.

The new Basel capital accord, adding a specific operational risk requirement and a full economic capital adjustment for capital management in the second pillar, sets better risk measurement standards for the financial industry, ultimately paving the way for improved control systems and returns.

Operational risks have always been controlled but more structured analysis and management has been encouraged by the introduction of the new Basel 2 Capital Accord. Dedicated risk management organizational units have been created and working in recent years to prepare UniCredit Group for an application to the regulators for the Advanced Measurement Approach, as soon as feasible.

Extensive testing of different modeling methodologies, discussions, and benchmarking inside and outside our organization ultimately led to a consensus that has now been implemented group-wide. Naturally, parts of these will be recognizable in this book.

One of the fundamental choices has been to use the loss distribution approach as the pivotal element to estimate the operational risk exposure, as opposed to a scenario-based approach. Based also on discussions with other banking groups, we found that there are common themes in the risk exposure between different banking institutions, but there are also unique characteristics that set one bank apart from the others. These differences originate in different organizational structures, processes, products, and markets. There are also cultural differences that influence behavior and the individual, historical experience of each bank. We reached the conclusion that by using actual incurred losses as the core modelling element, the individual characteristics and therefore the risk exposure would be best represented in the analyses. Logically, an important chapter (Chapter 2) is dedicated solely to the construction of the calculation dataset, with a focus on the internal loss data.

An approach for measuring operational risks based mainly on scenarios, in our view, presents several critical issues. A fundamental obstacle is how to ensure the objectivity of the results of the analyses, while, for example, for internal loss data, audited accounting data can be used to verify the data collection. In our experience, scenario analysis results can be heavily influenced by the personal experience of the people discussing the scenario. To simplify the concept, frequently a person that has experienced an operational problem in the past, tends to overestimate the risk of a reoccurrence, while a person that has never experienced that issue will underestimate the risk exposure. In real life the situation, of course, is more complex, but this risk is clearly present. Benchmarking exercises are helpful in reducing these biases, but in our view might not be sufficient.

The loss data approach is based on internal losses and, as UniCredit is a large, diversified banking group in terms of business, products, and territories, a wide and solid database is available for the operational risk assessment.

Although the internal data provide the fundamental element for the operational risk analysis, we are aware that these data are suboptimal. On one hand, they reflect what has happened in the past and therefore cannot take into account changes in processes and controls that are present today. Internal data can only reflect what has actually been incurred, rather than potential risks. This book describes what we believe is a rather pragmatic way of integrating the internal data in the risk exposure analysis, capturing potential losses and exposure in the evaluation. This is carried out including the analysis of losses incurred by other banking institutions, i.e. external losses, monitoring trends in internal indicators reflecting risk exposure and specific scenario analyses. These are used as 'worst-case scenarios' so that low-frequency/high-impact exposure are captured in the analysis.

Practical implementations of the operational risk modeling is insurance management. While in the past, insurance decisions were mainly based on simple claims/premium ratios and analysts experience, now a more detailed analysis supports the decision process. The impact of alternative insurance protection can be better analyzed, as more information is available.

We strongly believe insurance management has improved in terms of both risk coverage and cost efficiency, banks operational risk functions will be able to actively use insurance risk management. The modeling of insurance and the issues surrounding insurance management and risk transfer are illustrated in detail.

One of the lessons learned from the operational risk analysis in the past few years is, without doubt, that there are operational events imaginable.

Aldo Soprano
Bert Crielaard
Fabio Piacenza
Daniele Ruspantini

Acknowledgments

We wish to thank first and above all Elisabetta Magistretti, without whose vision and support throughout the years this book would likely have never been written. Special thanks also go to all our colleagues in UniCredit operational risk management *de facto* co-authors of this work: Davide Bazzarello, Fabio Monti, Loredana Demeo, Valeria De Mori, Chiara Ejbich, Angela Fortini, Rossella Galbiati, Monica Arrighi, Gabriele Maucci, Marco Penzo, Mario Prodi, Michael Brunner, and Riccardo Chiavolini.

We are particularly grateful to Eric Banks, who inspired us in writing it, Gunnar Krug, Nicoletta Ficca, Luana Spertini, Daniela Manzato, and Andrea Spanò, who helped us in reviewing the text and models, and Fitch Group's Algorithmics, for allowing us to use their international loss dataset – OpData d-base – in many examples.

We are very grateful to all of them and to the many colleagues and friends for their useful suggestions.

1

The development of ORM in UniCredit Group

1.1 A BRIEF HISTORY OF A FAST-GROWING GROUP

Nowadays, UniCredit Group is a large international banking group, serving millions of customers in many countries throughout the world. It provides full banking services and retail branches as well as wholesale commercial products for corporate clients, private banking, asset management and international investment banking. The group, though coming from one of the oldest Italian financial institutions, sustained major development from the mid-nineties, undertaking expansion into new markets, acquiring banks with a strong presence and deep roots. The changes have been so fast and continuous that UniCredit Group now can be included amongst one of the major banks in continental Europe and a leading player in many countries. The pace of change has been truly fast, and this has been possible thanks to a very clear strategy and execution capacity, as well as strong and experienced management. It has also been achieved, we believe, thanks to a strong risk management culture, with great attention to process control. This has been a key driver in the operational risk management process. UniCredit management has been and remains extremely focused on monitoring and risk assessment, and rather than hindering the development of operational risk control, starting from the top management levels, there has been immediate and full sponsorship of investment and strengthening of the operational risk management function. This has been a success factor in ensuring the highest quality service to clients, retaining them and gaining market share, adding to reputation and at the same time making sure that product distribution impacts in terms of costs and risk are available to business management.

UniCredit has incorporated many banks and financial service firms in recent years, creating a worldwide company that needs to control complex processes in a timely manner. Together with its development, it was necessary to ensure that operational risk was kept under control, so that strategy execution could be ensured. Especially under increasing market and regulatory scrutiny, ensuring operational risks were well managed became *paramount*. The difficulties of monitoring risk exposure in such a fast-changing and diversified group were compensated by an increased management need to ensure control and regular monitoring of operational risks. The investments necessary were, and remain, relevant, and we will describe these further on, but the Group management realized it was necessary, so the great difficulties and challenges we faced, and still are tackling, find strong support and commitment at the highest management level.

1.2 CREATING A NEW FUNCTION

For many financial institutions operational risk management has been a new requirement introduced with the 2001 Basel Capital Accord first consultative paper. It was then that banking regulators, reviewing banks' risk management requirements, introduced the operational risk concept. They proposed a definition, still subject to interpretation problems and open issues, as we will explain in the following chapter. It required that a dedicated operational risk control function was necessary. In many banks, operational risk control types were not concentrated and assigned to a unique function. Rather, operational risk control was assigned various processes and entailed the involvement of many functions. Internal auditors, information technology departments, security officers, credit underwriters, human resource managers, companies' own real estate administrations, accountants, planners and many others were managing operational risks. The new capital accord required that a dedicated process and function coordinate and monitor those types. With the exception of a few international banks, it meant for many financial institutions a brand new process, defining responsibilities, relations with other departments, developing control tools, recruiting and training staff. In short, building probably one of the most complex control processes, starting from zero and without any benchmark or reference to rely on. In the marketplace, advisory and experienced operational risk managers in the early years were not available, nor were there IT systems specifically designed for operational risk control.

The first problem to solve was identifying the new function's rules and responsibilities. We dedicated our very first efforts writing the operational risk management rulebook, indicating in detail the new risk manager tasks, the interactions with other functions and the Group headquarters risk department. For UniCredit group, it was paramount to outline the individual companies' operational risk manager interactions and responsibilities towards the Group risk management consolidating function. The rulebook, reviewed by internal audit and other internal functions responsible for compliance, was approved by the Group risk committee and Board of Directors as the first stepping stone in the new process.

1.3 DEVELOPING THE NEW CONTROL SYSTEM

Unlike market risk, for operational risk there was no JP Morgan's *Riskmetrics*, nor any commonly recognized benchmarking methodology available. The new Basel accord, unlike credit risk, didn't provide detailed instructions to banks on how to measure or control operational risk, provided an open approach, with generic requirements, principles more than specific rules. This was very stimulating and encouraging on one side, but left many uncertainties on how control processes and measuring methodologies should be developed. The lack of standard measurement methodologies and tested control tools benchmark control processes and specific literature on the subject was the common challenge for banks willing to adopt advanced measurement approaches for operational risk management. It also wasn't clear whether using advanced solutions would result in capital relief or actual control advantages. The sole indications available then were the first exercises performed by international regulators on operational loss data collection, *LDC*. These had been the foundations for the understanding of banks' operational risk exposure assessment by regulators, begun in 2001 and based on the assumption that a bank's operational risk is directly correlated to certain loss type. We will discuss and present our view on such assumption: one should take into account that the first LDC results were not quite satisfactory, as most banks started collecting operational loss types just after the New Basel Capital Accord first consultative paper in 2001.

The new operational risk function goal was to gather loss data, providing, indications to risk manager, audit, back office, HR, accountants, of what was needed. This was relatively straightforward for thefts, robberies, real estate damages, but it became a challenging and complex matter when we came to settlement losses or IT damage. The latter were small amount damages, often difficult to obtain or quantify.

1.4 CHALLENGES IN THE EARLY STAGES

We summarized the problems in the early stages of the operational risk framework development: no methodologies, no benchmarking approach, no experienced operational risk managers, no common understanding of how to set up the control process, no literature available, no specific indications from regulators, no tools available in the market, limited specialized consultancy. These factors combined made the start-up phase extremely complex, as it clearly demanding experienced project managers.

Ensuring regular control of operational risks for a group the size of UniCredit required a dedicated IT tool. In 2001 specific operational risk tools were not available in the market. We required a system that could gather information from UniCredit-specific procedures and databases. We opted then for an in-house software development solution operational risk management and control tool, with the related database. This resulted in a group wide application, distributed to all risk managers in all the countries and companies where UniCredit operates. The first application developed was engineered by the operational risk management team, supported by UniCredit IT development. The core architecture, still in the current operational risk system, defined distinct areas or modules, dedicated to loss data collection, risk indicators, scenario analysis, and operational process mapping. This then became an optional functionality, as we found the exercise of representing companies' processes cumbersome and difficult to maintain, with limited value added. The modules were released and distributed to operational risk managers at different stages, allowing feedback from users for further development.

1.5 METHODOLOGY TO MEASURE OPERATIONAL RISK

The greatest problem in measuring operational risk is that its very definition leaves lots of uncertainties on the interpretation of what constitutes operational risk and what it is instead, a credit market risk or simply a procedure adjustment (e.g. contra entries). We believe, this still represents the biggest challenge in measuring operational risk, as the final results will affect banks' capital. We perceive a rift between those convinced operational risk is correctly measured only based on losses, as these reflect entirely and completely a bank's exposure, and those believing operational losses are not actually either timely or fully indicative of the bank's operational risk, advocating other elements to be considered. We think that losses are usually only related to some of the operational risks, and very likely many operational problems do not translate into actual losses. We argue that accounted losses will be booked with significant delays to the events' occurrence, especially for large claims and major problems, the ones possibly having a major impact in determining the capital at risk. Some instead support their thesis on accounted operational loss validity, claiming that banks will gather years-long time series, allowing on one side the identification of reporting and booking delays, and on the other side permitting the improvement of timely booking.

1.6 TRAINING AND INTERNAL COMMUNICATION FOCUS

For us probably the greatest hurdle in the early stages was defining and explaining the operational risk concept. Often misunderstood as an additional further audit level, it required reiterated efforts to explain its peculiar role and identity. The internal communication was addressed at all levels proving to be a very time consuming exercise. There were no dedicated training courses available, so these also needed structuring: Training courses had to be designed to meet different types of requirements; providing introduction to the operational risk concept to all staff. We developed an entry level course accessible and easy to understand for people with very different working experience and know-how, from cashier to client relationship managers. We designed first a web-based introductory course, presenting key Basel concepts and then proceeding with an operational risk definition, the operational risk control function role, and its interaction with the other organizational structures. In the entry level course, provided to all Group's employees, the staff could learn the elementary operational risk concepts and foundations, including loss data collection, the course was then updated, but its purpose of providing a brief description of operational risk's, regulatory and process requirements still remains.

Once addressed the generic training for all employees, we provided specific training to the newly recruited operational risk managers. Again, there were no specific courses available, and we were actually developing measurement methodologies and control processes. The first specialized internal courses for operational risk managers focused on loss data classification and collection. Newly appointed operational risk managers were chosen amongst bankers with the most varied experience: internal audit, retail branch managers, trading, back office, accounting, etc. initially we asked them to analyze the profit & loss accounts booking and to identify and report operational type losses. For people who had never worked in accounting and weren't familiar with it, this wasn't an easy task, especially in a large group like UniCredit, with large retail branch operations, international investment banking, wholesale and asset management in many countries. Focus of our operational risk manager training is first to understand the profit & loss accounts logic, learning about IAS and IFRS principles and rules, consolidating accounting and general ledger. Rather than delegating it to the accounting department or some external consultants, we always preferred to assign these controls to the operational risk management. We attribute the greatest value to loss data completeness – we are convinced it helps to understand the company risk exposure and processes, it allows the operational risk managers to interact with many departments, and it gives an insight into possible operational exposures.

1.7 INTERNATIONAL REGULATORY CHALLENGES

UniCredit group is listed on Borsa Italiana, the Italian stock exchange, the consolidating regulator is the Bank of Italy, while the group controls, in its turn, banks and financial services in more than twenty countries, entailing very complex relations.

The new Basel capital accord implies that at individual country level there is an implementation directive, a regulation interpreting the Basel principles and guidelines, complying with national binding regulation and existing principles.

Ensuring consistent control over operational risks demands common methodologies, systems, rules, and standards. We believe the best approach was applying to controlled companies minimum common operational control standards, but allowing operational risk managers and companies to integrate these standards with additional specific controls like ad hoc reporting or analysis, when necessary for business or additional domestic regulatory requirements. This flexibility proved, a success factor: it allowed individual businesses to develop operational risk controls to reflect their peculiar structure and processes, bespoke analysis and reporting, providing also useful feedback and suggestions for improvement of the control framework. It also stimulated an open dialogue with regulators, facilitating integration of companies that already developed their own operational risk management framework.

An increasingly critical issue we faced was identifying the appropriate external loss data, given UniCredit group business structure and markets. We started with DIPO (Database Italiano di Perdite Operative), an Italian banks' loss data consortium. Even though still participating, as UniCredit became increasingly an international group, we needed a data source reflecting the operational risk exposure. We began collecting from publicly available data sources, newspapers, and internet newswire operational reported losses suffered by financial institutions. This was a repetitive and toilsome exercise, taking precious time away from staff. Eventually we decided on Algo operational loss data, an external provider. The data was provided by an international company, so ensuring service quality and reliability, also for auditing and validation guaranteeing loss data reporting independence.

1.8 REPUTATIONAL RISK MANAGEMENT

In recent times, with the increasing complexity of UniCredit Group and its growing. The operational risk management analyzed the reputational impacts of Group's products and businesses. Strictly linked to operational risk, the management of reputational risks hinges on internal process control, and the assessment of markets, clients' and communities' expectations. The focus on service efficiency takes into account long-term impact on results and environment; that's where we found useful the experience developed with operational risk control, applied to reputational impact.

Looking at international events that occurred to financial institutions, we found that many operational risks could have a paramount reputational impact, often larger than the loss or the inadequate service provided. Certain events could have major market and press relevance, with the company's management subject to unexpected levels of scrutiny, or the company's ethics or service quality. In recent years, due to major changes driven by consolidation and competition, the banking industry experienced increased attention by markets and media, sometimes questioning pricing and product distribution policy, risk appetite, and returns. As banks offer a service to markets and clients, experience high regulatory attention, being, are a structural component of this industry sector. As a consequence inadequate reputational risk control and management, relaxed or weak risk monitoring, can, sooner or later, be perceived by customers, resulting not in worse results but also damage to the company's reputation. Banks build their customer base on reputation, and it must be a management priority to maintain and enhance it.

2

The calculation dataset

2.1 DEFINITIONS

In operational risk modeling, special attention must be given to the *calculation dataset*, the subset of data from the overall operational risk management information available that is used for capital at risk estimates and measures. The criteria for data control and quality assessment, their updating to adjustments for business or process changes, the identification of relevant time series for risk calculation, are the pivotal components of our operational risk management framework. With a focus on risk assessment and impacts on estimates, we describe data treatment and recommend, based on our direct experience, desirable or preferred approaches. According to Basel 2 regulation, the calculation dataset must include internal losses, external data, business environment, internal control factors, and scenario analysis (see Figure 2.1). We cover these separately, presenting practical cases of classification and describing the problems we encountered.

We define the calculation dataset as the subset of operational risk information used for the measurement of capital at risk; this requires a distinction is made between the comprehensive operational risk information and the calculation dataset. Unlike market and credit risk that refer to specific portfolios or assets, operational risk exposure is extremely difficult to identify and isolate. Based on the Basel 2 definition, operational risk spans the whole organization and its processes (including credit and market risks). In our experience, when describing the calculation dataset characteristics, we focused on operational losses. It should be remembered that the operational risk exposure is not represented only by losses (we have never experienced losses for all processes exposed to operational risks). Inefficiencies can be captured by indicators, for example the number of end-of-day unsettled transactions or the number of times a software is unavailable.

We consider loss data the core element for capital at risk calculation, mainly because they are a requisite in the Basel 2 directive: financial institutions shall gather and report operational losses if they are willing

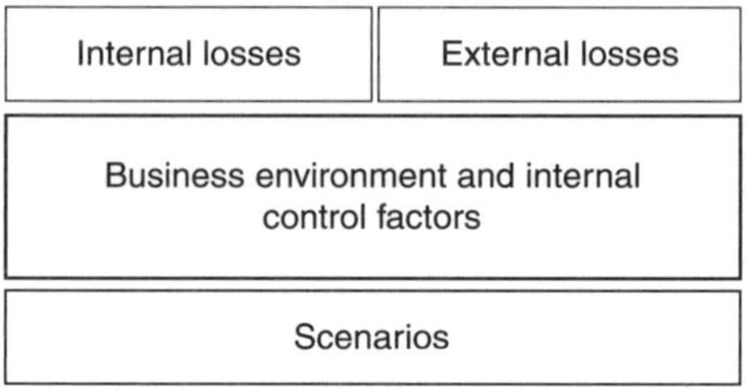

Figure 2.1 Four elements of Basel 2 AMA modeling

to apply for the standard (TSA) or advanced model (AMA). Operational losses are also required for capital at risk calculations for banks adopting AMA: they shall combine internal and external loss data, scenarios, and business environment and internal control factors. Scenarios will be included in the external data section of this chapter.

2.2 RULES OF THUMB

There are some general principles we suggest following when setting up operational risk data feeding and control process: we think these will allow greater control on quality, timeliness, and completeness of information gathered.

1. *Institutions should have a policy to identify when a loss or an event recorded in the internal loss event database is also to be included in the calculation dataset.*

   Linking or quoting the regulatory instructions or the new Basel capital accord isn't enough and will not ensure accurate and consistent data classification and treatment by operational risk manager. A detailed policy, describing with clear examples how loss cases must be treated, it is fundamental to ensure data quality and a reliable calculation dataset. The policy should provide consistent classification criteria of loss data. UniCredit Group have it approved by the management board of the holding company and individual controlled companies.
2. *Institutions must define appropriate minimum loss thresholds for the collection of the internal loss data.*

   Though we collect all losses for risk management and control purposes, this is less relevant for the calculation dataset, where a reasonable lower threshold simplifies control checks and possible integration with external data. The threshold will depend on the size of the company and its business complexity; we set it at €5000 but, in general, €10 000 could also be a good fit, very much depending on the internal data time series available. When modeling frequency, a higher threshold will quite likely exclude a significant amount of information, but this will not have a major impact in the final capital at risk results, especially when there are extremely infrequent high losses determining the capital at risk figures.

3. *Institutions shall use relevant external data, especially when there is reason to believe that they might be exposed to infrequent, yet potentially severe, losses.*

   Individual banks do not suffer major operational losses every year and for each event class. It will likely be necessary to integrate the internal dataset with external sources, for extreme, high-impact cases and classes that statistically do not experience many losses (event types like physical damage for example). When considering an external data source, we verify the existing quality control process and data validation, the time series length, the frequency by event type and country, the reporting threshold, and the event-updating mechanism. We found the latter the most relevant rule of thumb: considering very complex and high-impact operational losses, the actual amount is difficult to identify and tends to vary a lot in time. It will be necessary to verify how this is updated and, in public data sources, compare it with alternative sources, making sure these are consistently and correctly reported. External data sources often consider operational losses belonging to non financial industries. We think that, in constructing the calculation dataset, it is correct to consider only data belonging to the company sector, and we include only financial sector losses in the calculation dataset. We do not ignore other relevant information from external data sources, and use it to perform qualitative and quantitative analysis (e.g., scenario analysis).

4. *Institutions must have a policy for insurance elements and related data.*

   The insurance contract description and terms must be obtained and filed, ensuring full and correct elements for capital at risk modeling (see Chapter 4). As renewal takes place every year, and contract elements like deductibles and limits as well as clauses may vary from year to year, we check clauses and then set the model's parameters accordingly. We proceed likewise for all data on recoveries, time from claim and reimbursements, and related costs, all of which are reported and updated in the operational risk dataset, as these have a major impact on the final result.

5. *Regular training must be provided to operational risk managers on data classification.*

   A detailed data classification manual and a policy approved by the board are compulsory in UniCredit internal regulation for each controlled legal entity. Operational risk managers are responsible for data reporting and must apply common set standards and rules. It is paramount to provide consistent data reporting direct training to operational risk managers: internet solutions or class courses often prove insufficient. We believe training sessions on data classification must be repeated at least every year.

2.3 INTERNAL LOSS DATA

According to Basel 2 AMA regulation, a bank must consider internal loss data, applying loss-distribution or scenario-based approaches, or hybrid ones. Internal losses must be included in the operational risk management database and classified into a grid of given regulatory business lines and event types, as indicated in the new Basel capital accord paper. This is arguably the only very detailed regulatory rule imposed by the accord on financial institutions, which are otherwise given a significant freedom compared to the amount of detailed credit risk regulation.

2.3.1 Business Line Mapping

Basel 2 prescribes the data required for capital at risk calculation, this being either the relevant indicator (gross income) or operational losses. It is reclassified or mapped to eight business lines: corporate finance, trading and sales, retail banking, commercial banking, payment and settlement, agency services, asset management, and retail brokerage (Table 2.1). The accord specifies for each business line a subset of activities included. For corporate finance, these are municipal and government finance, merchant banking, advisory services, and corporate finance itself. Sales, market making, proprietary positions, and treasury are included for trading and sales. Retail banking, private banking, and card services are covered under retail banking. Commercial banking and payment and settlement don't have second level lists. Custody,

Table 2.1 Business lines

1	Corporate finance
2	Trading and sales
3	Retail banking
4	Commercial banking
5	Payment and settlement
6	Agency services
7	Asset management
8	Retail brokerage

corporate agency, and corporate trust make up agency services. Discretionary and nondiscretionary fund management are included under asset management. Retail brokerage again has no subcategories. The individual institution can decide to map data just to the first level categories or go further down to map to the second level categories or proprietary ones. We decided to apply the Basel 2 second level categories, as reconciliation with further internal categories would be cumbersome and wouldn't do much to enhance control capacity. One of the greatest challenges in classification, and implicitly for the capital at risk calculation, is represented by differences between the individual company's internal management information (especially for gross income) and regulatory business lines. This requires quite a substantial additional reclassification and regular updating exercises when there is a business restructuring, disposal, or acquisition. We set detailed rules of thumb for attribution in all cases where there will be multiple business line entities, for both the relevant indicator allocation and loss classification. This is a further critical issue in ensuring time series consistency and long-term adjustments.

We defined data classification rules to make sure that risk analysis and calculation can be performed in a consistent way over time, obtaining clear results (see also Section 2.9 on scaling):

1. a database must keep track of a company's ownership changes and business restructuring – the operational risk manager ought to maintain and file standardized documentation describing changes that have occurred together with any adjustment, such as scaling applied, rationale for intervening;
2. the time series aggregating date, when data from two or more companies are merged into another database, must also be reported and the original series must be traceable;

3. in cases where the operational risk manager cannot retrieve or obtain data, proforma financial statements should be used, allowing comparable and meaningful aggregation of gross income data;
4. rules of thumb applied over time for gross income allocation to business lines must also be recorded and available for future analysis.

We set detailed criteria for assigning loss data arising from events in a centralized function of activities that span more several business line.

2.3.2 Event Type Classifications

Internal losses must be mapped into seven regulatory types: we analyze these now, concentrating especially on the cases where attribution or classification might be problematic.

We shall introduce the concept of *boundary credit losses*, operational losses related to credit risk (or market risk). Boundary losses are recorded in the credit risk databases and are treated as credit risk for the purposes of calculating minimum regulatory capital, so that will not be subject to an additional operational risk capital charge. Banks must identify all material operational risk losses, including those related to credit risk, and report them separately in an internal operational risk database. Rules for identifying and treating operational related losses in the credit process are key to ensuring consistent classification and capital at risk results. Particularly relevant will be fraud cases which cause loans to default, and how events are attributed within the bank and in external databases (Table 2.2) (see also Section 2.4).

In our experience, one of the major sources of operational events is the Basel 2 category *clients, products, and business practices*, encompassing losses from inadequate product distribution to clients, without fraudulent intention; missing or interpreting incorrectly a legal requirement;

Table 2.2 Event types

1	Clients, products, and business practices
2	Damage to physical assets
3	Business disruption and IT systems failure
4	Execution, delivery, and process management
5	Internal fraud
6	External fraud
7	Employment practices and workplace safety

or not being fully compliant in applying regulations. The new accord identifies a set of subcategories in this group: one being *suitability, disclosure, and fiduciary losses*, such as fiduciary breaches, aggressive sales, account churning, and misuse of confidential information; then there are *improper business or market practices* for cases of losses coming from antitrust, improper trade, market manipulation, insider trading, money laundering; a further subcategory is the *product flaws* for defects and errors in the sold products; then we find *selection, sponsorship, and exposure* for cases of failure to provide guidelines to clients, or exceeding clients' mandates; there is also *advisory activities* for disputes over performance of advisory services. The following should be classified as improper business and market practice, rather than fraud: events of non compliance to regulations, infringement of antitrust laws; exclusive commercial agreements harmful to customers.

Losses caused by natural disasters or other events are included in *damage to physical assets*. We include havoc to branches and ATM machines and physical damage occurring to furniture and other hardware in the business's premises. In the case of partial or total destruction of property, the operational risk management quantifies the impact as the reconstruction value or the insured value or the latest available evaluation, irrespective of the remaining value to be amortized. The actual bank exposure will be the maximum real estate value of the business premises or other relevant properties in the portfolio: we shall verify whether an external database, including extreme real estate damage, might be applicable (see Section 2.5 on external data). As part of the business continuity plan, focus will be to ensure that key services are provided in cases of major disruption, for example in case of a terrorist attack. Full valuation and process hedging will be in the plan: in estimating the potential impact of extreme events for the physical assets class, this should also be included. Basel 2 doesn't indicate subcategories for this event class. We separate the branch network exposures, as these are exposed to typically high-frequency, low-severity damage, from the corporate headquarters.

Major source of operational risk arises from *business disruption and IT system failures*, operational losses related to information technology, related or caused by software or hardware problems. For such events, severity is often difficult to quantify, as they are tied to internal resources such as help desks and maintenance teams, and costs are directly billed or attributed to the affected function/unit as part of an overall service level agreement rather than on a one-by-one basis. Even in companies where this is the case, it might be done using estimates or service indicators, and the biggest problems or critical events are usually all fixed by internal staff. These events often have a severe impact on the company in terms of business disruption, and the service provided to clients, affecting reputation: the bank's image and market perception are extremely complicated to measure (see Chapter 5). It might be worthwhile, if not for capital at risk calculation then surely for management purposes, to develop a cost proxy model, estimating event impacts: resources needed to fix problems, service disruption impact, business effect, and client perception adjustment. We do not consider the cost of ordinary maintenance as an operational loss; instead, errors, contra entries, and losses from the migration of systems or programs are classified as IT losses. Likewise, errors in assignment of parameters or malfunctioning of programs are considered IT systems losses. Errors in data treatment, in our opinion, are also IT losses, while the losses caused by IT fraud, e.g. by phishing or hacking, are better attributed to external fraud. The business continuity plan costs will also be excluded from the loss data, unless an event occurs to trigger it, then the full impact will need reporting.

Processing trades and settlement, money transfers or cheques payments, filing and controlling credit documentation and covenants, phone banking transactions, and all back office activities generate thousands of errors, causing unsettled transactions, contra entries, manual entry mistakes, wrong customer information or delayed executions, leading to fines, or penalties, or claims. These are classified as *execution, delivery, and process management* losses from failed transaction processing or as a result of interaction with trade counterparties or clients. Basel 2 indicates seven subcategories for such types of operational events. There are, first of all, the losses caused by *transaction capture, execution, and maintenance* indicated as failed or incorrect communication of information to clients. This ought to be separated from cases involving clients' products and business practices, with involuntary execution errors. These must be treated and classified in the company's internal classifications regulation, so that data feeding is carried out consistently. Typical and frequent transaction errors are *entry, maintenance, or loading errors*, missed deadlines, and delivery failure like collateral management failures. Further cases are losses related to problems in *monitoring and reporting*, indicated as failed mandatory obligations or inaccurate external reports. Another class that will need classification rules is *customer intake and documentation* cases: as mentioned before, making sure the company obtains clients' permissions, and verifying contract documentation is complete, must be assigned to the correct loss type class, providing example lists, to avoid potential impacts on capital estimates. Losses caused by *client account management* are those related to clients' privacy and record management, such as wrongly kept clients' records and booking, or loss of clients' assets due to negligence. We are also exposed to losses caused by *trade counterparties* relationship management, generating potential disputes over performance quality and service execution. Process-related errors also include those arising from disputes between *vendors and suppliers*, and outsourcing disputes in general: these encompass both financial and nonfinancial counterparties, and must include internal and external service providers for banks relying on specialized process companies.

Operational risk includes exposure to fraud, a major source of losses, often with a heavy impact on a company's reputation. The *internal fraud* category, according to Basel 2, includes losses from stolen or misappropriated property, and due to breached regulations. Internal fraud is further divided into the subcategories of *unauthorized activities*, for transactions not reported intentionally, and deliberate, incorrect positions marking (this being potentially a market risk boundary case), and proper *theft or fraud*. In order to distinguish it from cases of external fraud, internal fraud is defined as all fraud where there is at least one employee involved. Events where there is an external accomplice will be treated as internal fraud. We treat fraud perpetrated by external financial agents working on an exclusive contract with one bank as internal, even though, technically, this is external fraud.

There are so many cases of *external fraud* that it is often considered the stereotype of operational risk: we found that cases of fraud are often boundary cases with credit risk. External fraud in Basel 2 is defined as losses originating from stolen or misappropriated property or action breaching the law perpetrated by a third party, without an internal accomplice. The subcategories here are *theft and fraud*, for cases of robbery, forgery, or check kiting, and *systems security*, for damages caused by hacking and theft of information. Hacking and other information technology driven crimes, such as phishing, should be considered external fraud rather than information technology related damages.

Problems due to incorrect or unfair staff management, or contractual inadequacy fall into the *employment practices and workplace safety* events class, these being the losses derived from noncompliance with working, health, or safety laws, employee injury claims, or from discrimination. Though a relevant operational risk with high reputational exposure, it could be a difficult information to obtain, for confidentiality reasons. We tend to require a minimum event description, ensuring privacy on one side and yet obtaining the necessary risk control and measurement information. Here, the subcategories include *employee relations*, for losses caused by compensation or benefit issues with employees, termination, and organized labor activity. Another one is the *safe working environment*, which covers a company's general liability, like compliance with health and safety regulations. There are also cases of *diversity and discrimination*, such as mobbing or physical abuse, or any form of unfair penalization based on politics, race, sexuality, age, creed, or nationality. We consider compensation interest, the amounts due for settlement, the interest on arrears for taxes in the position of a withholding agent, the legal expenses, and any other charges as a direct consequence of the event to be operational losses. Payments for anticipated retirement or severance pay, on the other hand, are not considered as operational losses.

2.3.3 Data Quality Analysis

We attribute the greatest importance to include as much information as possible on company's exposure to operational risk in the internal dataset, as this is used not just for capital at risk calculation. For each operational event we include a brief description of the causes, the business affected, and the geographical area, as different countries are exposed to specific risks.

The time lag between the occurrence date (when the event happened) and the observation date (when it was discovered) provides also interesting information for loss identification. We check the differences between the occurrence date and input date, the time elapsing before a loss is available for capital calculation.

2.3.4 Special Cases

There are cases we treat as special ones: these are *rapidly recovered losses, near misses, gain events, multiple time, and multiple effect losses* (definitions are reported in the CEBS CP10) (see Figure 2.2).

Figure 2.2 Economic manifestations

Rapidly recovered losses are operational events resulting in losses that are completely recovered in a very short period of time. CEBS doesn't specify what should be considered a short period of time: but we set it at five working days.

A *near miss* is an operational event that does not result in a loss. We don't have it in the calculation dataset, but we use it as a risk indicator for management purposes.

An operational risk *gain event* generates a profit. As for the near misses, we exclude gains from the calculation dataset, but are included in the operational management dataset, sometimes used for scaling data or scenario analysis.

Multiple time losses are a group of sequential losses occurring in different periods of time, relating to the same operational risk event. For example, a large number of incorrectly priced transactions from a single incorrect piece of reference data or from a scheme to defraud with many small transactions. We aggregate multiple time losses into a single loss event and include it in the calculation dataset.

Multiple effect losses are a group of linked losses suffered by different entities or business lines, units, or functions, generated by one root event. We add multiple effect losses into a single loss and then report it in the calculation dataset. For both multiple time and multiple effect losses, we record them individually, and then aggregate them.

We also monitor the *occurrence versus booking of an operational event*. A loss might occur on a certain date or period, but for some reasons may be booked later, sometimes even several years later. We ask operational risk managers to verify that events are booked as soon as they occur, and set maximum limits on event reporting.

2.4 MINIMUM LOSS THRESHOLD

The loss data threshold is the severity value over which losses will be included in the calculation dataset. We have different thresholds for loss reporting and capital at risk calculation. We define two distinct thresholds for many reasons:

- Different event types and/or businesses or countries where we operate might require an adjustment in the loss reporting threshold. Applying an identical limit could exclude all information on loss exposure for certain activities and countries. It would be very tiresome and demanding for areas where losses are very frequent and tend to span a wide range of severity levels.
- Controlling all losses levels irrespective of the risk calculation threshold, can be useful for service quality and efficiency verification.
- To support scenario analysis or risk indicator testing, the threshold for specific processes or businesses might be reviewed.

One could choose to have very low reporting thresholds, or none at all. For quality and complete assurance, we recommend that all losses, even the minor ones, are included. A varying threshold might result in varying frequency, affecting capital at risk distribution. In the new accord, an indicative level is set at \$10 000. This threshold should also be aligned to some external data consortia. External loss databases usually have a threshold higher than \$10 000: this might cause problems when integrating the information for the capital at risk calculation. The correct or adequate threshold should be the result of empirical testing, verifying the impact of different ones on the final capital at risk figures. It has a relevant impact for event types where there are very few losses and excluding a portion of the available information might hinder robust estimates. For certain event types (e.g. IT or personnel management related losses), available data are scarce and applying an identical limit to the other event classes might exclude precious data.

2.5 EXTERNAL DATA

In Basel 2 it is required that external data are used in the capital at risk calculation, but the means by which to do this isn't indicated. Banks that participate in consortia should provide data that are classified in a homogeneous manner and contain information that is comprehensive and reliable. Differences in the size of banks or other institution specific factors should be taken into account when incorporating external data for risk measurement.

There are three main external data source types currently available: public or external data sources, consortia, and internally generated scenario data. We decided to combine these three: generally, public sources have large quantities of data, especially when compared to internal scenarios; data from consortia can be too skewed to some countries or businesses.

2.5.1 Public or External Data Sources

These were the first to appear in the market, as the new Basel capital accord consultative paper was released in 2001. They gathered data for large historical losses, collected from newspapers or the internet, often including extreme and debated events that received significant media attention. Initially, providers thought these would be useful, especially to fill in time series gaps for capital at risk calculations. There were data going back sometimes 50 years, covering not only the financial industry but events of other industrial sectors. For these data we recommend to pay particular attention to some selection criteria, listed below.

- *Geographical span.* We verify the number of countries included in the set, checking if there is a special concentration in certain nations. This needs to be taken into account for risk measurement could have swing effects requiring gauging or weighting: for banks highly concentrated in certain countries or businesses, it could result in incorrect risk estimates, it would add inconsistent extremes where regulations and market practices, and conditions in terms of products and customers, can be very different.
- *Sector concentration.* Relevant data for capital at risk calculation of a bank should be a loss event suffered by a bank or a company in the financial sector: we check and exclude events from other industries. Loss events taken from unrelated sectors, such as manufacturing or the media, can be used for different purposes, but we exclude them from the capital at risk calculation, as the financial sector has a different operational risk exposure: assuming, for example, that a fraud is the same regardless of the type of company, it could be severely underestimating the differences in the control systems in place.
- *Time series length by event type.* Until recently, with a few exceptions, banks didn't have dedicated operational risk function (see Chapter 1). Many could only rely on a limited number of collected operational losses, and many started only a few years ago. The first risk estimates integrated limited internal data with external ones for most event types. Banks now rely on a significant amount of data, encompassing

all Basel 2 event types; some have recovered old events, so enriching the series. We check if the external sources are adequate in terms of the number of events, and whether there are sufficient or relevant high-severity losses for the various classes. It might be that precisely when one needs extreme or additional data, are missing also in the external provider.

- *Data classification and certification rules*. The bank internal classification rules can differ, sometimes significantly, from those of the external data provider. This could pose consistency problems: we found this often the case, for example, in boundary credit events and verify how events are updated. External providers rely on publicly available news for events updating: the media might report differing information, especially when it comes to severity. Likewise, it can prove difficult ensuring reliable data certification for updating; severe losses will require years before the final figures are determined and reported. We have special attention to quality control processes and rules applied by the provider. Typically, public data sources have high loss reporting thresholds, and also relevant in the selection process.

2.5.2 Consortium Data

Consortia are associations of banks exchanging operational losses, contributing to a pool of data that is then returned to the members. This is probably now the most widely used external loss data source. There are both international and national consortia, so offering a focused dataset, in particular for banks that have no, or limited, international operations: this ensures external data more consistent with a bank's risk exposure. There might be some concern that national consortia might be missing extreme events, as contribution remains a voluntary exercise. We feel there is also a potential risk of missing extreme losses using consortia's losses, but one might argue that identifying the applicable extreme is also questionable: a loss suffered by a large international bank might not be relevant to a small regional retail one, even scaled. In assessing whether to join a consortium we recommend analyzing:

- the number of banks participating and the countries where they operate;
- the reporting threshold. Consortia can have a far bigger bank of data than public sources, with implications for capital at risk modeling. Consortia have rules that often differ significantly from internal ones;

disclosure on individual events might be limited due to privacy agreements between member banks, far more than in public sources, a great constraint in verifying data classification accuracy.

2.5.3 Scenario Data

These are generated internally, and assess the potential impact of events in terms of loss frequency and severity. We perform regular scenario analysis, a pivotal element of UniCredit Group operational risk control framework. Scenarios could replace external data, though limitations remain, as we describe below.

- Scenario generation implies significant management and staff involvement, requiring repeated interviews and accurate controls on results consistency.
- Ensuring scenarios' estimates are correct in terms of frequency and severity.

We combine scenario, public, and consortia loss data: the operational risk manager will have more external information to integrate the internal time series. This also facilitates event comparison, benchmarking, and data scaling.

2.6 BUSINESS ENVIRONMENT AND INTERNAL CONTROL FACTORS

Basel 2 asks banks to monitor environmental and internal control factors (BECF) that could affect their operational risk profile. Such factors should be selected as meaningful drivers of risk that are translatable into quantitative measures, and should make banks' operational risk assessment more forward looking. We implemented BECF as a set of indicators, linked to processes and businesses in UniCredit. These vary from the fixed set of volume indicators, identical across businesses and processes, allowing benchmarking and comparison, to a fully bespoke set, varying from type of business and company and country. We select a limited or 'key' set of indicators both for capital at risk modeling and operational risk control. We found that too many indicators are costly and difficult to interpret for management and process owners. For capital at risk measurement, we believe easier to include a smaller set of indicators, treating a smaller amount of data and simplifying the explanation of the impact on capital at risk.

2.7 SCENARIOS

Scenarios are qualitative, reasoned impact assessments of severe losses. Sometimes, one may compensate for lack of data for specific event types, businesses, or processes by carrying out scenarios. We control the consistency of scenario assessment of similar businesses and event types throughout companies, managers, and time. We make sure that similar risk exposures are evenly measured. Some banks use the scenarios differently in capital at risk calculation, simulating the impact of rare and extreme conditions on the company, and adding internal estimates of tail events to external data sources.

2.8 INSURANCE INFORMATION

Banks have traditionally insured against operational risks, subscribing to specific policies, such as the BBB or similar ones, hedging fraud, directors' responsibilities, and company premises against fire or other damage, etc. Basel 2 recognizes their validity, provided these comply with a set of requirements (see Chapter 4). For capital at risk calculation purposes, we need a regular set of information on insurance.

- *Event types covered by an insurance policy.* The operational risk manager verifies which event types are covered and cases of exclusion in the contract.
- *Insurance policy terms and conditions and their compliance to regulatory standards for capital at risk recognition.* Common policies covering operational risk do not often comply with all the requisites.
- *Insurance limits and deductibles by event type, the upper and lower bounds for coverage application.* It will be the operational risk manager's responsibility, based on historical data and risk appetite, to set the right limit and deductible levels, optimizing the balance between premiums and hedging risk. In our experience, the more the operational risk manager is able to intervene in the process, engineering for standard loss reduction and control, the higher the deductible level, reducing insurance costs and improving control and process efficiency, and permitting higher limits for similar premium levels.
- *Statistics on recoveries from insurance and other sources by event type.* For each individual event type we report whether there is insurance coverage, deductibles, and limits, recovery expected and previously refunded sums, and any additional recovery. This information will be used for setting limits, deductibles, and insurance renewal convenience.

- *Statistical analysis on standards processing and payment times required by the insurance company.* At expiry, we assess whether it is convenient or preferable to go for a self-insurance solution or negotiate different conditions.
- *Details on damage covered by insurance and parts excluded, again a critical element.* With the support of other experts, we check that the final coverage is correctly and precisely understood and then embedded in the calculation.

We found, as insurance is usually provided by external companies, it is best to agree at the policy renewal the minimum dataflow requirement for the capital at risk calculation.

2.9 SCALING DATA

Often we have to integrate losses from a newly acquired company, external data from different sources, changes in internal business structure, disposal of activities or integration into others, changes in processes and information technology, all causing historical data structural changes. Internal and external information will then need adjustment before feeding the capital at risk calculation. Affected time series and individual data points could be scaled or removed.

- *Inflation scaling.* For time series sometimes spanning several decades, in particular for severe losses, we identify the appropriate inflation index to apply, especially when adjusting loss data from many countries.
- *External data scaling.* External data taken verbatim may incorrectly affect the capital at risk results. Limited information is often available for precise scaling, we use simple indicators like number of employees or branches, or the gross income. We often apply the gross income, rather than country or business-driven scaling factors, as this is easier to interpret.
- *Internal data scaling.* When we deal with the integration or disposal of companies and changes in businesses and processes, it is then necessary to decide whether the whole combined loss dataset shall remain untouched, or part of it (e.g. the part from the company that no longer exists and whose processes and systems have been migrated into new ones) should be scaled (the new target IT systems might show lower loss frequency and risk exposure), or even removed altogether. For the adjustments, we require the operational risk manager to document the amendments. For capital at risk measurement, extreme cases will be included in the calculation dataset, either as internal or as external

events. Keeping data will be down to the operational risk manager, balancing aim for accurate estimates with relevance in reflecting risk exposure.

2.10 THE UNICREDIT GROUP OPERATIONAL RISK DATABASE EVOLUTION

The operational risk calculation dataset, the subset of data from the overall operational risk management information available that is used to calculate the operational capital at risk, is a pivot element in operational risk modeling. Relying on a vast and sound dataset is paramount for the operational risk function. UniCredit Group was expanding and this has driven the database and operational risk software evolution.

In 2001, Group was mainly Italian and attention was focused on the loss data collection. This database was improved with new releases and with a group that was present in an ever-increasing number of European countries. We developed in 2005 a new operational risk software and database, replacing all previous ones. Today UniCredit Group relies on ARGO, an in-house solution, distributed and functioning in all companies controlled by the Group and every country. ARGO has also been validated by AMA regulations, and it is the tool for operational risk management and capital at risk calculation.

2.11 FINAL CONSIDERATIONS

Unlike other risk types relying on numerous vast time series and well-established modeling techniques, operational risk is still based on comparatively limited information. Bank consortia are strengthening, but indexes are missing, market providers are developing fast but still cannot fully answer all operational risk managers' data needs. Tremendous research advances and major leaps forward in modeling operational risk have been made, implementing more and new techniques or approaches, and showing fast developments but as yet unstable measurement approaches. There is still considerable freedom for banks to develop measurement models and thus set the operational capital at risk input data requirements. This leaves a vast amount of discretion to banks; substantial responsibility is given to each risk manager's own assessment, judging how the company's risk profile should be controlled and leaving to regulators the difficult task of ensuring a level playing field across institutions and countries.

3
Loss distribution approaches

In research literature and in the financial industry, operational risk measurement is still a relatively new discipline, experiencing rapid change. Two major measurement procedures are listed in the new Basel capital accord: the scenario-based and loss distribution approaches, respectively indicated here by SBA and LDA. A combination of these two is also allowed for regulatory capital purposes, effectively permitting a third category that we shall refer to as the hybrid approach (see Chapter 2). We believe that these three approaches or modeling techniques do not cover the full spectrum of possibilities for operational risk measurement and, as the financial industry is developing and testing new solutions, alternatives are already being applied while gauging current techniques. Our work does not cover alternative approaches to Basel 2, nor will it explore all three of the regulatory solutions indicated in the new accord; rather it will concentrate on and treat extensively LDA modeling, this being the one, in our experience, that holds very interesting properties, making it a very sound choice for regulatory capital measurement. Though operational risk modeling appeared quite recently in the literature, loss modeling has been a core research area for insurance purposes, and LDAs have been developed and used by actuaries for capital at risk calculation for many years, thus providing the bank's operational risk managers with plenty of modeling papers and case studies. In the previous chapter we described methods for developing an operational risk database. Here, the techniques to manage these data points are covered, including quantitative methods used to choose operational risk classes, techniques to determine the distributions that better fit these classes, the convolution method to calculate operational capital at risk. We will look at techniques to model operational losses, applying consolidated actuarial approaches, with exteme event modeling solutions and other current operational risk-specific solutions for aggregation and correlation.

We decided to opt for an LDA solution, weighing the advantages and weaknesses in comparison to SBAs. Although we believe the LDA constitutes a robust and valid estimate of operational risk exposure, it presents some difficulties and rigidities that can be easily solved with

SBAs. These offer more flexibility but presents additional problems to LDAs in justifying and ensuring the accuracy of results. Listing the major differences between the two approaches – LDAs and SBAs – we consider at least the points below:

1. Loss data completeness and therefore its certainty is a strength of LDAs, as the input is typically accounting data and these can be verified over time easily by auditors and regulators. It also presents the advantage of being fairly objective, which means that the information is neither originated by the operational risk management nor is it an estimate; it should be the direct result of profit and loss booking. SBAs might rely on judgments or estimated impacts that might involve additional effort to verify, so increasing the challenges for validation.
2. Integration of external loss data into the calculation dataset might be straightforward, likewise in combining these into the capital at risk calculation for LDAs.
3. Variation in the loss data structure over time is driven by profit and loss booking, so allowing the operational risk manager a clear, independent control position, directly showing the impact of dataset changes in the capital at risk results, and allowing identification of hedging or intervention if needed.
4. Time series adjustments and analysis are traceable and linked to processes and the business.
5. Data feeding can easily be automated, (at least to a reasonable extent).

LDAs might prove a viable solution, favorable in terms of auditing review, internal and external benchmarking. We found LDAs particularly rigid if we wanted to obtain risk measures for single companies, products, or processes where internal and external loss data weren't available or were limited. Likewise, capital at risk on a stand alone basis using LDAs will be robust only where there are statistically sufficient time series, (so allowing for often limited possibilities and sometimes statistically weak results when existing data are scarce). Generally, SBAs produce more consistent results for individual companies or businesses than LDAs.

We will describe a robust operational loss modeling for capital at risk measurement, looking at calculation dataset building, risk class homogeneity, severity distribution and frequency distribution, aggregation, correlation, business environment and risk control factors, adjustments, insurance hedging and their combination into a Value at Risk measure.

3.1 CALCULATION DATASET BUILDING

The term calculation dataset identifies that part of the operational risk data used for the calculation of capital requirement. The calculation dataset has been described in Chapter 2. Some settings are defined by regulation (e.g. at least five years, no credit cross-border cases) others are more company specific. Hence, part of the proposed implementation comes from our experience.

To comply with regulatory requirements (see references 1 and 2 on page 193), the calculation dataset should be articulated in the four parts:

1. Internal dataset.
2. External dataset.
3. Scenario-generated dataset.
4. Risk indicators dataset.

3.1.1 Internal Calculation Dataset

The internal dataset includes at least the following information:

- event description;
- legal entity (or other structures like sub-holding and division);
- total loss;
- occurrence date;
- observation date;
- accounting date;
- Basel business line (1st level);
- Basel event type;
- Cross-border (i.e. market risk, credit risk, or not cross border);
- Insurance coverage (Yes or No);
- Insurance recovery.

The internal calculation dataset encompasses elementary operational risk data: e.g. loss, provision, funds release, contra entry, gain, estimated loss, insurance recovery, other recovery. Each data point in the calculation dataset represents an operational event.

We define observation period as the time range considered to include operational events in the calculation dataset. The occurrence date and accounting date of each operational event must fall in the observation period. The length of the observation period must be at least five years (three years in the start-up period). Banks can set the observation period longer for risk classes with low frequency.

There are different types of dates referring to the operational event (i.e. occurrence date, observation date, accounting date, date of capture in operational risk database). There is no common agreement industry-wide on which date should be used as correct observation period. The occurrence date better reflects the bank's risk profile but some relevant loss data may not be included, if there is a long lawsuit for an internal fraud, could elapse many years between the occurrence and the date on which the loss is realized. If this period is longer than five years, the event will never be included in the calculation. The observation and accounting date may be more convenient the observation date is more difficult to ascertain with high confidence, whereas the accounting date can always be found. Using accounting dates is very conservative: one could also include events that occurred a long time ago, misrepresenting the risk profile. In this case, it may be useful to set some longer limit for the occurrence date (e.g. 10–15 years).

The bank could have loss data from several countries; loss amounts have to be converted into a common currency (e.g. the Euro), using the exchange rate at the time of the loss accounting date.

Operational losses should be aggregated in certain cases for capital at risk calculation.

1. Only losses for internally validated events should be considered. The bank should have in place some process for checking and validating collected data.
2. All losses with accounting dates in the observation period are considered.
3. The amount of each loss is adjusted for inflation, applying a set inflation index. The adjustment is based on the accounting date.
4. The total loss for each operational event is calculated as the sum of losses, provisions, fund uses, timing impacts, and other recoveries, considering losses, provisions, and timing impacts as positive and fund uses and other recoveries as negative. This way, multiple time losses are aggregated into a single total loss. Other recovery is defined as all recoveries that are not insurance recoveries. Timing impacts, defined as fully corrected temporary distortions of the profit and loss accounts in a particularly reporting period, are taken into account with their amount multiplied by the payout ratio, when they affect the reporting of two distinct calendar years.

   If an operational event affects more than one company, the operational risk function must present its own data: those reported by several companies must be aggregated into one single operational event with a single total loss calculated as the sum of each loss (multiple effect losses case). Likewise, operational events with strong cross dependencies have to be aggregated into a single data point. Single operational events belonging to different risk classes (see section 3.3) should not be aggregated.

5. After each loss process, operational events with adjusted total losses higher than or equal to the minimum threshold are selected.
6. Insurance recoveries are aggregated and considered separately.
7. Credit boundary events are excluded.

3.1.2 External Calculation Dataset

External data events are operational losses of other financial institutions and banks. External data are used to integrate the low-frequency/high-severity events, when internal data alone are not sufficient. We gather external data from either:

- consortium data;
- public data.

Examples of consortium databases are DIPO (the Italian Operational Risk Data Consortium) and ORX (Operational Risk eXchange, a consortium on an international level), whereas a source of public data is the Algo OpData database.

We use public losses only to integrate low-frequency/high-severity events.

The exchange rate used for external events should be based on the accounting date; if this is not available, the discovery date can be used, or the occurrence date.

External data can be considered relevant for the calculation dataset if they comply with the following:

1. Only loss data from closed events are included, estimated losses are excluded.
2. Only losses incurred by financial companies are considered; losses from nonfinancial companies can be taken into account only for scenario analysis or stress testing.
3. Financial losses incurred by insurance companies are not considered.
4. Losses that led to bankruptcy are not considered.

5. Credit risk boundary events are excluded.
6. The observation period is ten years based on occurrence date. Where occurrence date is not available the discovery date is used (e.g. date of settlement in case of public data).

3.1.3 Scenario-generated Calculation Dataset

Scenario data are fictitious events used to integrate internal and external loss data in the high-impact/low-frequency area. The operational risk function can identify the relevant scenarios considering historical events or specifying a new scenario. This requires verifying the impact of scenarios in case such events occur looking at processes involved, the controls in place, and the reporting procedures. The operational risk function will check the impact of a selected scenario by interviewing process managers. Data for each scenario will be included in the observation period with a length of five years. Only validated scenarios are considered for quantification purposes.

3.1.4 Risk Indicators Calculation Dataset

Indicators are data reflecting operational risk exposure: the value of an indicator should be correlated to changes in risk levels. Using operational risk indicators to adjust capital at risk based on internal, external, and scenario data adds a forward-looking effect to the estimates. The selection of relevant operational risk indicators should be based on the relevance for risk warning.

According to our methodology, risk indicators adjusting the capital at risk should satisfy the following requirements:

- updated data is available monthly or quarterly;
- more than one year of data is available (at least the last 13 months must be available for monthly data and at least the last five quarters must be available for quarterly data).

3.2 GENERAL LDA FRAMEWORK

In this section, we introduce the concepts of LDA for modeling operational loss data (see Figure 3.1). Loss amounts $x_1, \ldots, x_n$ are supposed to be realizations of independent and identically distributed (i.i.d.) random

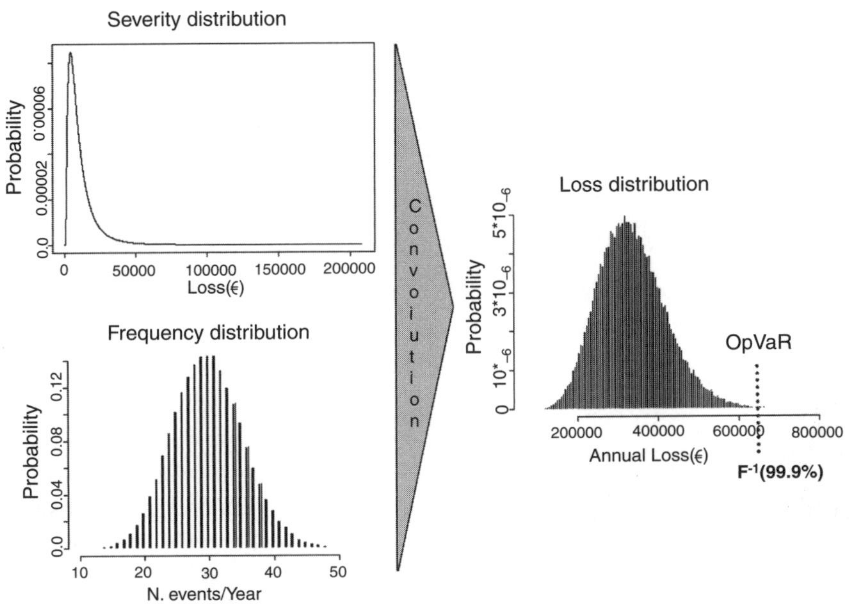

Figure 3.1 Loss distribution approach framework

variables $X_1, \ldots, X_n$. The losses are seen as independent realizations of a random variable X identifying the loss severity. Losses are considered to be positive real numbers, so the random variable X is continuous and positive. The probability density function of X is denoted by f_X and the probability distribution function F_X identifies the loss severity distribution. f_X and F_X are continuous functions defined only for positive values.

We assume that the number of loss events, n, between times t and $t + \Delta t$ is a realization of a random variable N. For operational risk, the value Δt is considered equal to one year. The positive and discrete random variable N describes the loss frequency. The probability mass function of N is identified by p and the probability distribution function P is defined as:

$$P(n) = \sum_{k=0}^{n} p(k) \tag{3.1}$$

The function P identifies the loss frequency distribution.

The severity X and the frequency N are supposed to be independent.

The aggregated loss amount between times t and $t + \Delta t$ can be described by the following random variable:

$$S = \sum_{i=1}^{N} X_i \tag{3.2}$$

The probability distribution function F_S is a compound distribution:

$$F_S(x) = \begin{cases} \mathbb{P}(S \leq x) = \sum\limits_{n=0}^{\infty} p(n) \cdot \mathbb{P}(S \leq x | N = n) & \\ \qquad\qquad\; = \sum\limits_{n=0}^{\infty} p(n) \cdot F_X^{*n}(x), & x > 0 \\ p(0), & x = 0 \end{cases}$$

where $*$ is the operator *convolution* and F_X^{*n} is the n-fold convolution of distribution function F_X:

$$F_X^{*n}(x) = \int_0^x F_X^{*(n-1)}(x - y) f_X(y)\, \mathrm{d}y \tag{3.3}$$

The 2-fold convolution is the probability distribution function of two random variables that are independent and identically distributed:

$$F_X^{*2}(x) = \mathbb{P}(X_1 + X_2 \leq x) = \int_0^x F_{X_1}(x - y) f_{X_2}(y)\, \mathrm{d}y \tag{3.4}$$

The starting point is:

$$F_X^{*1}(x) = \int_0^x F_X^{*(0)}(x - y) f_X(y)\, \mathrm{d}y = F_X(x) = \int_0^x f_X(y)\, \mathrm{d}y \tag{3.5}$$

Hence:

$$F_X^{*0}(0) = 1 \tag{3.6}$$

Once the loss distribution is determined, the capital at risk (or capital charge) can be calculated applying a risk measure. The most used risk measure in financial applications is *Value at Risk* (VaR).[1] The Value at

[1] Other risk measures have been proposed, such as expected shortfall and median shortfall (see reference 3 on page 193).

Risk at confidence level α is defined as the quantile of level α ($0 < \alpha < 1$):

$$\text{VaR}(\alpha) = F_S^{-1}(\alpha) \tag{3.7}$$

According to Basel 2, for operational risk, the capital at risk has to be calculated considering one year as the holding period and 99.9% as the confidence level. Hence, the capital at risk can be determined as the VaR at confidence level $\alpha = 99.9\%$ calculated on the annual loss distribution.

3.3 OPERATIONAL RISK CLASSES

We define an operational risk class an homogeneous risk category in terms of risks covered and data available. In reference 4 on page 193, several examples of risk classes are reported:

- event type
- business line
- a combination of event type/business line
- a legal entity class
- a cause class.

As described in Section 3.2, LDAs ought to satisfy the hypothesis of independence and identical distribution (i.i.d.). In both the new Basel capital accord (see reference 2) and the CEBS's (Committee of European Banking Supervisors) CP10 (see reference 4), financial institutions shall test the hypothesis that data belonging to a risk class are independent and identically distributed, prerequisite for robust modeling.

We now look at some techniques to verify that a risk class is independent and identically distributed, analyzing identical distribution first. We consider only business lines and event types as plausible risk categories. We apply a simple method to test the merits of both alternatives in terms of data homogeneity in each risk class.

3.3.1 Identically Distributed Risk Classes

An operational risk class should be a data-homogeneous risk category. The trade-off between data homogeneity and data availability should be analyzed:

- increasing the number of classes improves the homogeneity, but smaller amounts of data will be available to model each class;
- decreasing the number of classes improves the data availability, but data for every class will be less homogeneous.

We define as a minimal risk class the combination of an individual business line with one event type (BL × ET), ensuring a high degree of homogeneity. The operational risk manager will likely face difficulties related to small amount of data available for certain classes (these, typically, will be the same within the company and external data sources, see Chapter 2). Alternatively, considering as risk classes some aggregations of business lines or event types, one could experience cases of extensive or adequate data available, but with a very low degree of homogeneity. The operational risk manager shall assess the trade-off, based on data availability, management requirements, and business structure.

To satisfy the requirement of identical distribution of risk classes, we set the business line by event type cells as minimal classes, then tests the degree of homogeneity, of both the business lines and the event types. Considering one of these two classifications as risk class setting, data availability is no longer critical, leaving only the problem of testing data homogeneity. In order to verify data homogeneity for business lines as risk class, the level of aggregation of the minimal member of classes that gets to each single business line is verified. Similarly, if event types were set as risk classes, then analogous analysis should be carried out. We tested this using an agglomerative cluster analysis (see reference 5).

This is a statistical method used to assign multivariate entities to a few, rather than *a priori* set, categories. Some of the most used cluster analysis techniques are:

- *hierarchical analysis*, where each class belongs to a different, larger one;
- *non-hierarchical analysis*, in which non-hierarchical groups are created, and therefore the number of groups must be decided beforehand.

A cluster hierarchical analysis can be carried out by applying one of several techniques; one of the most used is the agglomerative, where one sets at the beginning each element as a single risk class and after $n - 1$ subsequent aggregations, a unique cluster is obtained. A metric that measures the differences (i.e. the dissimilarities) between the elements is applied.

The metric we use to calculate the dissimilarities between the generic i and j elements is:

$$d(i, j) = 1 - pv(i, j) \tag{3.8}$$

where $pv(i, j)$ represents the p-value of the Kolmogorov–Smirnov test applied to the samples i and j. This test, in its two-sample version, analyzes whether two samples belong to the same probability distribution function, testing the hypotheses:

- $H_0 : F_1(x) = F_2(x) \, \forall x$
- $H_1 : F_1(x) \neq F_2(x)$ for at least one value of x.

The Kolmogorov–Smirnov two-sample test applies the statistic $T = \sup_x |F_1(x) - F_2(x)|$, which is the maximum vertical distance between the two distributions.

Applying the agglomerative algorithm, in each of the $n - 1$ iterations, the distances between the residual clusters are determined and clusters presenting the minimum value are combined to form one larger cluster. Distances are calculated among clusters applying the *group average method*, where the distance between two clusters is the average of the dissimilarities between the elements in one cluster and the elements in the other. For example, if we have a cluster composed of the cells BL1/ET2 and BL4/ET2, and another cluster including the cells BL3/ET2 and BL2/ET2, the distance between these two is obtained as:

$$\begin{aligned} & d((\text{BL1/ET2}, \text{BL4/ET2}); (\text{BL3/ET2}, \text{BL2/ET2})) \\ & = \frac{1}{4} d((\text{BL1/ET2}, \text{BL3/ET2}) + d(\text{BL1/ET2}, \text{BL2/ET2}) \\ & \quad + d(\text{BL4/ET2}, \text{BL3/ET2}) + d(\text{BL4/ET2}, \text{BL2/ET2})) \end{aligned}$$

Analysis results can be graphically represented by trees, as shown in Figure 3.2.

In order to choose between business lines and event types, we have to test the level of aggregation of BL × ET, for all the business lines and the event types;

1. Business lines are considered as risk classes. The aim is to determine the level of total aggregation of the cells 'business line/event type' that form each single business line.
2. Event types are considered as risk classes. The aim is to determine the level of aggregation of the cells 'business line/event type' for each event type.

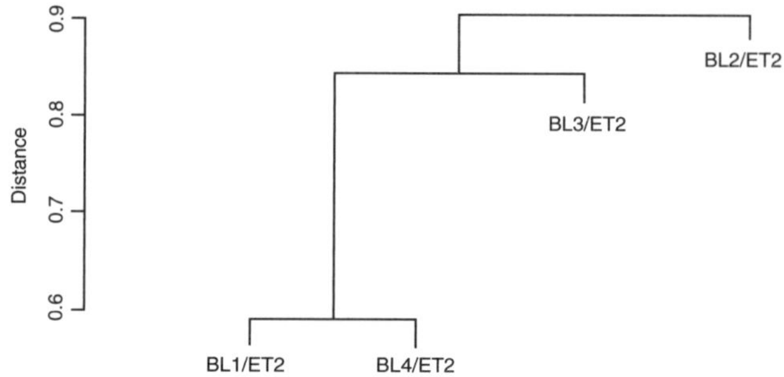

Figure 3.2 Aggregation of cells BL/ET inside the class 'External fraud'

We obtained the distance levels of complete aggregation for event types $(d_1^{\text{et}}, \ldots, d_7^{\text{et}})$ and for business lines $(d_1^{\text{bl}}, \ldots, d_8^{\text{bl}})$. Once these values are calculated, a criterion to get the best risk class is defined. We compare the maximum among the distances obtained for the event type aggregations and the maximum among the distances obtained for the business line aggregations.

Finally, the event type classification will be chosen if:

$$\max(d_1^{\text{et}}, \ldots, d_7^{\text{et}}) < \max(d_1^{\text{bl}}, \ldots, d_8^{\text{bl}}). \tag{3.9}$$

Vice versa, the business lines are selected.

3.3.2 Inflation Adjustment

In order to assure data homogeneity, we consider effects of inflation. Considering inflation effects, all available data can be included and compared. But it should be considered for a sound calculation dataset set-up. Every loss amount included in the calculation dataset can be adjusted for inflation applying a yearly CPI (consumer price index). The accounting date is recommended as the reference date for the adjustment. If this is unavailable, the event occurrence or observation date could do as a proxy. The inflation adjustment can be calculated as:

$$A_{\text{adjusted}} = A \cdot \frac{\text{CPI}(Y_{\text{RD}})}{\text{CPI}(Y_{\text{AD}})} \tag{3.10}$$

where

A is the original amount of the loss;

A_{adjusted} is the inflation-adjusted loss amount;

Y_{RD} is the reference date year (i.e. last year of the observation period);

Y_{AD} is the accounting date year;

$\mathrm{CPI}(Y_{\mathrm{RD}})$ is the value of CPI referenced to the year Y_{RD};

$\mathrm{CPI}(Y_{\mathrm{AD}})$ is the value of CPI referenced to the year Y_{AD}.

We consider a yearly CPI but, alternatively, the index could be applied on a monthly basis for a more granular adjustment.

3.3.3 Data Independence

Once the data homogeneity of risk classes has been verified, the operational risk manager should proceed to check data independence. The degree of dependence within a class is assessed. In operational risk, this is also called *implicit correlation*, not to be confused with the dependency amongst different classes, the *explicit correlation*. It is interesting to note that, intuitively, dependency within a risk class is higher than dependency amongst different classes, as loss data in the same category are clearly more similar and originated by the same event types. Research literature and banking regulators assign higher weights to dependency between different classes.

A commonly used method to check data independence are the autocorrelation plots. Autocorrelation (or serial correlation) measures how much each observation is correlated to previous ones. Let $x_1, \ldots, x_n$ be a sample of losses, seen as realizations of random variables $X_1, \ldots, X_n$, increasing in order by date, with mean μ and variance σ^2. The autocovariance function of $x_i, i = 1, \ldots, n$ at lag k is defined as:

$$\gamma(k) = \mathbb{E}(X_i - \mu)(x_{i+k} - \mu) \tag{3.11}$$

The autocorrelation function at lag k is defined as the standardized version of the autocovariance function:

$$\rho(k) = \frac{\gamma(k)}{\gamma(0)} = \frac{\gamma(k)}{\sigma} \tag{3.12}$$

The autocovariance function estimate at lag k is:

$$\hat{\gamma}(k) = \frac{1}{n} \sum_{i=1}^{n-k} (x_1 - \bar{x})(x_{i+k} - \bar{x}) \tag{3.13}$$

where:

$$\bar{x} = \frac{1}{n}\sum_{i=1}^{n} x_i \tag{3.14}$$

is the sample mean.

The autocorrelation function estimate at lag k is:

$$\hat{\rho}(k) = \frac{\hat{\gamma}(k)}{\hat{\gamma}(0)} \tag{3.15}$$

Usually, the analysis of autocorrelation is graphically supported. The autocorrelation plot function is built by plotting the autocorrelation estimates for the lags $k = 1, \ldots, M$, which is:

$$\{(k, \hat{\rho}(k)) : k = 1, \ldots, M\} \tag{3.16}$$

Clearly we obtain $\hat{\rho}(0) = 1$, this being the correlation of a loss sample with itself. If losses $x_1, \ldots, x_n$ are independent, $\hat{\rho}(k) = 0$ for $k = 1, \ldots, M$, whereas if the losses are dependent, $\hat{\rho}(k)$ for $k = 1, \ldots, M$ is significantly different from zero.

Figure 3.3 shows an example of an autocorrelation plot analysis. The horizontal band around zero represents the 95% confidence limits for

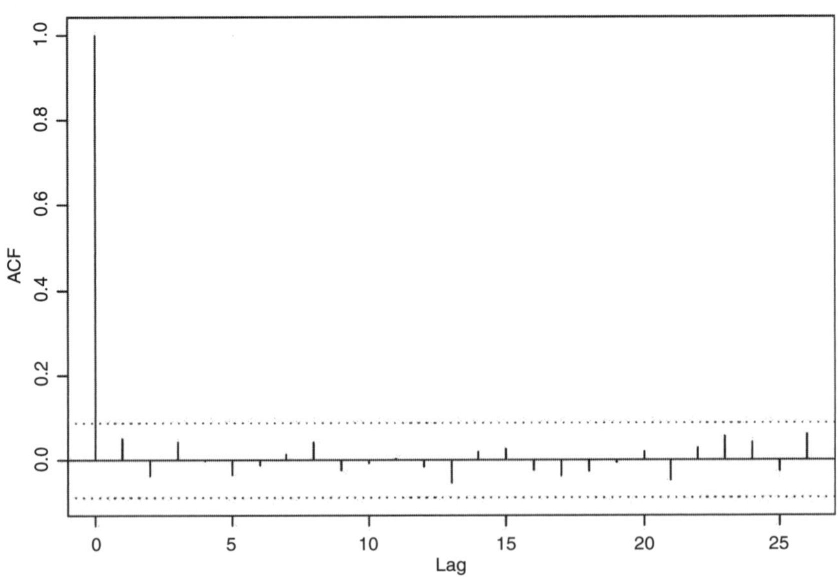

Figure 3.3 Example of autocorrelation analysis

the hypothesis $H_0 : \rho = 0$. If no autocorrelation estimate falls outside the confidence interval defined by the two dotted lines in Figure 3.3, we assume that there is no serial correlation.

In our test, we created such plots for loss data ordered by date for each risk class. For cases where loss data present a high level of autocorrelation for specific lags, a qualitative analysis is necessary. If there is cross-dependence for some operational events, these will be aggregated into a single gross loss to comply with regulations.

Once completed, we have verified the independent identical distribution condition and can now proceed to the actual loss distribution modeling.

3.4 PARAMETRIC ESTIMATION AND GOODNESS-OF-FIT TECHNIQUES

Once the correct risk classes are identified, we shall determine which statistical distributions best describe the severity and frequency of each individual risk class identified. We describe the parametric estimation techniques that we use to model loss data, and goodness-of-fit methods to select the appropriate distribution.

3.4.1 Severity Distributions

Losses $x_1, \ldots, x_n$ are seen as realizations of independent and identically distributed (i.i.d.) random variables $X_1, \ldots, X_n$.

The severity is represented as a continuous random variable X, and it can be described with a probability density function $f_X(x, \theta)$ where θ is the parameter or the vector of parameters.

In order to estimate parameters, the maximum likelihood method is applied. The likelihood function is defined as:

$$L(x_1, \ldots, x_n, \theta) = \prod_{i=1}^{n} f(x_i, \theta) \tag{3.17}$$

This is the probability that, given a certain value for the parameter θ, the realizations $x_1, \ldots, x_n$ of the random variables $X_1, \ldots, X_n$ occurred. The maximum likelihood estimator, $\hat{\theta}$, maximizes the likelihood function. It verifies that:

$$\frac{\partial L(x_1, \ldots, x_n, \theta)}{\partial \theta} = 0 \tag{3.18}$$

Once the values $x_1, \ldots, x_n$ are set, the maximum likelihood estimator, $\hat{\theta}$, maximizes the probability of that realization. The log-likelihood function could also be considered:

$$\ln L(x_1, \ldots, x_n, \theta) = \ln \prod_{i=1}^{n} f(x_i, \theta) = \sum_{i=1}^{n} \ln f(x_i, \theta) \qquad (3.19)$$

Hence:

$$\frac{\partial \ln L(x_1, \ldots, x_n, \theta)}{\partial \theta} = \frac{\partial}{\partial \theta} \ln \prod_{i=1}^{n} f(x_i, \theta) = \frac{\partial}{\partial \theta} \sum_{i=1}^{n} \ln f(x_i, \theta) = 0 \qquad (3.20)$$

As in banks operational losses are typically reported only above a minimum threshold H, a conditioned density function $f_X^*(x, \theta)$ must be considered to avoid or minimize the risk of biased estimates:

$$\begin{aligned} f^*(x, \theta) = f(x, \theta | x \geq H) &= \frac{f(x, \theta)}{1 - \mathbb{P}(x \leq H)} \\ &= \frac{f(x, \theta)}{1 - F(H, \theta)}, \quad x \geq H \end{aligned} \qquad (3.21)$$

where

θ is the parameter or the vector of parameters;

H is the threshold;

$f(x, \theta)$ is the probability density function;

$F(x, \theta) = \mathbb{P}(X \leq x)$ is the probability distribution function.

The log-likelihood function is

$$l(\theta) = \sum_{i=1}^{n} \ln(f^*(x_i, \theta))$$

The parameters are obtained by maximizing l:

$$\hat{\theta} = \frac{\arg\max l(\theta)}{\theta} \qquad (3.22)$$

Usually, the maximum likelihood estimation does not have a closed form, especially if truncation is applied. Parameter estimates are obtained by applying numerical methods.

Our modelling technique considers a set of distributions including those listed in Table 3.1 (a detailed description, including properties and best application, is provided in reference 6 on page 193). Even if,

Table 3.1 Probability distribution list

Name of distribution	Density function
Lognormal (μ, σ)	$f(x;\mu,\sigma) = \frac{1}{x\sigma\sqrt{2\pi}} \exp\left(-\frac{(\ln(x)-\mu)^2}{2\sigma^2}\right)$
Exponential (θ)	$f(x;\theta) = \theta \exp(-\theta x)$
Pareto (α, θ)	$f(x;\alpha,\theta) = \frac{\alpha\theta^\alpha}{(x+\theta)^{\alpha+1}}$
Weibull (θ, τ)	$f(x;\theta,\tau) = \frac{\tau(x/\theta)^\tau \exp(-(x/\theta)^\tau)}{x}$
Gamma (α, θ)	$f(x;\alpha,\theta) = \frac{(x/\theta)^\alpha \exp(-x/\theta)}{x\Gamma(\alpha)}$
Loglogistic (γ, θ)	$f(x;\gamma,\theta) = \frac{\gamma(x/\theta)^\gamma}{x[1+(x/\theta)^\gamma]}$

from exercises performed over many years, we noted that the lognormal distribution is the one distribution showing the most satisfactory results in almost all cases (see Figure 3.4), we strongly believe it is necessary to test many distributions each time. In verifying the available distributions we consider both graphical methods and analytical methods: greatest attention is directed towards the graphical methods, which allow a better understanding of the behavior.

Bearing these in mind, we can argue that, in performing a best-fit analysis, a purely automated solution cannot be implemented.

From the distributions listed in Table 3.1, the Pareto provides the heaviest tail, the Weibull has the thinnest tail; the lognormal, exponential, and gamma all show a medium-sized tail shape.

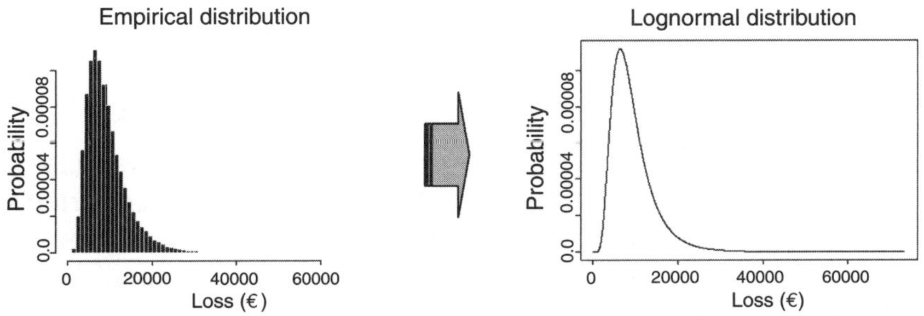

Figure 3.4 Example of parametric estimation

3.4.2 Graphical Methods

One of the most common graphical methods is the quantile–quantile plot or q–q plot. This allows observation of the goodness of fit on the tail of the distribution and a graphical comparison between empirical and estimated quantiles. Given the sorted sample of losses $x_{(1)} \leq x_{(2)} \leq \ldots x_{(n)}$, a graph is built by plotting the following points:

$$\left\{\left(x_{(i)}, F^{-1}\left(\frac{i}{n+1}\right)\right) : i = 1, \ldots, n\right\}$$

If the points are near the bisettrix, then the fit can be considered satisfactory. If loss data are collected only over a minimum threshold H, the points are:

$$\left\{\left(x_{(i)}, F^{*^{-1}}\left(\frac{i}{n+1}\right)\right) : i = 1, \ldots, n\right\} \tag{3.23}$$

where:

$$F^*(x) = \begin{cases} \dfrac{F(x) - F(H)}{1 - F(H)}, & x \geq H \\ 0, & x < H \end{cases}$$

is the truncated probability distribution function, while:

$$F^{*^{-1}}(p) = F^{-1}(p(1 - F(H)) + F(H)), \quad 0 \leq p \leq 1 \tag{3.24}$$

is the truncated quantile function.

A q–q plot is a very useful means of assessing the goodness of fit in the tail region. Consider the example in Figure 3.5. The distribution seems to adequately fit the data apart from the two biggest points, which are slightly overestimated.

Similarly, the probability–probability plot (p–p plot) compares the probabilities; in this case the following points will be plotted:

$$\left\{\left(\frac{i}{n+1}, F(x_i)\right) : i = 1, \ldots, n\right\} \tag{3.25}$$

3.4.3 Analytical Methods

Analytical methods are statistical tests of goodness of fit, like those defined by Kolmogorov–Smirnov and Anderson–Darling.[2] Supposing

[2] Other goodness-of-fit tests are Cramer–von Mises and Kuiper.

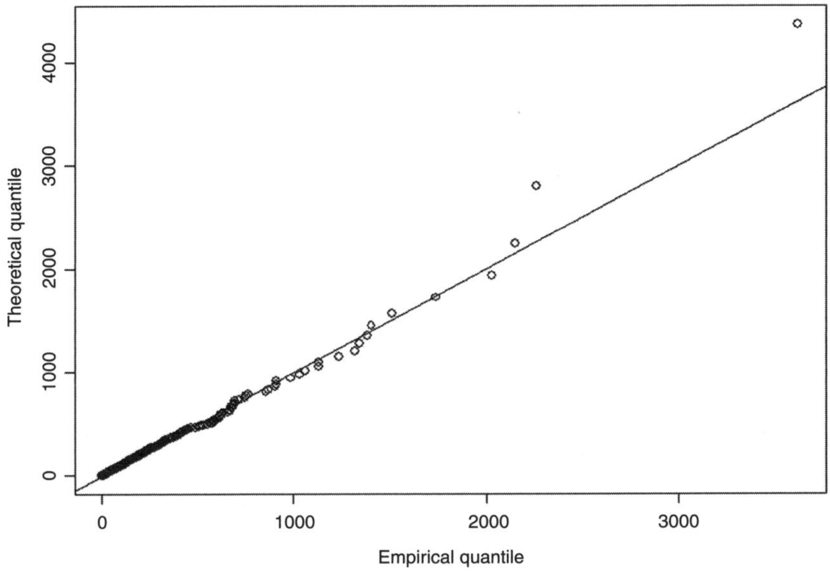

Figure 3.5 Example of a q–q plot

that the sample $x_1, \ldots, x_n$ is a realization of a set of random variables i.i.d. with probability distribution function $F(x)$, then the following hypotheses are tested:

H_0: sample follows the distribution $F(x)$;
H_1: sample does not follow the distribution $F(x)$.

The statistic of the test is a measure of the distance between empirical and estimated probability distribution functions: the lower the value of the result statistic, the better the fit.

Kolmogorov–Smirnov Test

The test statistic of Kolmogorov–Smirnov is:

$$D = \max_{1 \leq i \leq n} \left| F(x_i) - \frac{i}{n} \right| \tag{3.26}$$

where $x_1 \leq x_1 \leq \ldots \leq x_n$ is the sorted sample. It is a measure of the maximal difference between the empirical and theoretical distribution functions.

Anderson–Darling Test

The test statistic of Anderson–Darling is:

$$A^2 = n \int_{-\infty}^{+\infty} \frac{[F_n(x) - F(x)]^2}{[F(x)(1 - F(x))]} \mathrm{d}F(x) \tag{3.27}$$

where

$F(x)$ is the theoretical distribution function;

$F_n(x_i) = \dfrac{n - i + 0.5}{n}$ is the empirical distribution function.

The calculation formula for the Anderson–Darling test statistic is as follows:

$$A^2 = -n - \sum_{i=1}^{n} \frac{(2i - 1)}{n} [\ln F(x_i) + \ln(1 - F(x_{n+1-i}))] \tag{3.28}$$

where $x_1 \leq x_2 \leq \ldots \leq x_n$ is the sorted sample.

If loss data are truncated over a minimum threshold H, the probability distribution function F is replaced by the truncated distribution function F^*.

We found the Anderson–Darling to be more useful than the Kolmogorov–Smirnov, as it gives a higher weight to the tail of a distribution.

p-value Calculation

For each test, the p-value is calculated; the value (1 − (p-value)) is the maximum confidence level for which it is possible to reject the null hypothesis. Then the p-value is maximized.

The null hypothesis is rejected if the p-value is lower than the level α, usually from 5% to 10%. If D is the observed value of a goodness-of-fit statistic (such as Kolmogorov–Smirnov or Anderson–Darling) and d is the critical value for a given level, then the p-value is computed as p-value $= \mathbb{P}(D \geq d)$.

A possible alternative for computing the p-value and the critical values would be to perform Monte Carlo simulation for every hypothesized distribution: the observed value D is thus computed. Then, for a given level α, the steps listed below are carried out:

1. We generate a large number of samples (e.g. $I = 1000$) from the fitted truncated distribution of size n equal to the number of observed data (such that all these points are above or equal to H).
2. We fit the truncated distribution and estimate conditional parameters for each sample $i = 1, \ldots, I$.
3. We estimate the goodness-of-fit statistic value for each sample $i = 1, \ldots, I$.
4. We calculate the p-value as the proportion of the number of times the sample statistic values exceed the observed value D of the original sample.
5. We reject H_0 if the p-value $< \alpha$.

A p-value of, for example, 0.3 implies that the test statistic value was higher than in the original sample in 30% of similar sized samples obtained from simulation applied to the very same distribution and using an identical parameter estimation procedure.

The Schwarz Bayesian Criterion

There is an alternative approach to the formal hypothesis test, for comparing the goodness of fit given by several distributions: methods applying the likelihood value and then adjusting it to take into account the sample size and the number of parameters.

The Schwarz Bayesian Criterion (SBC):

$$SBC = NLL + r \cdot \ln(n/2\pi) \tag{3.29}$$

applies the negative logarithm of the likelihood function, NLL, and adds $r \cdot \ln(n/2\pi)$, where r is the number of estimated parameters and n is the sample size. Accordingly, the best model will have the smallest SBC value. We note that, as the sample size increases, the penalty for an extra parameter also increases. With a large sample it should be possible to correctly estimate a few more parameters, justifying a more complex solution. Hypothesis tests become more powerful as the sample size increases and alternative hypotheses tend to be selected even if they are only slightly more accurate descriptions of the population. For models with similar numbers of parameters, the one with the smallest negative loglikelihood will be prefered.

3.4.4 Frequency Distributions

The annual loss frequency can be represented with a positive and discrete random variable N with probability mass function denoted with p and probability distribution function P. Several distributions can be used to model the frequency of operational losses, in particular the Poisson, geometric, binomial, and hypergeometric distributions. Among these distributions, the Poisson distribution is the most commonly used.

A random discrete variable N is defined as a Poisson variable with parameter λ, and is written as $N \sim \text{Po}(\lambda)$, when the following probability distribution function applies:

$$\mathbb{P}(N = n) = p_n = \mathrm{e}^{-\lambda}\frac{\lambda^n}{n!} \quad n = 0, 1, 2, \ldots \tag{3.30}$$

The sample estimation of the Poisson distribution parameter (λ_{sample}) is given by the empirical mean of the annual loss number, considering losses whose values are greater than or equal to the minimum threshold H:

$$\hat{\lambda}_{\text{sample}} = \frac{1}{t}\sum_{i=1}^{n} n_i \tag{3.31}$$

where

n_i is the number of losses that occurred in the year i;

t is the length of the observation period, measured in years.

As with severity, the frequency distribution is affected by reporting bias if only losses above a certain threshold are considered. If, for some bank, the reporting cut-off is set at a high level, then the average number of reported events will be low. This simply means that the average number of events must be corrected for reporting bias as well.

Adjustment of the frequency distribution for reporting bias forms a further analysis after adjusting the severity distribution.

If only losses above a threshold H are included, then estimates will have a bias and a correction is needed. The relationship between the estimate of the sample and the real dataset is given by the probability of obtaining a loss higher than the observed threshold. The frequency parameter is adjusted to obtain the estimate considering the whole range of positive losses:

$$\hat{\lambda} = \frac{\hat{\lambda}_{\text{sample}}}{\mathbb{P}(X > H)} = \frac{\hat{\lambda}_{\text{sample}}}{1 - F(H)} \tag{3.32}$$

where

$\hat{\lambda}$ is the estimate of the Poisson distribution parameter for the whole range of positive losses ($x > 0$);

$\hat{\lambda}_{\text{sample}}$ is the sample estimate of the Poisson distribution parameter ($x > H$);

F is the probability distribution function of severity.

The use of the Poisson distribution can be explained as it requires the estimate of only one parameter and has an equal mean and variance. However, this distribution has some limitations as it assumes a constant rate of loss occurrence over time. In reality, the frequency of operational losses is not constant and the negative binomial distribution could be used to model the frequency of operational losses. This distribution is a generalization of the Poisson process and it requires the estimate of two parameters, allowing flexibility in the shape of the distribution compared to the Poisson. Results of empirical studies on the quantification of operational risk (see references 7 and 3 on page 193) have shown that the negative binomial distribution provides a good fit to the frequency of operational losses. The negative binomial distribution has the following probability mass function:

$$p(n; \alpha, \beta) = \binom{n + \alpha - 1}{n} \left(\frac{1}{1+\beta}\right)^{\alpha} \left(\frac{\beta}{1+\beta}\right)^{n} \quad n = 0, 1, 2, \ldots \tag{3.33}$$

where $\alpha > 0$ and $\beta > 0$. The maximum likelihood of parameters can be obtained by solving the following system of equations:

$$\begin{cases} \alpha\beta = \mu_{\text{sample}} \\ \alpha\beta(1 + \beta) = \sigma^2_{\text{sample}} \end{cases}$$

where μ_{sample} and σ^2_{sample} are the empirical mean and the variance respectively.

Also for the negative binomial distribution, when just losses above a threshold H are included, then estimates need adjusting for reporting bias. Parameters are given by the following system of equations:

$$\begin{cases} \alpha\beta = \dfrac{\mu_{\text{sample}}}{1 - F(H)} \\ \alpha\beta(1+\beta) = \dfrac{\sigma^2_{\text{sample}}}{(1 - F(H))^2} \end{cases}$$

where F is the probability distribution function of severity.

3.5 APPLYING EXTREME VALUE THEORY

When modelling operational loss severity, it is very hard to find a distribution to adequately fit data for low and high values. The operational risk losses dataset includes two distinct parts: high-frequency and low-impact losses, the body of the distribution; low-frequency and high-impact losses, the tail of the distribution.

These two subsets will need different distributions for appropriate fitting and robust results. Techniques from *Extreme Value Theory (EVT)* are thus applied in our model (Figure 3.6).

Given a threshold u, the data above this value are defined as extreme. Let X be a random value with distribution function F. The conditional distribution will be:

$$F_u(y) = \mathbb{P}(X - u \leq y | X > u) \tag{3.34}$$

This is the excess distribution function of value X above threshold u.

For a wide range of distribution classes F, the limit distribution $(u \to \infty)$ of the excess distribution function will be identified by the

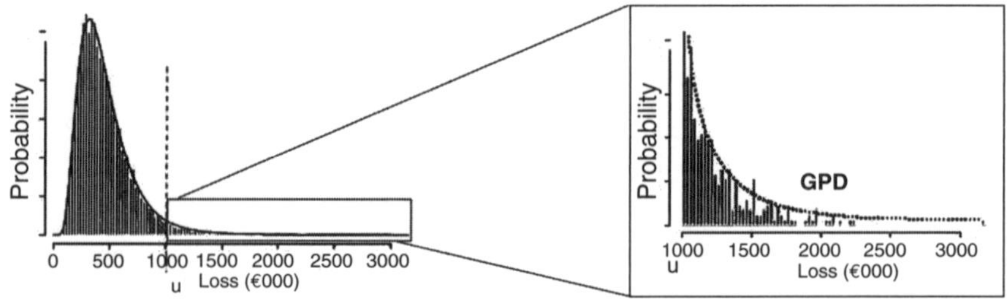

Figure 3.6 Extreme value theory

following distribution,[3] called the generalized Pareto distribution (GPD):

$$G_{\xi,\beta(y)} = \begin{cases} 1 - \left(1 + \xi \dfrac{y}{\beta}\right)^{-\frac{1}{\xi}}, & \text{if } \xi \neq 0; \\ 1 - \exp\left(-\dfrac{y}{\beta}\right), & \text{if } \xi = 0. \end{cases} \tag{3.35}$$

where $y \geq 0$ if $\xi \geq 0$ and $0 \leq y \leq -\beta/\xi$ if $\xi < 0$.

$\xi \in \mathbb{R}$ and $\beta > 0$ are the respective shape and scale parameters. If $\xi > 0$, the distribution will behave as a fat tail; that is, the tail of the distribution decays slower than the exponential one.[4]

As X has been defined as $X = u + y$, the GPD can be defined in terms of X, i.e.:

$$G_{\xi,\beta}(x - u) = 1 - \left(1 + \xi \frac{x - u}{\beta}\right)^{-\frac{1}{\xi}} \tag{3.36}$$

Considering the definition of conditional probability, the excess distribution function $F_u(y)$ will be:

$$F_u(y) = \frac{F(y + u) - F(u)}{1 - F(u)} \tag{3.37}$$

The tail of the distribution of X can be defined as follows:

$$F(x) \cong (1 - F(u))\, G_{\xi,\beta}(x - u) + F(u), x > u \tag{3.38}$$

For the high threshold u, $F(u)$ can be determined with an empirical estimator[5] $(n - N_u)/n$, where N_u is the number of extreme data points and n is the sample size.

The tail estimator is therefore:

$$\hat{F}(x) = 1 - \frac{N_u}{n}\left(1 + \xi \frac{x - u}{\beta}\right)^{-\frac{1}{\xi}} \quad \text{for} \quad x > u \tag{3.39}$$

For a given probability $q > F(u)$, the percentile $\hat{F}^{-1}(q)$ the tail can be obtained inverting the tail estimator:

$$\hat{F}^{-1}(q) = u + \frac{\beta}{\xi}\left[\left(\frac{n}{N}(1 - q)\right)^{-\xi} - 1\right] \tag{3.40}$$

---

[3] From the theorem of Pickands, Balkema and de Haan.

[4] Typically, this is the case for operational loss data.

[5] Or through a parametric estimate (e.g. lognormal).

Once the threshold u is defined, the GPD parameters are estimated on the data falling above the threshold. A common method for GPD parameter estimation is the maximum likelihood.

The GPD has the following density function:

$$g_{\xi,\beta}(y) = \begin{cases} \dfrac{1}{\beta}\left(1+\xi\dfrac{y}{\beta}\right)^{-\frac{1}{\xi}-1}, & \text{if } \xi \neq 0 \\ \dfrac{1}{\beta}\exp\left(-\dfrac{y}{\beta}\right), & \text{otherwise.} \end{cases} \tag{3.41}$$

Having defined $y_1, \ldots, y_{N_u}$ as the excess data above the threshold, the log-likelihood function will be:

$$l(\xi, \beta) = \sum_{i=1}^{N_u} \ln\left(g_{\xi,\beta}(y_i)\right) \tag{3.42}$$

allowing us to obtain the estimate of the parameters:

$$\left(\hat{\xi}, \hat{\beta}\right) = \arg\max_{\xi,\beta} l\left(\xi, \beta\right) \tag{3.43}$$

The choice of the threshold is fundamental as it defines:

- the quantity of data to be modeled;
- the quality of the data above the threshold.

A low threshold will include a relevant number of data, but does not ensure these data are extreme; a high threshold guarantees more data are effectively extreme, but a lower number reduces the quality of estimates, thus increasing variance.

We choose the threshold u using graphical analysis: the random excess-data mean approach. The random excess-data mean function $e(u)$ is analytically represented as:

$$e(u) = \mathbb{E}(X - u | X > u) \tag{3.44}$$

and is empirically estimated as the ratio between the sum of the excess data above threshold u and the number of excess data points:

$$e(u) = \frac{1}{N_u}\sum_{i=1}^{N_u} y_i \tag{3.45}$$

If the plot of the empirical mean excess function seems to traces a straight line above a value for u, the excess data above the threshold are

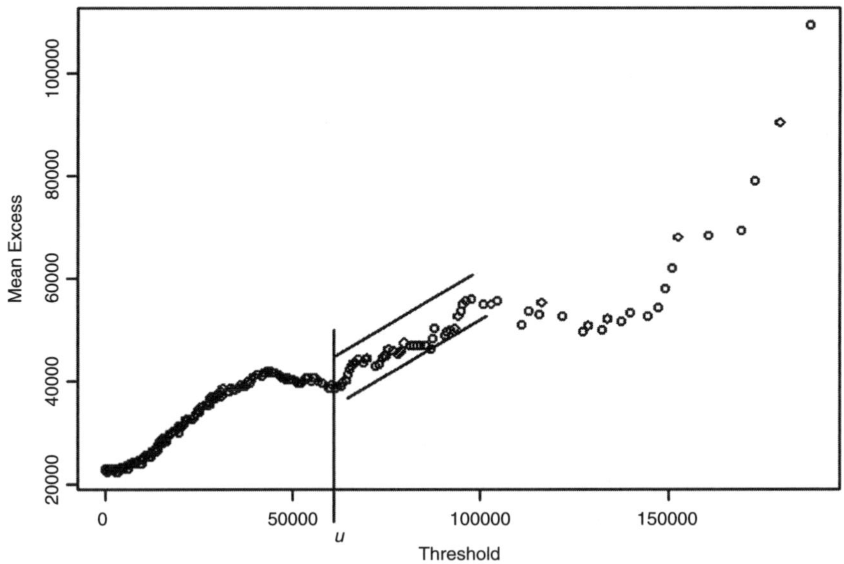

Figure 3.7 Threshold analysis through the mean excess function

distributed like a GPD (see the example in Figure 3.7). We know this can be a critical choice. In our experience, the analysis of the same plot, performed by different analysts, can result in different values u.

If the distribution behaves like a GPD with shape parameter ξ and scale parameter β, then the mean excess function will be a linear function of the threshold:

$$e(u) = \frac{\beta + \xi u}{1 - \xi} \tag{3.46}$$

If the line has a positive slope, then the GPD will have a positive shape parameter. If the line is flat, the distribution is exponential. Once the parameters for the shape and scale of the GPD are found, further graphical analysis is used to confirm the soundness of the threshold, testing the stability of the shape parameter varying the threshold.

3.6 *g-and-h* DISTRIBUTION THEORY

We looked at an alternative distribution named *g-and-h* for operational loss data modeling (see references 8, 9 and 10 on page 193).

The *g-and-h* distribution was defined for the first time by Tukey (see references 11 on page 193).

Let $Z \sim N(0, 1)$ be a standardized normal random variable. The transformation:

$$X = A + B\frac{e^{gZ} - 1}{g}e^{\frac{1}{2}hZ^2} \quad (A, B, g, h \in \mathbb{R}) \tag{3.47}$$

generates a random variable X that has a *g-and-h* distribution.

The random variable X has support on $\mathbb{R}$, and so it allows both positive and negative values. In particular, if $h = 0$, the transformation for the *g-and-h* is:

$$X = A + B\frac{e^{gZ} - 1}{g} \tag{3.48}$$

and X assumes the g distribution. In the same way, if $g = 0$, the transformation for the *g-and-h* is:

$$X = A + Be^{\frac{1}{2}hZ^2} \tag{3.49}$$

and X adopts the h distribution.

When $g = 0$ and $h = 0$, the random variable X follows the distribution of the standardized normal random variable.

The parameters A and B are less critical in the characterization of the *g-and-h* distribution because they are a simple component of linear transformation.

As the *g-and-h* is a function of four parameters, it allows many distributional forms, including the GPD.

An important characteristic of *g-and-h* is that the function:

$$k(x) = \frac{e^{gx} - 1}{g}e^{\frac{1}{2}hx^2} \tag{3.50}$$

increases for $h > 0$; so, the probability distribution function of a random variable X is a *g-and-h* and we can write:

$$F(x) = \Phi(k^{-1}(x)) \tag{3.51}$$

where Φ is the probability distribution function of a standardized normal random variable.

Assuming the properties listed above apply, if the parameters $A, B, g \in \mathbb{R}$ and $h \in \mathbb{R}^+$ are known, in theory it's possible to calculate the quantile, α, of the distribution, as:

$$q_\alpha = F^{-1}(\alpha) = k(\Phi^{-1}(\alpha)), \quad 0 < \alpha < 1 \tag{3.52}$$

The main hurdle in the analysis of such distribution is the huge computational complexity of the cumulative distribution function of the *g-and-h*. The function $k^{-1}(x)$ in fact does not have an explicit form.

It's possible to calculate $k^{-1}(x)$ using a numerical optimization that, given X, minimizes the function of Z:

$$w(Z) = \left| X - \left(A + B \frac{e^{gZ} - 1}{g} e^{\frac{1}{2}hZ^2} \right) \right| \tag{3.53}$$

This optimization can be carried out only when the parameters $A, B, g \in \mathbb{R}$ and $h \in \mathbb{R}^+$ are known.

As often the parameters are not known, it is necessary to implement a procedure to estimate their values.

The maximum likelihood method is not used to estimate the values of the parameters because the calculation would be very complex from a computational point of view.

In fact, the distribution function of the variable *g-and-h* can be written as:

$$\frac{\mathrm{d}F(x; A, B, g, h)}{\mathrm{d}x} = \frac{\Phi\left(k^{-1}(x; A, B, g, h)\right)}{k'\left(k^{-1}(x; A, B, g, h); A, B, g, h\right)} \tag{3.54}$$

where $k'(z)$ is the derivative with respect to z of the function $k(z)$, and A, B, g, h are the parameters of the *g-and-h* distribution.

To maximize the likelihood, we need to maximize the value:

$$L(A, B, g, h) = \prod_{i=1}^{n} \frac{\Phi\left(k^{-1}(x; A, B, g, h)\right)}{k'(k^{-1}(x; A, B, g, h); A, B, g, h)} \tag{3.55}$$

(where n is the sample size) or its logarithm. The derivative of functions, which can be computed only numerically, would be required and numerical error could be difficult to check.

We suggest minimizing the *Anderson–Darling statistic*. This is a particular case of a generic approach based on the minimization of divergence measures. The approach enables a robust, consistent, and asymtotical normal valuation of the parameters (see reference 12 on page 193).

The Anderson–Darling statistic is:

$$\mathrm{d}\,(F_n, F_\Theta) = \int_{-\infty}^{\infty} [F_n(x) - F_\Theta(x)]^2\,[F_n(x)(1 - F_\Theta(x))]^{-1}\,\mathrm{d}F_\Theta(x) \tag{3.56}$$

where F_Θ is the theoretical probability distribution function with the parameter Θ (in this case, the vector of parameters A, B, g, h), and F_n is the empirical probability distribution function evaluated on n observations.

The minimum of Equation (3.56) is calculated as the minimization of:

$$\hat{\mathrm{d}}\,(F_n, F_\Theta) = -\frac{1}{n^2}\sum_{i=1}^{n}(2i-1)\,[\ln F_\theta(x_i) + \ln(1 - F_\Theta(x_{n+1-i}))] - 1 \tag{3.57}$$

where n is the sample size and x_i is the value of the i-th ordered observation of the sample $(x_1 \leq x_2 \leq \cdots \leq x_{n-1} \leq x_n)$.

The value $\hat{\theta}$ minimizing $\hat{\mathrm{d}}(F_n, F_\Theta)$ is the estimate of parameter $\Theta = (A, B, g, h)$.

If we are interested in this procedure, we should consider the possibility of using truncated data, as observations lower than the threshold could be missing. Considering that we are not using the maximum likelihood method, truncated distributions cannot be used as described in Section 3.4. In this case, we could use shifted distributions. If we have the loss sample $x_1, x_2, \ldots, x_n$ collected over the minimum threshold $H > 0$, we apply the estimation procedure on the sample $x_1 - H$, $x_2 - H, \ldots, x_n - H$, with a threshold equal to zero. When values are simulated from the estimated shifted distribution, these will be added to H.

3.7 CALCULATING OPERATIONAL CAPITAL AT RISK

In previous sections we have looked at a general LDA framework (see Section 3.2) and some techniques used to estimate the severity distribution (see Sections 3.4, 3.5, and 3.6). Now we will present a complete practical application of LDA including EVT, as we have in our operational risk capital at risk model.

When applying a calculation method as described in Section 3.2, for each operational risk class we consider and model separately frequency and severity.

Applying the extreme value theory technique, we estimate separately the body and the tail. The body is modeled using one of the distributions shown in Table 3.1, while for the tail, we use a generalized Pareto distribution.

Just as for the severity distribution, we have to consider separately a body and a tail and apply two frequency distributions. In both cases, frequency is modeled through a Poisson distribution.

The Value at Risk (VaR) is obtained applying the Monte Carlo algorithm. In our experience, 1 000 000 simulations should be performed to obtain the distribution of the annual aggregated losses and the VaR with a sufficient level of accuracy. Increasing the number of simulations performed, we obtain an improvement in the robustness of the results. But increasing the number of simulations also increases the computational time. We performed tests on the robustness of results and we think that 1 000 000 can be considered a minimum number to obtain sufficiently accurate results at the required confidence level. The VaR is calculated as the 99.9% quantile of the resulting distribution, as prescribed in the new Basel capital accord for advanced model approaches (see reference 2). We apply it in its standard form to all the chosen risk classes not covered (or only partially covered) by insurance policies. For risk classes hedged instead by insurance, mitigating effects are considered when performing Monte Carlo simulations (see Section 3.8).

Once obtained the capital at risk, we adjust to take into account the operational business environment and internal control factors (see Section 3.9 on the key risk indicators): we calculate a scaling coefficient and apply it to the VaR. In our model the scaling coefficient allows to correct the VaR according to risk indicators trends.

Once the VaR and the annual loss distribution for each risk class are obtained, we calculate the overall capital:

- summing up the values already obtained – that is, to assume that risk classes are perfectly dependent and comonotone; or
- using copula-based methods (see Section 3.10), taking into account diversification effects.

We strongly believe the second option is the best: taking into consideration diversification effects enables a better description of the bank's risk exposure.

3.7.1 Loss Severity Distribution

The severity distribution is the probability distribution function of an individual loss amount. Applying EVT, the severity is obtained estimating separately the distribution's body below threshold u and the tail of the distribution above threshold. We estimate the body of the distribution by considering only internal loss data, while estimating the tail we consider internal, external, and scenario-generated data. For losses lower than u, we use a parametric approach; for losses higher than the threshold, extreme value theory (EVT) is applied. We set the threshold at the value resulting from balancing data homogeneity of different data sources and availability, also applying the graphical techniques explained in Section 3.5. The density function of severity random variable X is then:

$$f_X(x) = \begin{cases} \omega \cdot f^*_{\text{body}}(x), & x < u \\ (1-\omega) \cdot f^*_{\text{tail}}(x) & x \geq u \end{cases}$$

where

$f^*_{\text{body}}(x) = \dfrac{f_{\text{body}}(x)}{F_{\text{body}}(u)}$ is the probability density function of the body distribution truncated under threshold u;

$f^*_{\text{tail}}(x) = \dfrac{f_{\text{tail}}(x)}{1 - F_{\text{tail}}(u)}$ is the probability density function of the tail distribution truncated over threshold u;

$\omega, 1-\omega$ are the weights of the body and the tail of the severity distribution.

We define $\omega = F_{\text{body}}(u)$.

Body Distribution

We believe that the body of the severity distribution must be estimated using only internal data: this way, the result will be as risk sensitive as possible. We know that there may not be enough data available, but we decided not to include external data in modeling the body of the loss severity distribution. This issue doesn't concern a relevant international bank like UniCredit so we decided not to include external data in the modeling of the body distribution.

As mentioned before, we regularly test the distributions listed in Table 3.1 and when choosing the distribution for single risk classes we take into account goodness-of-fit results, properties of distributions, and reasonableness of capital figures. Based on our experience, the lognormal distribution seems the best in almost all cases.

We estimate the parameters with maximum likelihood technique conditioned to truncation over minimum threshold, H, of the operational losses. The probability density function conditioned to truncation is the following (see Equation 3.21):

$$f_X^*(x, \theta) = f(x, \theta | x \geq H) = \frac{f(x, \theta)}{1 - \mathbb{P}(x \leq H)} = \frac{f(x, \theta)}{1 - F(H, \theta)}, \quad x \geq H \tag{3.58}$$

where

θ is the vector including the parameters of the distribution (e.g. lognormal $\theta = (\mu, \sigma)$);

H is the minimum threshold and $f(x, \theta)$ is the probability density function.

In case of lognormal distribution, we get:

$$f(x, \theta) = f_{\mathrm{LN}}(x; \mu, \sigma) = \frac{1}{x\sigma\sqrt{2\pi}} \exp\left(-\frac{(\ln(x) - \mu)^2}{2\sigma^2}\right) \tag{3.59}$$

Proceeding as described in Section 3.4 and given the losses $x_1, \ldots, x_n$, the log-likelihood function is:

$$l(\theta) = \sum_{i=1}^{n} \ln\left(f^*(x_i, \theta)\right) \tag{3.60}$$

The parameter estimate is obtained through maximization of the log-likelihood function:

$$\theta = \frac{\mathrm{argmax} l(\theta)}{\theta} \tag{3.61}$$

For the lognormal distribution $\hat{\theta} = (\mu, \sigma)$ and $f_{\mathrm{body}}(x) = f_{\mathrm{LN}}(x; \mu, \sigma)$. Hence, the body of the distribution becomes:

$$f^*_{\mathrm{body}}(x) = \frac{f_{\mathrm{body}}(x)}{F_{\mathrm{body}}(u)} = \frac{f_{\mathrm{LN}}(x; \mu, \sigma)}{F_{\mathrm{LN}}(u; \mu, \sigma)} \tag{3.62}$$

Tail Distribution

The sample size of internal loss data is often not sufficient for consistent and robust estimation in the tail part; in such cases, integration with other data sources may be required: we decided to model the tail of the severity distribution by combining internal, external, and scenario-generated data.[6] A more advanced method to combine internal, external, and scenario-generated data is using Bayesian techniques (see reference 14). We used the first option because of his simplicity, however we are doing extensive research to move to the more advanced solution. The threshold value is chosen to ensure a balance between data homogeneity and availability.

Applying extreme value theory, values over a high threshold u are estimated through the generalized Pareto distribution (GPD).

The probability distribution function of loss data truncated above the threshold u is:[7]

$$G_{\xi,\mu,\beta}(x) = \begin{cases} 1 - \left(1 + \xi \dfrac{x-\mu}{\beta}\right)^{-\frac{1}{\xi}}, & \text{if } \xi = 0; \\ 1 - \exp\left(-\dfrac{x-\mu}{\beta}\right), & \text{otherwise.} \end{cases} \tag{3.63}$$

and the probability density function is:

$$g_{\xi,\mu,\beta}(x) = \begin{cases} \dfrac{1}{\beta}\left(1 + \xi \dfrac{x-\mu}{\beta}\right)^{-\frac{1}{\xi}-1}, & \text{if } \xi = 0; \\ \dfrac{1}{\beta}\exp\left(-\dfrac{x-\mu}{\beta}\right), & \text{otherwise.} \end{cases} \tag{3.64}$$

where $x \geq 0$ if $\xi \geq 0$ and $0 \leq x \leq \mu - \frac{\beta}{\xi}$ if $\xi < 0$, and where ξ and β are, respectively, the shape and scale parameters. μ is the location parameter set to the threshold u ($\hat{\mu} = u$).

The parameters of the GPD can be estimated by the maximum likelihood method (see Section 3.5).

The tail distribution results are:

$$f^*_{\text{tail}} = \frac{f_{\text{tail}}(x)}{1 - F_{\text{tail}}(u)} = \frac{g_{\xi,\mu=u,\beta}(x)}{1 - G_{\xi,\mu=u,\beta}(u)} = g_{\xi,\mu=u,\beta}(x) \tag{3.65}$$

---

[6] A trivial technique to combine internal, external, and scenario-generated data is simply mixing them into a unique sample over the same threshold. In this case, we suppose they have the same probability distribution function (see reference 13).

[7] Note that the loss amount above the threshold u is modeled by the three-parameter GPD form.

3.7.2 Loss Frequency Distribution

The frequency distribution is the probability distribution function of the number of losses in a time period of one year. The distribution is estimated using internal data, the relevant source we can use. The frequency of annual losses is assumed to follow a Poisson distribution with parameter λ: a random discrete variable N is defined as a Poisson variable with parameter λ and is written as $N \sim \text{Po}(\lambda)$, when the following probability mass function applies:

$$\mathbb{P}(N = n) = p_n = \mathrm{e}^{-\lambda}\frac{\lambda^n}{n!} \qquad n = 0, 1, 2, \ldots \tag{3.66}$$

The sample estimation of the Poisson distribution parameter (λ_{sample}) is given by the empirical mean of the annual loss number, considering losses greater than or equal to the minimum threshold H:

$$\hat{\lambda}_{\text{sample}} = \frac{1}{t}\sum_{i=1}^{n} n_i \tag{3.67}$$

where

n_i is the number of losses occurring in the year i;

t is the length of the observation period, measured in years.

As already observed in the Section 3.4.4, if only losses above threshold H are included, the estimates will be biased and a correction needed. The relationship between the estimate from the sample and real data is given by the probability of obtaining a loss higher than observed threshold. The frequency parameter is adjusted considering the whole range of positive losses:

$$\hat{\lambda} = \frac{\hat{\lambda}_{\text{sample}}}{\mathbb{P}(X > H)} = \frac{\hat{\lambda}_{\text{sample}}}{1 - F(H)} \tag{3.68}$$

where

$\hat{\lambda}$ is the estimate of the Poisson distribution parameter for the whole range of positive losses ($x > 0$);

$\hat{\lambda}_{\text{sample}}$ is the sample estimate of the Poisson distribution parameter ($x > H$);

F is the probability distribution function of severity.

As we split the severity distribution into two parts, we do likewise for frequency.[8]

Using the following property of the Poisson distribution:

$$\text{Po}(\lambda_1 + \lambda_2) = \text{Po}(\lambda_1) + \text{Po}(\lambda_2) \tag{3.69}$$

supposing that $\text{Po}(\lambda_1)$ and $\text{Po}(\lambda_2)$ are independent, parameters of frequency distributions related to each section of the severity distribution are then estimated:

$$\hat{\lambda}_{\text{body}\,(x<u)} = \hat{\lambda} \cdot \mathbb{P}(x < u) = \hat{\lambda} \cdot \omega \tag{3.70}$$

and

$$\hat{\lambda}_{\text{tail}\,(x \geq u)} = \hat{\lambda} \cdot \mathbb{P}(x \geq u) = \hat{\lambda} \cdot (1 - \omega) \tag{3.71}$$

where

$\hat{\lambda}_{\text{body}\,(x<u)}$ is the parameter of the frequency distribution of losses lower than u;

$\hat{\lambda}_{\text{tail}(x \geq u)}$ is the parameter of the frequency distribution of losses higher than u;

$\omega, 1 - \omega$ are the weights of the body and the tail of the severity distribution.

Considering that the body of the severity distribution is estimated on losses greater than or equal to the minimum threshold H, there is no evidence of the reliability of the distribution under this threshold. If $F(H)$ is near 1, we may obtain a very high value for λ and then for $\lambda_{\text{body}\,(x<u)}$: consequently the computational time for a Monte Carlo simulation to obtain the annual loss distribution (see Section 3.7.3) becomes very long. Computational time increases virtually linearly with λ.[9] According to the properties of distributions used to model operational risk, we experience a negligible impact on capital at risk given by losses simulated under the minimum threshold with (see Section 3.11 for a theoretical proof):[10] simulating losses under the minimum threshold Monte Carlo procedure is not helpful.

---

[8] This technique is not compulsory but it is useful from a computational point of view.

[9] On the basis of our experience, using a Pentium 4 3Ghz processor with 1GB RAM, computational time to perform one million Monte Carlo simulations with $\lambda = 1000$ is 380 seconds without insurance modeling. Including insurance the computational time is 510 seconds.

[10] This is a property of subexponential distributions that are typically used to model operational risk (see reference 15 on page 193 for details).

A solution is to adjust $\lambda_{\text{body}\,(x<u)}$ considering losses higher than the minimum threshold H:

$$\hat{\lambda}_{\text{body}(H \le x \le u)} = \hat{\lambda}_{\text{body}(x<u)} \cdot \frac{\mathbb{P}(H < x < u)}{\mathbb{P}(x < u)} = \hat{\lambda}_{\text{body}(x<u)} \cdot \frac{F(u) - F(H)}{F(u)} \tag{3.72}$$

In this case, the Monte Carlo simulation for the body of the severity distribution must be implemented, sampling losses between the thresholds H and u.

3.7.3 Annual Loss Distribution

The annual loss distribution is obtained through convolution. This is the distribution of total loss S in the holding time period, given by the aggregation of severities X of the single losses:

$$S = \sum_{i=1}^{N} X_i \tag{3.73}$$

The probability distribution function of random variable S is given by:

$$\begin{aligned} F_S(x) = \mathbb{P}(S \le x) &= \sum_{n=0}^{\infty} p(n) \cdot \mathbb{P}(S \le x | N = n) \\ &= \sum_{n=0}^{\infty} p(n) \cdot F_X^{*n}(x), \quad x > 0 \end{aligned} \tag{3.74}$$

where $F_X^{*n}(x)$ is the n-fold convolution of distribution function F_X of severities, as described in Section 3.2.

Bearing in mind that, usually, it's not possible to find a closed form for F_S, numerical methods are used. Some available approaches are:

- Monte Carlo method;
- Panjer's recursion;
- Fast Fourier transforms (FFT).

We implemented Monte Carlo techniques: although this option is very demanding in terms of computational time, it ensures soundness and it is easier to apply. Panjer's recursion and FFT tend to underflow or overflow for inappropriate initial setting.

Monte Carlo method proceeds by steps:

1. The number n_j of losses that occurred in the year j is estimated by sampling from the frequency distribution.
2. n_j independent realizations, representing the values of the losses that occurred in the year j, are drawn from the severity distribution.
3. The annual loss for the year j is the sum of the n_j values simulated in the previous step.

Steps 1–3 are repeated for J realizations.

The higher J, the better the accuracy of estimation. Generally, we recommend at least $J = 1\,000\,000$, but this value should be increased until $J = 10\,000\,000$ to obtain a negligible numerical sampling error.

One way of understanding the variability of results using Monte Carlo it is to repeat the procedure several times and calculate the variance of the obtained estimates. A technique to reduce variance is to calculate the final result as the average or median of estimates in repeated Monte Carlo simulations.

Once applied EVT techniques, the body and tail of the severity and frequency distributions are estimated separately. So we apply Monte Carlo to each part of the distribution. Given λ_{body} and λ_{tail} (the $\lambda_{\text{body}(H \leq x < u)}$ and $\lambda_{\text{tail}(x \geq u)}$ previously estimated), the following realizations are carried out:

$n_j^{\text{body}}\ j = 1, 2, \ldots, J$ from a Poisson distribution with parameter λ_{body}

$n_j^{\text{tail}}\ j = 1, 2, \ldots, J$ from a Poisson distribution with parameter λ_{tail}

Modeling the body of the severity distribution, for each year $j = 1, 2, \ldots, J$, n_j^{body} losses between the thresholds H and u are simulated from the estimated distribution (e.g. lognormal). J annual losses are equal to J sums of the n_j^{body} simulated losses:

$$s_j^{\text{body}} = \sum_{i=1}^{n_j^{\text{body}}} x_{ij}^{\text{body}} \qquad j = 1, 2, \ldots, J \tag{3.75}$$

where

s_j^{body} is the annual loss under the threshold in the *j*th step;

x_{ij}^{body} is the *i*th loss simulated in the *j*th step from the body of the severity distribution;

j is the number of step.

As observed in section 3.7.2, extending the parametric body distribution to values smaller than the minimum threshold could lead to implausible results for the frequencies and huge increase of the computational time, so we don't model losses below H. However, if we had a sufficiently sound data collection below the minimum threshold, we could consider these losses simply summing up their average annual value to each annual loss sampled from the body distribution. In this way, the losses below H would be considered without affecting the parameters estimation with their potential bias.

Hence, the J annual losses referred to the body region are (loss amount lower than u):

$$s_j^{\text{body}} = s_{x<H} + \sum_{i=1}^{n_j^{\text{body}}} x_{ij}^{\text{body}} \quad j = 1, 2, \ldots, J$$

where the value $s_{x<H}$ is obtained by summing over all losses that are below the minimum threshold, normalizing to the one year holding period (i.e. average annual amount).

When modeling the tail of the severity distribution, for every year $j = 1, 2, \ldots, J$, n_j^{tail} losses over threshold u are simulated from the estimated GPD. J annual losses over the threshold are equal to J sums of the simulated losses:

$$s_j^{\text{tail}} = \sum_{i=1}^{n_j^{\text{tail}}} x_{ij}^{\text{tail}} \quad j = 1, 2, \ldots, J \tag{3.76}$$

where

s_j^{body} is the annual loss under the threshold in the jth step;

x_{ij}^{body} is the ith loss simulated in the jth step from the tail of the severity distribution;

j is the number of the step.

The sum of the J annual losses under threshold s_j^{body} and over the threshold s_j^{tail} is a sample of simulated annual losses marked as a sample:

$$[s_1, s_2, \ldots, s_n] \tag{3.77}$$

where:

$$s_j = s_j^{\text{body}} + s_j^{\text{tail}}, \quad j = 1, \ldots J. \tag{3.78}$$

3.7.4 Single Class Capital at Risk

The Value at Risk of the loss distribution representing a single risk class is the quantile at a confidence level α (i.e. $\alpha = 99.9\%$); that is, provided the losses $s_j,\ j = 1, \ldots, J$, are sorted in increasing order:

$$s_{1:J} \leq s_{2:J} \leq \ldots \leq s_{J:J} \tag{3.79}$$

The VaR is obtained as:

$$VaR_{99.9\%} = F_s^{-1}(99.9\%) = \inf\left\{ s_{j:J} : \frac{j}{J} \geq 99.9\% \right\} \tag{3.80}$$

But VaR can also be defined as the sum of expected loss (EL) and unexpected loss (UL); that is

$$VaR = EL + UL \tag{3.81}$$

where:

$$EL = \mathbb{E}(S) = \frac{1}{J}\sum_{j=1}^{J} s_j \tag{3.82}$$

Expected loss can be deducted from capital at risk if regulatory requirements are satisfied (see references 1, 2 and 4). The easiest way to define expected loss is to consider the mean of the annual loss distribution, though this this statistic could give too sensitive a result with extreme losses that cannot be classified as expected. For this reason we apply the median instead of the mean: this way we obtain a more stable and robust estimation of the expected loss (EL):

$$EL = F_s^{-1}(50\%) \tag{3.83}$$

3.8 INSURANCE MODELING

Insurance contracts can be considered in the operational risk modeling assessing the effects of insurance contracts on individual risk classes. This is a reasonable proxy of insurance protection, as it takes into account individual insurance contract conditions, deductibles, and set limits. Stochastic factors such as payment uncertainty and counterparty default risk should also be considered explicitly (see reference 16).

Suppose that the insurance policy covers exactly a risk class, complying with regulatory requirements (see references 1, 2 and 4). If we set the deductibles as d and the policy limit as m for each single loss event, the insurance recovery on loss x_{ij} will be given by:

$$R_{d,m}(x_{ij}) = \min(\max(x_{ij} - d, 0), m) \quad i = 1, \ldots, n_j \quad j = 1, \ldots, J \tag{3.84}$$

where

n_j is drawn from the frequency distribution; it is the number of losses in the year j;

x_{ij} is the ith loss drawn from the severity distribution in the year j;

J is the number of simulated annual losses.

Then the value of the net loss is modified as follows:

$$\tilde{x}_{ij} = x_{ij} - R_{d,m}(x_{ij}), \quad i = 1, \ldots, n_j, \quad j = 1, \ldots, J \tag{3.85}$$

and the net annual loss becomes:

$$\tilde{s}_{ij} = \sum_{i=1}^{n_j} x_{ij} - \sum_{i=1}^{n_j} R_{d,m}(x_{ij}), \quad j = 1, \ldots, J \tag{3.86}$$

Setting the deductibles as D and the policy limit as M aggregated on an annual basis,[11] one we adjust the annual loss distribution. Recovery on annual loss becomes:

$$R_{d,m,D,M}(s_j) = \min\left(\max\left(\sum_{i=1}^{n_j} R_{d,m}(x_{ij}) - D, 0\right), M\right), \quad j = 1, \ldots, J \tag{3.87}$$

where s_j is the jth simulated annual loss such that $s_j = x_{1j} + \cdots + x_{nj}$. Then, the net annual loss is:

$$\tilde{s}_j = s_j - R_{d,m,D,M}(s_j), \quad j = 1, \ldots, J \tag{3.88}$$

Risk measures after insurance coverage are then calculated on the sample $[s_1, \ldots, s_J]$. Let's remember that complying with Basel 2 AMA requirements involves:

- appropriate haircuts reflecting the policy's declining residual term;
- the payment uncertainty due, for example, to mismatches between insurance policy coverage and the analyzed operational risk class;[12]
- the recognition of counterparty risk in the creditworthiness of the insurers and potential concentration risk of insurance providers.

[11] These conditions are not applied on each single loss amount, but instead on the whole set of annual losses.

[12] For example, when considering external fraud, only robberies are insured by a BBB policy.

3.8.1 Appropriate Haircuts Reflecting the Policy's Declining Residual Term

The insurance policy must have an initial expiration term longer than one year. For policies with initial terms shorter than one year, the bank should make haircuts reflecting the shorter time horizon, up to 100% haircut for policies lasting 90 days or less. The recovered annual loss should be modified:

$$R_{d,m,D,M}(s_j) = \alpha \cdot \min\left(\max\left(\sum_{i=1}^{n_j} R_{d,m}(x_{ij}) - D, 0\right), M\right)$$
$$j = 1, \dots, J \tag{3.89}$$

where:

$$\alpha = \begin{cases} \dfrac{\min(\text{remaining days}, 365)}{365} & \text{if remaining days} > 90 \\ 0 & \text{otherwise} \end{cases} \tag{3.90}$$

Similar methodology can be applied to the terms of cancellation.

3.8.2 Payment Uncertainty

We modeled payment uncertainties of mismatches between insurance contracts and the risk classes.

Each operational loss, independently, is supposed to be insured with probability p $(0 \leq p \leq 1)$. This implies that the annual number of insured losses is the sum of Bernoulli trial results. Then, the frequency of insured losses, $\tilde{N}$, will follow a binomial distribution ($\tilde{N} = B(n, p)$), and its probability mass function will be:

$$\mathbb{P}(\tilde{N} = \tilde{n}) = \binom{n}{\tilde{n}} p^{\tilde{n}}(1-p)^{n-\tilde{n}} \tag{3.91}$$

where

$\tilde{n}$ is the number of annual insured losses;

n is the total annual number of losses obtained from the frequency distribution;

p is the probability that a loss is insured.

The probability p can be estimated on internal data[13] as the ratio:

$$p = \frac{\#\text{insured losses}}{\#\text{losses}} \tag{3.92}$$

where

#insured losses is the number of insured losses;

#losses is the total number of losses.[14]

We model uncertainty using Monte Carlo methods where the number of annual losses n_j is drawn from the frequency distribution, obtaining the frequency $\tilde{n}_j$ from a binomial distribution $B(n_j, p)$. In the annual losses with size n_j, a size $\tilde{n}_j$ subset is insured and a size $n_j - \tilde{n}_j$ subset is not recovered; the losses belonging to the size $n_j - \tilde{n}_j$ subset are the gross loss amount.

The probability p was considered so far to be constant. Empirical evidence shows that p depends on the loss amount. This probability is better represented by specific probability for ranges of loss amount. Suppose we have K probabilities $p_1, \ldots, p_K$ defined on ranges of loss amount, delimited by $K-1$ thresholds $u_1, \ldots, u_{K-1}$ $(u_1 \leq \ldots \leq u_{K-1})$; that is:

$$p = \begin{cases} p_1 & \text{if } x < u_1 \\ p_k & \text{if } u_{k-1} \leq x < u_k \quad k = 2, \ldots, K-1 \\ p_K & \text{if } x \geq u_{K-1} \end{cases} \tag{3.93}$$

where $p_k \leq p_{k-1}$, $k = 2, \ldots, K-1$. The probability that a loss is insured is obtained applying a non-increasing step function.[15]

For each range k, a simulation is performed, with probability p_k to get a sample of annual losses $[\tilde{s}_1^k, \ldots, \tilde{s}_j^k]$, resulting in the annual loss distribution.[16] The total annual loss distribution is obtained adding the non-ordered samples $[\tilde{s}_1^k, \ldots, \tilde{s}_J^k]$:

$$\tilde{s}_j = \sum_{k=1}^{K-1} \tilde{s}_j^k, \quad j = 1, \ldots, J \tag{3.94}$$

[13] In the absence of internal data, system estimates can be used.

[14] The probability p can be adjusted, taking into account the probability that an insured loss doesn't get recovered because of litigation. This probability could be estimated through the ratio: $p = \frac{\#\text{insured losses without litigation}}{\#\text{losses}}$.

[15] p could also be considered a non-increasing continuous function of the loss amount, $p = p(x)$, with $\frac{\mathrm{d}p}{\mathrm{d}x} \leq 0$.

[16] To obtain the annual loss distribution of a single range, one needs to estimate the frequency for losses included in the range and simulate from severity in the range.

Deviations from full recovery can be included discounting the insurance payments with a specific factor:

$$R_{d,m,D,M}(s_j) = \beta \cdot \alpha \cdot \min\left(\max\left(\sum_{i=1}^{n_j} R_{d,m}(x_{ij}) - D, 0\right), M\right)$$
$$j = 1, \ldots, J \qquad (3.95)$$

where β $(0 \leq \beta \leq 1)$ is the average recovery rate resulting from the ratio of actual recovered and potentially recovered amounts. The factor β may be estimated from internal loss data:

$$\beta = \frac{\text{Actual recovered loss amount}}{\text{Potential recovered loss amount}} \qquad (3.96)$$

The recovery rate is likely to be a function of the loss amount. Then, β can be modeled using a non-increasing step function:

$$\beta = \begin{cases} \beta_1 & \text{if } x < u_1 \\ \beta_k & \text{if } u_{k-1} \leq x \leq u_k \quad k = 2, \ldots, K-1 \\ \beta_K & \text{if } x \geq u_{K-1} \end{cases} \qquad (3.97)$$

where $\beta_k \leq \beta_{k-1}, k = 2, \ldots, K - 1$.

Recoveries can be affected by payment delays, especially for large claims. Recoveries suffering delays longer than one year should not be considered, as they exceed the BIS2 holding time period. This can be taken into account in the β calculation:

$$\beta = \frac{\text{Actual recovered loss amount in one year}}{\text{Potential recovered loss amount}}$$

For over one year reimbursement recognition, payment delays may be considered discounting the recovery with an average delay.

Generalizing to the case of multiple insurance policies for same risk class,[17] we suppose this is covered by policies with single and aggregated deductibles and limits $(d_h, m_h, D_h, M_h, h = 1, \ldots, H)$, with given probabilities $(p_h, h = 1, \ldots, H$ with $p_1 + \cdots + p_H \leq 1)$ and given average recovery ratios $(\beta_h, h = 1, \ldots, H)$. The probability that no insurance is applied will be:

$$p_{\text{no insurance}} = 1 - (p_1 + \cdots + p_H) \qquad (3.98)$$

[17] In this case, we consider p to be a constant function of the loss amount.

The number of losses covered by each insurance contract is supposed to follow a multinomial distribution. The probability that $\tilde{n}_1, \tilde{n}_2, \ldots, \tilde{n}_H$ losses are insured by policies $1, 2, \ldots, H$, is given by:

$$\mathbb{P}(\tilde{N}_1 = \tilde{n}_1, \ldots, \tilde{N}_H = \tilde{n}_H) = \frac{n!}{\tilde{n}_1! \cdots \tilde{n}_H \cdot (n - \tilde{n}_1 - \cdots - \tilde{n}_H)!} \cdot p_1^{\tilde{n}_1} \cdots p_H^{\tilde{n}_H} \cdot p_{\text{no insurance}}^{n-\tilde{n}_1-\cdots-\tilde{n}_H}$$

where n is the number of losses simulated for one year.

When the number of losses n_j for $j = 1, \ldots, J$ is drawn from the frequency distribution, the numbers of insured losses $\tilde{n}_{1j}, \ldots, \tilde{n}_{H_j}$ will be simulated from a multinomial distribution. For each run of the Monte Carlo simulation ($j = 1, \ldots, J$), n_{hj} ($h = 1, \ldots, H$) losses are drawn from the severity distribution, applying the coverage conditions d_h, m_h, D_h, $M_h (h = 1, \ldots, H)$. Recoveries are discounted using the factor $\beta_h (h = 1, \ldots, H)$ and added, obtaining the net annual loss.

3.8.3 Counterparty Risk

We define counterparty risk as the possibility that the insurer defaults or incurs severe liquidity constraints, failing to meet its payment obligations. Counterparty risk can be modeled considering the probability of default $pd (0 \leq pd \leq 1)$ of the counterparty's rating and the recovered loss given default $rlgd (0 \leq rlgd \leq 1)$. Full insurance recoveries can be obtained only when the insurer has not defaulted. If J annual losses are simulated using Monte Carlo methods, then the full insurance recoveries are obtained only for $(1 - pd) \cdot J$ years. For the remaining $(pd \cdot J)$ years, insurance recoveries must be discounted using the factor $rlgd$. The recovery on annual loss[18] will be:

$$R_{d,m,D,M}(s_j) = \begin{cases} rlgd \cdot \beta \cdot \alpha \cdot \min\left(\max\left(\sum_{i=1}^{n_j} R_{d,m}(x_{ij}) - D, 0\right), M\right) & \text{if } j \in YD \\ \beta \cdot \alpha \cdot \min\left(\max\left(\sum_{i=1}^{n_j} R_{d,m}(x_{ij}) - D, 0\right), M\right) & \text{if } j \in YND \end{cases} \quad (3.99)$$

$$j = 1, \ldots, J \quad (3.100)$$

[18] The average value of the recovery on annual loss, i.e. $\frac{1}{J} \sum_{j=1}^{J} R_{d,m,D,M}(s_j)$, can be used as estimate of the pure theoretical premium referred to the insurance contract.

where

YD is the set of simulated years where the insurer defaults ($\#YD = pd \cdot J$);[19]

YND is the set of simulated years where the insurer does not default ($\#YND = (1 - pd) \cdot J$).

This is a conservative approach, as a default could occur at any time throughout the year, and a relevant percentage of losses could result in a full recovery even in the case of default.

3.8.4 Application of Insurance

The approach presented will now be applied to external fraud losses. This risk class is usually hedged by the robbery section of standard policies (such as the BBB policy, see Chapter 4). The capital charge for external fraud is estimated applying the LDA model: severity is supposed to follow a lognormal distribution with parameters 9 and 2 (the mean and variance of log-losses); frequency a Poisson distribution with parameter 200 (the average number of losses in one year). These parameters are assumed to apply to a generic domestic bank with a gross income in the range of €2–4 billion. The annual loss distribution is obtained using Monte Carlo techniques. We assume the insurance hedge terms are:

- deductible on a single loss, $d = €1\,000\,000$;
- limit on a single loss, $m = €15\,000\,000$;
- no deductible on annual loss ($D = €0$);
- limit on annual loss, $M = €30\,000\,000$.

The probability that a loss is insured is set at 80%, and the average recovery rate is 73%. The probability of default is supposed to be 0.1%, while the recovered loss given default set at 0%. EL and UL are reported in the following cases:

1. No insurance.
2. Insurance without random effects on recoveries ($p = 100\%$, $\beta = 100\%$, $pd = 0\%$, $rlgd = 0\%$).
3. Insurance with random effects on recoveries ($p = 80\%$, $\beta = 73\%$, $pd = 0,1\%$, $rlgd = 0\%$).

[19] The function $f(x) = [x]$ represents the integer part of x.

Table 3.2 Results in €'000

	No insurance	Insurance $p = 100\%$; $\beta = 100\%$; $pd = 0\%$; $rlgd = 0\%$	Insurance $p = 80\%$; $\beta = 73\%$; $pd = 0.1\%$; $rlgd = 0\%$
Expected loss	11.975	9.692	10.638
Unexpected loss	56.622	40.578	47.230

We see from the results reported in Table 3.2 that random effects on recoveries may have relevant impacts on operational risk measures. Recoveries with random effects accounted for little more than half of recoveries without random effects, with a significant impact on expected and unexpected loss. We note that the insurance offset on the capital charge without random effects exceeds 20%, but the external fraud sample is only a subset and the maximum offset should be considered on the total capital at risk charge.

3.9 ADJUSTMENT FOR RISK INDICATORS

Capital at risk for each risk class, calculated on actual and scenario-generated loss data (indicated as $OpVaR^{\text{LDA}}$), should also consider the business environment and internal control factors, adding a forward-looking effect. We obtained this adjusting the capital at risk using operational risk indicators (key operational risk indicators, KoRI):

$$OpVaR = OpVaR^{\text{LDA}} \cdot C^{\text{KoRI}} \tag{3.101}$$

According to our operational risk indicators are data reflecting operational risk exposure, as the value of an indicator should be correlated to changes in risk levels. We believe that monitoring operational risk using indicators provides early risk warning signals.

Each indicator is linked to a specific process and we rely on an extensive library of KoRIs. It is important to stress that not all the indicators are considered in capital calculation: we identify a list of significant indicators.

In our model, the scaling coefficient for risk indicator i is the ratio of last year level and the average value of all years considered in the observation period:

$$C_i^{\text{KoRI}} = \frac{KoRI_i^t}{\overline{KoRI}_i^{t-1,t-2,\ldots,1}}. \tag{3.102}$$

where

C_i^{KoRI} is the coefficient of adjustment for indicator i;

$KoRI_i^t$ is the value of the ith indicator in the last year;

$\overline{KoRI}_i^{t-1,t-2,\ldots,1}$ is the average annual value of the ith indicator on the full observation period.

Before a scaling coefficient is calculated, risk indicators should be scaled to become comparable: if a threshold is defined, the ratio between the indicator value and the threshold is computed.

Considering that risk indicators are available monthly or quarterly, the annual value of the risk indicator is the average of data in the actual year: for monthly risk indicators, the annual value is the average over 12 months, for quarterly indicators, the average calculated over four quarters.

In the calculation of C_i^{KoRI}, the denominator $\overline{KoRI}_i^{t-1,t-2,\ldots,1}$ is the average of all annual values included in the observation period. Given the frequent data shortage, a solution would be to calculate $\overline{KoRI}_i^{t-1,t-2,\ldots,1}$ as the average of all observations. For monthly available indicators, $\overline{KoRI}_i^{t-1,t-2,\ldots,1}$ is the average of all monthly values and for quarterly, $\overline{KoRI}_i^{t-1,t-2,\ldots,1}$ the average of all quarterly values.

A relevant set of indicators is selected by the operational risk manager based on their relevance for early risk warning.

The overall risk indicator coefficient is the average of coefficients for every indicator i:

$$C^{\text{KoRI}} = \frac{1}{n}\sum_{i=1}^{n} C_i^{\text{KoRI}} \tag{3.103}$$

where

n is the number of selected risk indicators;

C_i^{KoRI} is the coefficient of adjustment of the indicator i;

C^{KoRI} is the overall risk indicator coefficient of adjustment.

We have decided to cap the overall coefficient C^{KoRI} in order to obtain a bounded variation, for example, of 5% (i.e. $95\% \leq C_i^{\text{KoRI}} \leq 105\%$). If we obtain a value for C^{KoRI} higher than 105%, the definitive value is set at 105% and if we get a value lower than 95%, the value is set at 95%.

The annual loss distribution of the risk class combining loss data and risk indicators is obtained multiplying each simulated annual loss by C^{KoRI}:

$$\left| C^{\text{KoRI}} \cdot s_1, C^{\text{KoRI}} \cdot s_2, \ldots, C^{\text{KoRI}} \cdot s_j \right| \tag{3.104}$$

3.10 OPERATIONAL RISK CLASS AGGREGATION

Operational Value at Risk can be calculated simply as the sum of different Values at Risk for single risk class. If we have H operational risk classes, we define

$$OpVaR(S_h) \quad h = 1, \ldots, H \tag{3.105}$$

as the Value at Risk calculated on loss distribution S_h relating to risk class h at the 99.9% percentile; i.e.

$$OpVaR(S) = \sum_{h=1}^{H} OpVaR(S_h) \tag{3.106}$$

we assume that the S_h, $h = 1, \ldots, H$, are perfectly dependent and comonotone.[20]

This hypothesis may be too conservative, we want to understand the real correlation structure among risk classes. The *VaR* is not always subadditive,[21] i.e. the following inequality

$$VaR_{99.9\%}(S) = VaR_{99.9\%}\left(\sum_{h=1}^{H} S_h\right) \leq \sum_{h=1}^{H} VaR_{99.9\%}(S_h) \tag{3.107}$$

may reverse (see reference 17 on page 194). This happens if the random variables S_h have particular dependence or the underlying distribution functions are very skewed or heavy-tailed.

Methods based on copula functions,[22] (see Section 3.10.1) such as the Gaussian, t-Student (see Section 3.10.2), or Archimedean (see Section 3.10.3), are useful to incorporate the diversification effect.

Monte Carlo methods can be used to determine the overall risk estimate, with the proper dependence structure among risk classes, using copulae. Suppose we have distribution functions $F_{S(h)}$, $h = 1, \ldots, H$

[20] S_h, $h = 1, \ldots, H$, are comonotone if there exist increasing functions $f_1, \ldots, f_H$ and a random variable X such that $S_h = f_h(X)$, $h = 1, \ldots, H$.

[21] Subadditivity means that aggregating individual risks does not increase overall risk.

[22] Perfect dependence case is equivalent to using the upper Fréchet bound copula C^+.

of annual losses for each single risk class. The distribution function of overall annual losses is obtained repeating the following three steps many times (at least $J = 10^6$):

1. We simulate a realization of a multivariate random vector $\bar{u} = (u_1, \ldots, u_H)$ with marginals uniformly distributed on [0, 1] from a defined copula C.
2. We obtain a loss scenario for each risk class $s_j(h)$, $h = 1, \ldots, H$, applying to each uniformly distributed realization (simulated in the previous step), the inverse of the cumulative distribution function $F_{S(h)}\big(s_j(h) = F^{-1}_{S(h)}(u_h)\big)$.
3. We obtain a total loss scenario, s_j, summing losses $s_j(h)$ for each $h = 1, \ldots, H$:

$$s_j = \sum_{h=1}^{H} s_j(h) \tag{3.108}$$

The simulated empirical distribution function of the institution's overall loss is obtained. Overall VaR is calculated as the quantile at 99.9%. The expected loss can be deducted to obtain the overall capital at risk:

$$OpVaR = VaR - EL$$

The value EL must be seen as an upper limit, which may be subtracted from the Value at Risk provided that, in the observation period, there are enough available provisions covering it. The latter can be defined:

$$EL_{\text{av}} = \sum_{\text{obs.period}} \text{provisions} \tag{3.109}$$

This information should be available in the operational risk database, considering provisions that are not still used to cover actualized losses.

Finally, the overall capital at risk calculated considering available provisions (*OpVaR*) is defined as:

$$OpVaR^{\text{LDA}} = VaR - \min(EL, EL_{\text{av}}) \tag{3.110}$$

In the following section, we look at copulae function theory.

3.10.1 Copulae Functions

Copulae are uniform distributions which enable to extract the dependence structure from joint probability distribution function of a set of random variables and, at the same time, to separate the dependence structure from the univariate marginal behavior.

Define $\mathbf{X} = (X_1, \ldots, X_n)$ as the random vector,[23] with marginal distribution functions $F_1, \ldots, F_n$; the multivariate distribution function

$$F(x_1, \ldots, x_n) = \mathbb{P}[X_1 \leq x_1, \ldots, x_n \leq x_n] \quad (3.111)$$

defines entirely the dependence structure of the random variables $X_1, \ldots, X_n$. This analytical function may be practically impossible to estimate.

Applying a copula function is a useful means for estimating the multivariate distribution function. We can separate the analysis into two parts:

1. Defining the marginal distribution functions $F_1, \ldots, F_n$, representing the distribution for every class.
2. Defining the dependence structure of the random variables $X_1, \ldots, X_n$ identifying a correct copula function.

Defining the Copula Function

An n-dimensional copula[24] is a multivariate distribution function, C, with marginal functions distributed uniformly in $[0, 1]$ $(U(0, 1))$ such that:

1. $C : [0, 1]^n \rightarrow [0, 1]$
2. C has marginal functions C_i such that:

$$C_i(u) = C(1, \ldots, 1, u, 1, \ldots, 1) = u, \quad \forall u \in [0, 1] \quad (3.112)$$

consequently, if $F_1, \ldots, F_n$ are univariate distribution functions, then $C(F_1(x_1), \ldots, F_n(x_n))$ is a multivariate distribution function with marginal functions $F_1, \ldots, F_n$ because $U_i = F_i(X_i)$, $i = 1, \ldots, n$ is a uniform random variable. Hence, copula functions can be used to estimate and simulate multivariate distributions once marginal distributions have been determined.

Copulae are invariant under strictly increasing transformations of the underlying random variables; they are uniformly continuous and hence their derivatives exist almost everywhere.

[23] In our case, the components of $\mathbf{X}$ represent the n risk classes.

[24] This is the original definition by Sklar (see reference 18 on page 194).

The following theorem is of key importance when dealing with copula functions, as it is used in all practical applications.

Sklar's Theorem

Let F be an n-dimensional distribution function with continuous marginal functions $F_1, \ldots, F_n$, then there exists a unique representation through the copula function:

$$F(x_1, \ldots, x_n) = C(F_1(x_1), \ldots, F_n(x_n)) \tag{3.113}$$

Following Sklar's theorem, one observes that, for multivariate continuous distribution functions, the marginal univariate functions and the multivariate dependence structure can be separated. The dependence structure can be represented as an appropriate copula function. From Sklar's theorem, the following corollary may be derived.

Corollary to Sklar's Theorem Let F be an n-dimensional distribution function with marginal continuous functions $F_1, \ldots, F_n$ and copula C (that satisfies Equation (3.113)). Then:

$$\begin{aligned} C(u_1, \ldots, u_n) &= F(F_1^{-1}(u_1), \ldots, F_n^{-1}(u_n)) \\ \forall u &= (u_1, \ldots, u_n) \in [0, 1]^n \end{aligned} \tag{3.114}$$

where F_i^{-1} is the inverse of F_i.

3.10.2 Elliptical Copulae

Elliptical copulae are those relating to elliptical distributions. Simulation from elliptical copulae is easy; rank correlation and tail dependence coefficients can be calculated easily for these copulae, but they do not have closed-form expressions and are restricted to radial symmetry. Examples of elliptical copulae are Gaussian and Student-t copulae.

Gaussian Copula

The Gaussian copula (or normal copula) is the copula of the multivariate normal distribution. If the random vector $\mathbf{X} = (X_1, \ldots, X_n)$ is made of independent variables with a normal distribution, then:

1. The univariate marginal functions $F_1, \ldots, F_n$ are Gauss functions.
2. The dependence structure among the marginal distributions is described by a unique copula function $C_{\boldsymbol{R}}^{\mathrm{Ga}}$ (the Gaussian copula) such that[25]

$$C_{\boldsymbol{R}}^{\mathrm{Ga}} = \Phi_{\boldsymbol{R}}\left(\phi^{-1}(u_1), \ldots, \phi^{-1}(u_n)\right) \tag{3.115}$$

where

$\Phi_{\boldsymbol{R}}$ is the normal standard multivariate distribution function with correlation matrix $\boldsymbol{R} = \{\rho_{i,j}\}$;

ϕ^{-1} is the inverse of Gauss's standard univariate distribution function.

The parameter for the Gaussian copula can be estimated from Kendall's correlation coefficients (see Section 3.10.4) applying the following transformation:

$$\rho = \sin\left(\frac{\pi}{2}\rho_\tau\right) \tag{3.116}$$

where ρ_τ is Kendall's rank correlation coefficient and ρ is the coefficient used for the Gaussian copula. The matrix obtained is a symmetric of pairwise correlation estimates with unit diagonal entries and off-diagonal entries in $[-1, 1]$ that may not be positive semidefinite. To ensure that the matrix is positive semidefinite, a transformation based on the eigenvalue method is applied (see reference 19).

In order to simulate random variables from the Gaussian copula, the following procedure is carried out. If the matrix $\boldsymbol{R}$ is positive definite, then there exists a matrix $\boldsymbol{A}$ of dimensions $n \times n$ such that $\boldsymbol{R} = \boldsymbol{A}\boldsymbol{A}^{\mathrm{T}}$. It is then assumed that the random variables $Z_1, \ldots, Z_n$ are normal standard independent. Given the vector $\mu \in \mathbb{R}^n$, the random vector $\mu + \boldsymbol{A}\boldsymbol{Z}$ (where $\boldsymbol{Z} = (Z_1, \ldots, Z_n)^{\mathrm{T}}$) is multinormal, with mean vector μ and covariance matrix $\boldsymbol{R}$. The matrix $\boldsymbol{A}$ can be determined through the Cholesky's decomposition of matrix $\boldsymbol{R}$. This decomposition is the sole

[25] This can be deduced easily from Equation (3.113).

triangular matrix inferior to $\boldsymbol{L}$ such that $\boldsymbol{L}\boldsymbol{L}^{\mathrm{T}} = \boldsymbol{R}$. Therefore, random variables can be generated from the Gaussian n-dimensional copula:

- defining the Cholesky decomposition $\boldsymbol{A}$ of matrix $\boldsymbol{R}$;
- simulating n random normal standard independent variables $z_1, \ldots, z_n$;
- compute $\boldsymbol{x} = \boldsymbol{A}z$;
- determining the components $u_i = \phi(x_i)$, $i = 1, \ldots, n$;
- the resulting vector, $(u_1, \ldots, u_n)^{\mathrm{T}}$, is a realization of the n-dimensional Gaussian copula $C_{\boldsymbol{R}}^{\mathrm{Ga}}$.

Student-t Copula

The Student-t copula (or t-copula) is the copula of the t distribution. Unlike the Gaussian copula, it better captures tail dependencies and may be more suitable to describe operational risk data. If the number of degrees of freedom becomes large, the t-copula behaves like the Gaussian one.

Let $\boldsymbol{X} = (X_1, \ldots, X_n)$ be a vector with a multivariate t distribution with ν degrees of freedom. The copula of vector $\boldsymbol{X}$ can be analytically represented in the form:

$$C_{\nu,\boldsymbol{R}}^{t}(u_1, \ldots, u_n) = t_{\nu,\boldsymbol{R}}^{n}(t_{\nu}^{-1}(u_1), \ldots, t_{\nu}^{-1}(u_n)) \tag{3.117}$$

and where $t_{\nu,\boldsymbol{R}}^{n}$ denotes the multivariate probability distribution function of the random vector $\sqrt{\nu}Y/\sqrt{S}$, where the random variable $S \sim \chi_{\nu}^{2}$ and the random vector $\boldsymbol{Y}$ are independent. t_{ν} denotes the margins of $t_{\nu,\boldsymbol{R}}^{n}$.

Correlation matrix $\boldsymbol{R}$ for the Student-t copula is estimated like the Gaussian copula, whereas the number of degrees of freedom, ν, is estimated with a maximum likelihood procedure.[26] To simulate random variates from the Student-t copula:

- we define the Cholesky decomposition $\boldsymbol{A}$ of matrix $\boldsymbol{R}$;
- we simulate n independent random variates $z_1, \ldots, z_n$ from the standard normal distribution;
- we simulate a variate s from a chi-square distribution with ν degrees of freedom, independent of $z_1, \ldots, z_n$;
- we determine the vector $\mathbf{y} = \boldsymbol{A}z$;

[26] An alternative procedure involves using the maximum likelihood method to estimate both parameters $\boldsymbol{R}$ and ν.

- we set $x = \frac{\sqrt{\nu}}{s}\mathbf{y}$
- we determine the components $u_i = t_\nu(x_i); i = 1, \ldots, n$;
- the resulting vector, $(u_1, \ldots, u_n)^\mathrm{T}$ is a realization of the n-dimensional t-copula $C^t_{\nu,\boldsymbol{R}}$.

3.10.3 Archimedean Copulae

Archimedean copulae usually describe stronger dependence between extreme data. Archimedean copulae are easy to construct and they have simple closed-form expressions.

A two-dimensional Archimedean copula can be written in the form:

$$C_\alpha(u, v) = \varphi_\alpha^{-1}(\varphi_\alpha(u) + \varphi_\alpha(v)) \quad \forall (u, v) \in [0, 1]^2 \tag{3.118}$$

for all $0 \le (u, v) \le 1$ and where φ_α is the generator function of the copula with dependence parameter α satisfying:

- $\varphi_\alpha(1) = 0$;
- $\varphi'_\alpha(t) < 0$ for all $t \in [0, 1]$; that is to say, φ_α is decreasing;
- $\varphi''_\alpha(t) \ge 0$ for all $t \in [0, 1]$; that is to say, φ_α is convex.

As the generator uniquely determines an Archimedean copula, different choices of generator yield many families of copulae that differ in the number and the range of dependence parameters.

The dependence parameters are linked to the measures of association, like the Kendall's tau and Spearman's rho. For the Archimedean copulae, Kendall's tau (τ) can be evaluated directly from the generator:

$$\tau = 1 + 4\int_0^1 \frac{\varphi_\alpha(t)}{\varphi'_\alpha(t)}\mathrm{d}t \tag{3.119}$$

To construct the estimate of α, it is common practice to base the estimation procedure on the observed value of Kendall's tau.[27]

A multivariate Archimedean copula is defined below:

$$C_\alpha(u_1, \ldots, u_n) = \varphi_\alpha^{-1}(\varphi_\alpha(u_1) + \cdots + \varphi_\alpha(u_n)) \\ \forall u = (u_1, \ldots, u_n) \in [0, 1]^n \tag{3.120}$$

for all $0 \le (u_1, \ldots, u_n) \le 1$, and where φ_α is the generator function of the copula satisfying the listed conditions.

[27] An alternative approach to estimating α involves a maximum likelihood procedure.

Archimedean copulae seem to fit bivariate return distributions well but are extremely restrictive in the higher-dimensional case, requiring a single parameter capturing all dependencies among the random variables and imply exchangeability, hence equicorrelated ranks.

Gumbel Copulae

Although many parametric families of Archimedean copulae exist (e.g. Clayton, Frank, and Gumbel), we focus on the Gumbel–Hougaard copula. The Gumbel–Hougaard copula, proposed by Gumbel 20 and discussed by Hougaard (see reference 20 and 21 on page 194), combines upper tail dependence and non-negative association.

The generator function is given by $\varphi_\alpha(u) = (-\ln(u))^\alpha$ with $\alpha \geq 1$ and its inverse takes the following form:

$$\varphi_\alpha^{-1}(t) = \exp\left(-\ln\left(t^{\frac{1}{\alpha}}\right)\right) \tag{3.121}$$

The form of the Gumbel copula in the bivariate case is:

$$C_\alpha^{\mathrm{Gu}}(u, v) = \exp\left\{-\left[(-\ln u)^\alpha + (-\ln v)^\alpha\right]^{\frac{1}{\alpha}}\right\} \tag{3.122}$$

where $\alpha \in [1, +\infty)$ defines the degree of dependence between the variables, $\alpha = 1$ would imply independent variables and $\alpha \to +\infty$ means perfect dependence.

α can be estimated through a non parametric approach from the observed value of Kendall's tau. In case of Gumbel copula, the α estimate has a simple closed form:

$$\alpha = \frac{1}{1-\tau} \tag{3.123}$$

The multivariate extension is defined as:

$$C_\alpha^{\mathrm{Gu}}(u_1, \ldots, u_n) = \exp\left\{-\left[\sum_{j=1}^{n}(-\ln u_j)^\alpha\right]^{\frac{1}{\alpha}}\right\} \tag{3.124}$$

We consider the Kendall's rank correlation averaged over all pairs of data of risk classes to be the Gumbel copula parameter.

The Gumbel copula is relevant as it exhibits a strong tail dependence and because it is directly related to multivariate extensions of extreme value theory.

In order to simulate random variates from the Gumbel copula, we proceed by steps:

As the inverse of the generator function φ is equal to the Laplace transform of a positive stable variate from the $X \sim \text{St}\left(\frac{1}{\alpha}, 1, \gamma, 0\right)$ distribution, where

$$\gamma = \left(\cos\left(\frac{\pi}{2\alpha}\right)\right)^{\alpha} \quad \alpha > 1 \tag{3.125}$$

we can then:

- simulate a positive stable variate $X \sim \text{St}\left(\frac{1}{\alpha}, 1, \gamma, 0\right)$;
- simulate n independent standard uniform variables $V_1, \ldots, V_n$;
- determine

$$U = \left(\exp\left(-\left(-\frac{\ln V_1}{X}\right)^{\frac{1}{\alpha}}\right), \ldots, \exp\left(-\left(-\frac{\ln V_n}{X}\right)^{\frac{1}{\alpha}}\right)\right) \tag{3.126}$$

Since the positive stable distribution is not well known as other distributions, an algorithm for simulating a stable random variate $X \sim \text{St}\left(\frac{1}{\alpha}, 1, \gamma, 0\right)$ requires:

- to simulate a uniform variable $\theta \sim U\left(-\frac{\pi}{2}, \frac{\pi}{2}\right)$;
- to simulate an exponentially distributed variable W with mean 1 independent of θ;
- to set $\theta_0 = \arctan\left(\beta \tan\left(\frac{\pi\alpha}{2}\right)\right)/\alpha$;
- to compute $Z \sim \text{St}(\alpha, \beta, 1, 0)$:

$$Z = \frac{\sin\alpha\,(\theta_0 + \theta)}{(\cos\alpha\theta_0 \cos\theta)^{1/\alpha}} \left[\frac{\cos(\alpha\theta_0 + (\alpha - 1)\theta)}{W}\right]^{(1-\alpha)/\alpha} \qquad \alpha \neq 1$$

$$Z = \frac{2}{\pi}\left[\left(\frac{\pi}{2} + \beta\theta\right)\tan\theta - \beta \ln\left(\frac{\frac{\pi}{2} W \cos\theta}{\frac{\pi}{2} + \beta\theta}\right)\right] \qquad \alpha = 1$$

- to compute $X \sim \text{St}(\alpha, \beta, \gamma, \delta)$:

$$X = \gamma Z + \delta \qquad \alpha \neq 1$$

$$X = \gamma Z + \left(\delta + \beta \frac{2}{\pi} \gamma \ln(\gamma)\right) \qquad \alpha = 1$$

3.10.4 Choice of Copula

A number of papers have shown that the empirical fit of the Student-t copula is generally better than the Gaussian copula, the dependence structure of the multivariate normal distribution. Gumbel and Student-t copulae, in contrast with the Gaussian one, are able to model tail dependence. However, the Gumbel copula is very restrictive on its multivariate extension because a single parameter is used to capture the entire correlation structure among all risk classes. Hence, the Student-t copula may be considered a better solution to model the dependence structure for operational risk data.

The choice of the best copula can also be made by minimizing the distance to the empirical copula of the data or by maximizing the likelihood function value (see references 22 and 23 on page 194).

3.10.5 Correlation Coefficients

Gaussian and Student-t copulae are parameterized from the correlation matrix. The latter also requires the estimation of the degrees of freedom.

There are different types of correlation measure, such as Pearson's linear correlation, Kendall's, and Spearman's rank correlation.

Pearson's Linear Correlation

Let X and Y be two real-valued, non-zero random variables with finite variance. *Pearson's correlation coefficient* is defined as:

$$\rho(X,Y) = \frac{\mathrm{Cov}(X,Y)}{\sqrt{\mathrm{Var}(X)\cdot \mathrm{Var}(Y)}} \tag{3.127}$$

where $\mathrm{Cov}(X,Y) = E(XY) - E(X)E(Y)$.

This is a measure of linear dependence. If X and Y are independent random variables, then $\rho(X,Y) = 0$ since $\mathrm{Cov}(X,Y) = 0$. If there is perfect linear dependence, that is $Y = aX + b$ almost surely and $a \neq 0$, then $\rho(X,Y) = \mathrm{sgn}(a)$. In the case of imperfect linear correlation, $-1 < \rho < 1$. Correlation fulfills the linearity property:

$$\rho(aX + b, cY + d) = \mathrm{sgn}(a \cdot c)\rho(X,Y) \tag{3.128}$$

when $a, c \neq 0$. It is thus invariant under strictly increasing linear transformations.

If $\mathbf{X} = (X_1, \ldots, X_n)$ and $\mathbf{Y} = (Y_1, \ldots Y_n)$, all pairwise correlations can be summarized in a symmetric and positive semidefinite $n \times n$ matrix $\boldsymbol{R}$ with:

$$R_{ij} = \rho(X_i, X_j) \quad 1 \le i, j \le n \tag{3.129}$$

Spearman's Rank Correlation

Let X and Y be random variables with distribution functions F_1 and F_2 and joint distribution function F. *Spearman's rank correlation* is given by:

$$\rho_s = \rho\,(F_1(X), F_2(Y)) \tag{3.130}$$

where ρ is the usual linear correlation coefficient.

Kendall's Rank Correlation

Let (X_1, X_2) a random vector and (Y_1, Y_2) an independent copy having the same distribution, then *Kendall's rank correlation* is defined by:

$$\begin{aligned}\rho_\tau(X_1, Y_2) = {} & \mathbb{P}\,((X_1 - X_2)\,(Y_1 - Y_2) > 0) \\ & - \mathbb{P}\,((X_1 - X_2)\,(Y_1 - Y_2) < 0)\end{aligned} \tag{3.131}$$

that is, the probability of concordance minus the probability of discordance.

The main advantage of rank correlation over linear correlation is the invariance under monotonic transformations and the sensible handling of perfect dependence; the drawback is calculation time, since rank correlation coefficients are not moment-based.

Correlation Estimation

The dependent structure among data should be reviewed yearly, but if data use insufficient for robust estimates then the correlations are calculated among the monthly losses of the risk classes. If there is not any dependence between observations of a single risk class dataset at monthly aggregated level, the same observed dependence structure can be transposed at yearly level. To verify if this transposition can be actually done, an autocorrelation analysis can be performed on monthly aggregated loss of each risk class. In any case, given that losses tend to be accounted at the same times of the year (i.e. end of 1st semester, end of year), we deem that estimating correlation on monthly accounted losses is very conservative.

3.11 THE CLOSED-FORM APPROXIMATION FOR OpVaR

Typically the severity of operational losses is modeled through a so-called subexponential distribution such as the Weibull, Pareto, or generalized Pareto distribution (GPD), meaning that data distribution tails decay more slowly than the exponential tail distribution.

The defining property of subexponential distributions is that the distribution tail of the sum of n subexponential random variables has the same order of magnitude as the distribution tail of the maximum variable amongst them; more precisely:

$$\lim_{x \to +\infty} \frac{\mathbb{P}(X_1 + \ldots + X_n > x)}{\mathbb{P}(\max(X_1, \ldots, X_n) > x)} = 1 \quad \text{for} \quad n \geq 2 \tag{3.132}$$

This means that severe annual losses are mainly driven single big loss rather than accumulated small independent losses. From an analytical point of view, the 'real' operational risk is the risk of incurring a single huge loss like.

A consequence of this property is that, for confidence levels near to 1, we can approximate the OpVaR calculated on the aggregated annual loss distribution with a certain quantile of the severity distribution (see reference 24 on page 194):

$$OpVaR(\alpha) \cong F_X^{-1}\left(1 - \frac{1-\alpha}{\mathbb{E}(N)}\right) \tag{3.133}$$

where

F_X^{-1} is the quantile function of the severity distribution;

α is the confidence level of the OpVaR calculation $0 < \alpha < 1$;

$\mathbb{E}(N)$ is the expected value of the frequency distribution ($E(N) = \lambda$ if the frequency is modeled using a Poisson distribution).

Given that we are estimating the OpVaR through a quantile of the severity distribution, the closed form is also called a *one-event approximation*.

If we model the severity distribution using a generalized Pareto (GPD), we obtain the approximation (see reference 25 on page 194):

$$OpVaR(\alpha) \cong u + \frac{\beta}{\xi}\left[\left(\frac{(1-\omega)\mathbb{E}(N)}{1-\alpha}\right)^{\xi} - 1\right] \tag{3.134}$$

where

u is the body–tail threshold;

ξ and β are, respectively, the shape and scale parameters of the generalized Pareto distribution;

$\mathbb{E}(N)$ is the average of the frequency distribution;

$1-\omega$ is the weight of the tail in the severity distribution.

Hence, $(1-\omega)\cdot\mathbb{E}(N)$ is the expected annual number of losses above u. If the frequency is modeled applying a Poisson distribution:

$$(1-\omega)\cdot\mathbb{E}(N) = (1-\omega)\cdot\lambda = \lambda_{\text{tail}} \tag{3.135}$$

Therefore, we have:

$$OpVaR(\alpha) \cong u + \frac{\beta}{\xi}\left[\left(\frac{\lambda_{\text{tail}}}{1-\alpha}\right)^{\xi} - 1\right] \tag{3.136}$$

We can consider OpVaR the difference between the quantile 99.9% of the annual loss distribution and the expected loss. In fact, as shown in reference 26 on page 194, the quantile of the annual loss distribution is better approximated as:

$$F_S^{-1}(\alpha) \cong F_X^{-1}\left(1 - \frac{1-\alpha}{\mathbb{E}(N)}\right) + (\mathbb{E}(N)-1)\cdot\mathbb{E}(X) \tag{3.137}$$

where

F_S^{-1} is the quantile function of the annual loss distribution;

$\mathbb{E}(N)$ is the expected value of the frequency distribution;

$\mathbb{E}(X)$ is the expected value of the severity distribution.

If $\mathbb{E}(N) \gg 1 (\lambda \gg 1$ in the case of a Poisson distribution), then:

$$(\mathbb{E}(N)-1)\cdot\mathbb{E}(X) \cong \mathbb{E}(N)\cdot\mathbb{E}(X) = EL \tag{3.138}$$

Hence, we have:

$$F_S^{-1}(\alpha) \cong F_X^{-1}\left(1 - \frac{1-\alpha}{\mathbb{E}(N)}\right) + EL \tag{3.139}$$

and we obtain:

$$OpVaR(\alpha) = F_S^{-1}(\alpha) - EL \cong F_X^{-1}\left(1 - \frac{1-\alpha}{\mathbb{E}(N)}\right) \tag{3.140}$$

From our analysis, compared to the results of Monte Carlo simulations, this approximation of OpVaR is accurate, especially when the generalized Pareto distribution is used to model severity of losses. This closed-form approximation still cannot replace Monte Carlo methodology for several reasons:

- we need the annual loss distribution for each risk class to calculate the overall capital at risk through the copula function;
- we cannot apply our methodology to quantify the insurance effect;
- if the expected loss is defined as the median in place of the mean and/or the expected loss is bounded by the available provisions, we get some differences.

We have to use the Monte Carlo simulation as we need the annual loss distribution and not only the OpVaR for each risk class. In any case, the results reported in this section are useful allowing us to perform repeated tests on the LDA model without performing time-consuming calculations and, most importantly, they give an idea of the interaction between model parameters and final results.

3.11.1 Effect of the Minimum Threshold on Capital at Risk

This closed-form approximation is also useful to understand the effect of excluding losses below a minimum threshold. In our methodology, severity estimation is conditioned to left truncation; we also suppose that frequency is estimated only on losses greater than or equal to a minimum threshold (e.g. €5000). Applying Monte Carlo simulation, losses would be drawn from the severity distribution over the minimum threshold (see Section 3.7.2) and each simulated annual loss does not consider the sum of single losses under €5000 referenced to the simulated year. This quantity should have a negligible effect on capital at risk intended as unexpected loss. This can be shown from a theoretical point using the closed-form approximation. For subexponential distributions (e.g. lognormal, GPD), the OpVaR can be approximated by:

$$OpVaR(\alpha) \cong F_X^{-1}\left(1 - \frac{1-\alpha}{\mathbb{E}(N)}\right) \tag{3.141}$$

It can be proved that the closed-form approximation is insensitive to the minimum threshold. The left-truncated version of F_X over the threshold u is:

$$F_X^*(x) = \frac{F_X(x) - F_X(u)}{1 - F_X(u)} \tag{3.142}$$

The Poisson parameter truncated over the threshold u is:

$$\lambda^* = \lambda \cdot (1 - F_X(u)) \tag{3.143}$$

Taking F_X^* to be subexponential, the closed form approximation can be applied:

$$F_X^*(x) \cong 1 - \frac{1-\alpha}{\lambda} \tag{3.144}$$

Hence:

$$\begin{aligned} OpVaR(u) &\cong F_X^{*-1}\left(1 - \frac{1-\alpha}{\lambda^*}\right) \\ &= F_X^{-1}\left([1 - F_X(u)]\left(1 - \frac{1-\alpha}{[1 - F_X(u)]\,\lambda}\right) + F_X(u)\right) \\ &= F_X^{-1}\left(1 - \frac{1-\alpha}{\lambda}\right) \cong OpVaR \end{aligned}$$

3.12 CONFIDENCE BAND FOR CAPITAL AT RISK

Applying bootstrap techniques, we determine a confidence band for OpVaR for every risk class. The bootstrap method implies certain procedures are repeated a high number of times (e.g. 10 000):

1. A sample with the same size of loss data is drawn with replacement.
2. Parameters of severity and frequency are estimated on the sample.

Hence, we get an empirical distribution for parameters of severity and frequency.

Next, we repeat, a number of times, the following:

1. Parameters of the severity and frequency distributions are drawn from the respective distributions;
2. Capital at risk is calculated from the drawn parameters, taking into account the risk indicator adjustment.

A sample of capital at risk is obtained, representing the empirical distribution function of capital at risk:

$$[OpVaR_1, OpVaR_2, \ldots, OpVaR_{10\,000}] \tag{3.145}$$

Repeating Monte Carlo simulation for each step of the bootstrapping to measure each OpVaR can very computational intensive. Calculating the OpVaR using a closed-form approximation (see references 24 and 25), as described in Section 3.11, it is a useful way to reduce computational time:

$$OpVaR \cong u + \frac{\beta}{\xi}\left[\left(\frac{\lambda_{\text{tail}}}{1-\alpha}\right)^{\xi} - 1\right], \quad \text{where } \alpha = 99.9\% \tag{3.146}$$

As the capital at risk distribution is calculated, we get a confidence band with the desired confidence level p, with $0 < p < 1$ (e.g. 90%):

$$Op\hat{V}aR \in \left[F^{-1}_{OpVaR}\left(\frac{1-p}{2}\right), F^{-1}_{OpVaR}\left(\frac{1+p}{2}\right)\right] \tag{3.147}$$

where F_{OpVaR} is the empirical distribution function of OpVaR.

Once confidence bands have been obtained for every risk class, the confidence band for the overall capital at risk can be calculated: the lower bound is the sum of lower bounds of every risk class, while the higher bound is the sum of all risk classes' higher bounds.

Assessing the estimates' accuracy, the confidence band allows to check whether the number of losses is sufficient for OpVaR the calculation, for example:

$$\mathbb{P}((1-c)\cdot OpVaR \leq Op\hat{V}ar \leq (1+c)\cdot OpVaR) < \varepsilon \text{ with } c = 30\% \text{ and } \varepsilon = 90\% \tag{3.148}$$

That is, the sample size is considered sufficient if the range $((1-c)\cdot OpVaR, (1+c)\cdot OpVaR)$ is included in the confidence band.

3.13 STRESS TESTING

According to AMA regulatory requirements, stress tests should be performed on a regular basis to address model robustness and stability. We observe a variation in results when a single very high loss or a set of high losses is included in the historical dataset. For every risk class, losses may be chosen from external public data, considering operational events with maximal loss amounts. To ensure consistency with internal data, the stressed loss should be selected from events with occurrence dates falling in the observation period.

3.14 LOSS DATA MINIMUM THRESHOLD SETTING

We use internal data for the capital charge calculation only if the loss amount is higher than the threshold H, as we believe:

- it is not realistic to collect and model all operational loss data independently from the loss amount;
- the effect of the losses under the threshold on capital calculation is negligible.

If the severity follows, for example, a lognormal distribution, using the left-truncated density function:

$$f_X^*(x, \boldsymbol{\theta}) = f(x, \theta | x \geq H) = \frac{f(x, \boldsymbol{\theta})}{1 - \mathbb{P}(x \leq H)} = \frac{f(x, \boldsymbol{\theta})}{1 - F(H, \boldsymbol{\theta})}, \quad x \geq H \tag{3.149}$$

where

$\theta = (\mu, \sigma)$ is the vector including the parameters of the lognormal distribution;

H is the minimum threshold;

$f_X(x, \boldsymbol{\theta}) = f_{\mathrm{LN}}(x; \mu, \sigma) = \dfrac{1}{x\sigma\sqrt{2\pi}} \exp\left(-\dfrac{(\ln(x) - \mu)^2}{2\sigma^2}\right)$ is the probability density function of the lognormal distribution.

We assume the frequency of the annual losses follow a Poisson distribution of parameter λ. The maximum likelihood estimate of λ is given by the empirical average of the annual loss frequency. If losses with minimum threshold H are taken, the estimate will be biased and to correct for it we use:

$$\hat{\lambda} = \frac{\hat{\lambda}_{\text{sample}}}{\mathbb{P}(x > H)} = \frac{\hat{\lambda}_{\text{sample}}}{1 - F_X(H)} \tag{3.150}$$

where

$\hat{\lambda}$ is the estimate of the Poisson distribution parameter for the whole range of positive losses ($x > 0$);

$\hat{\lambda}_{\text{sample}}$ is the sample estimate of the Poisson distribution parameter (loss $> H$);

F_X is the probability distribution function of severity.

Given the losses $x_1, \ldots, x_n$, the log-likelihood function becomes:

$$l(\theta) = \sum_{i=1}^{n} \ln f^*(x_i, \theta) \tag{3.151}$$

The parameter estimate is obtained through maximization of the log-likelihood function $\hat{\theta} = \arg\max_\theta l(\theta)$.

We determine a threshold H consistent with distributional hypothesis, and use the following iterative procedure (see reference 27 on page 194):

1. Parameters are estimated for each value of $H \geq 0$;
2. Graphs for the following functions are drawn: $H \mapsto \mu(H)$, $H \mapsto \sigma(H)$, and $H \mapsto \lambda(H)$.
3. The threshold $\hat{H}$ is set as the minimum value over which $\mu(H)$, $\sigma(H)$ and $\lambda(H)$ are approximately constant.

According to the distributional hypothesis, the estimations we calculated with thresholds lower than $\hat{H}$ are affected by bias.

3.15 EMPIRICAL APPLICATION ON ALGO OpData

OpData is a database of worldwide operational risk events provided by Algorithmics (UK) Limited (© Algorithmics Software LLC). As of December 2006, it included over 11 000 events dating back to 1990. The database tracks primarily operational risk events. Boundary events (credit/market/strategic risk) are also included and identified under the category *other*.

To qualify for OpData, an event must be closed and settled: the loss must be known (finite) and an agreement must been reached to pay a fine, to finalize a settlement, or to write down a loss. The loss impact must be USD $1 million or more (or the equivalent in another currency) at the time the loss amount is publicly available.

OpData database is updated with new set of records every six months, and includes an audit trail and CPI worksheet. Every record corresponds to an operational event, the OpData record categories are listed in Table 3.3.

United States Consumer Price Index (CPI) data are provided to get the current value, based on loss amount (loss amount is as of the Settlement date).

Table 3.3 OpData record categories

Column name	Data type	Comments
OpData Event ID	number	Unique identifier
FIRST Event ID	number	cross-reference to linked FIRST case, where available
BIS Event Type – Level 1	BIS index	Top-level BIS indexing. Example 'Internal Fraud'
BIS Event Type – Level 2	BIS index	Mid-level BIS indexing. Example 'Theft and Fraud'
BIS Event Type – Level 3	BIS index	Bottom-level BIS indexing. Example 'Theft/extortion/embezzlement/robbery'
Organization	OpData index	Identifies the legal entity, topmost business entity, or government entity. Example: 'Citigroup'
Firm Name	OpData index	Identifies a subordinate unit of Organization. Example 'Citibank'
Description of Event	Free text	Synopsis of loss event, dates, and names of relevant parties.
Loss Amount in Local Currency (mln)	amount (millions)	Loss amount in the currency in which the amount was reported, as of Settlement Date.
Loss Amount (USD $mln)	amount (millions)	Loss amount in US dollars as of Settlement Date.
Current Value (USD $mln)	amount (millions)	Loss amount in US dollars as of Settlement Date, scaled to the present date using CPI scaling factor.
Settlement Date	date	Date on which the Loss Amount was made public.
Industry (Sector) SIC	index	Industry/Sector of Organization, under Standard Industrial Classification (SIC).

Some data fields are obtained from the bankscope database: these are total assets, total equity, employees, total deposits, and total revenue (these could be used as scaling factors in capital modelling).

OpData events are collected with standard research tools, such as Factiva and Lexis/Nexis: research staff read press reports and websites of financial regulatory institutions. Every event requires at least two press sources or one regulatory source to be included. Researchers collect further information on each case as needed to establish the correct loss amount. When sources disagree, further research may be needed. In some cases, where loss amounts are not public, an estimate of the loss is reported: for example, the middle of a range.

We apply our LDA model, as described in the previous paragraphs, to Algo OpData. The calculation dataset is obtained by applying the following criteria:

- only losses incurred by financial companies are considered;
- financial losses incurred by insurance companies are not considered;
- credit risk boundary events are excluded.

For the analysis, current loss amounts based on the CPI are considered: this is converted to Euros and values greater than or equal to €1 000 000 are selected. We obtain a hypothetical internal calculation dataset, scaling losses, dividing each amount by 200. This way, results a dataset with a minimum threshold of €5000. LDA is then applied, using the BIS event type level 1 as risk classification.

As part of the analysis, results we report:

- descriptive statistics;
- autocorrelation analysis;
- estimation of capital at risk through parametric models;
- estimation of capital at risk through EVT model;
- estimation of capital at risk through *g-and-h* distribution;
- application of copula functions to obtain the overall capital at risk.

If we suppose that the dataset obtained represents a time series with length of one year, we can assume this represents a very large internationally active bank. In fact, we have 122 losses over one million and, from, an average internationally active bank should have from 50 to 80 losses over this threshold. In the reported average gross income for an internationally active bank is around 10 billion Euros (see reference 3). Hence, we can assume that the analysis refers to an internationally active bank, with gross income of around 20 billion Euros.

Table 3.4 Descriptive statistics for Algo OpData (€'000)

EventType	Number	Mean	StDev	Min	q025	q050	q075	Max
Internal fraud	1037	210	662	5	13	36	127	8889
External fraud	335	101	265	5	9	21	73	2202
Employment	138	89	221	5	9	19	64	1943
Clients	1254	232	839	5	14	39	136	10 754
Physical assets	11	1031	1625	22	73	254	1115	5105
IT system	19	147	356	5	10	28	75	1528
Process management	235	108	294	5	10	27	82	3773
Total	3029	196	688	5	12	33	118	10 754

3.15.1 Descriptive Statistics

Table 3.4 reports a series of descriptive statistics for each event type.

3.15.2 Autocorrelation Analysis

Autocorrelation plots for each risk class are reported in Figures 3.8–3.14.

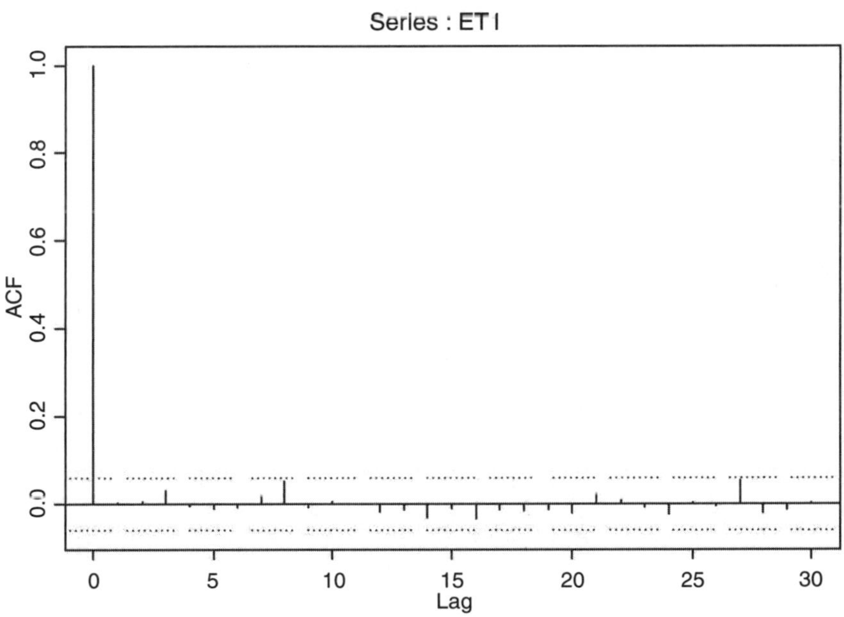

Figure 3.8 Autocorrelation plot for internal fraud

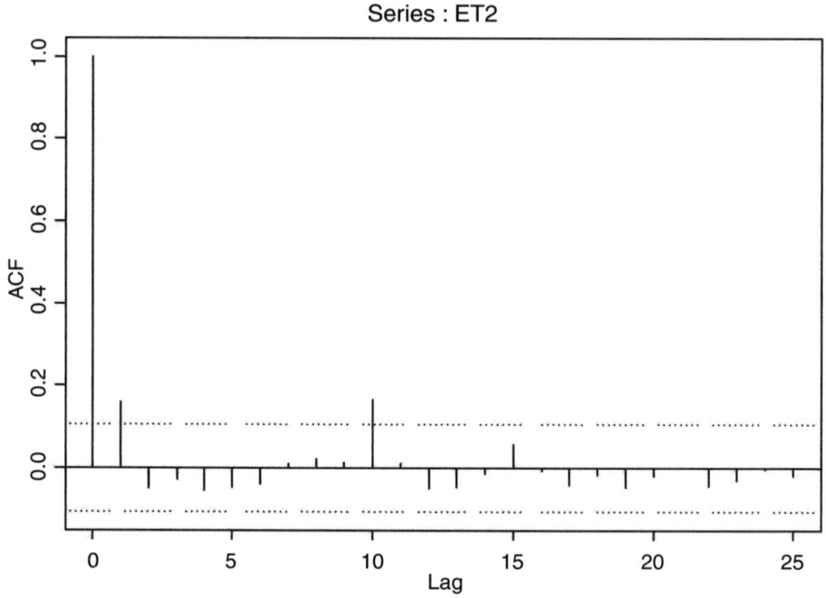

Figure 3.9 Autocorrelation plot for external fraud

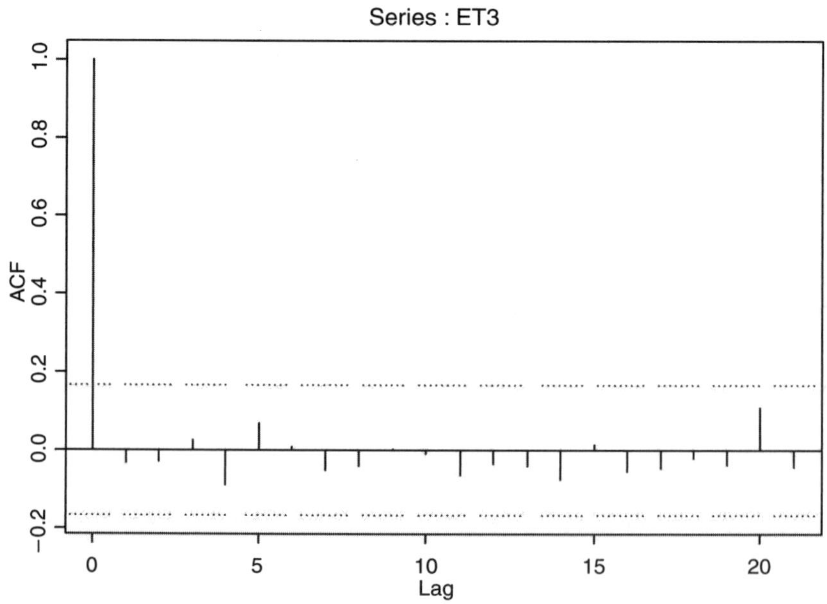

Figure 3.10 Autocorrelation plot for employment problems

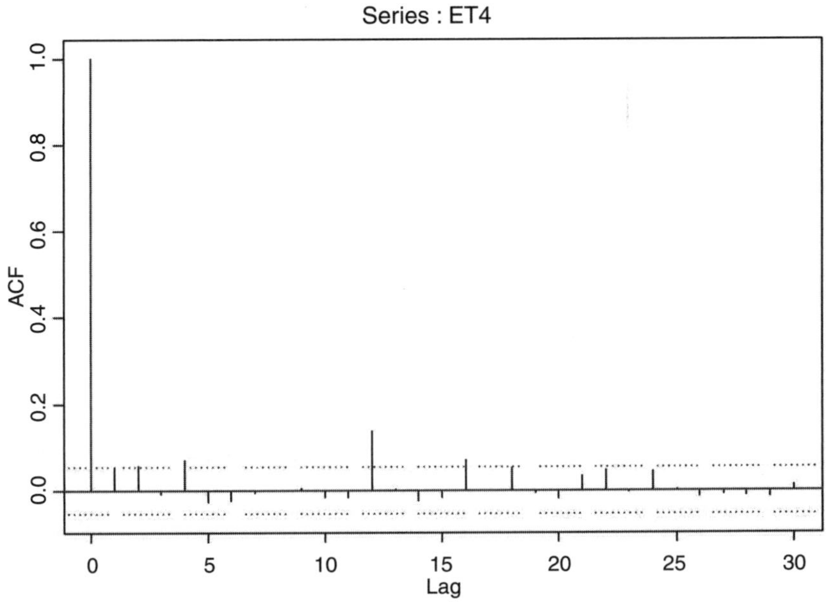

Figure 3.11 Autocorrelation plot for clients claims

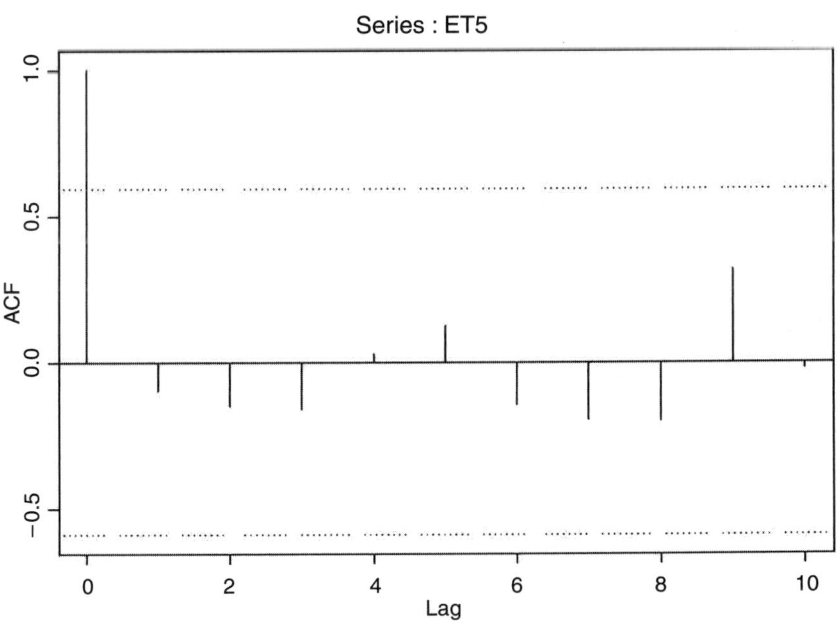

Figure 3.12 Autocorrelation plot for physical asset losses

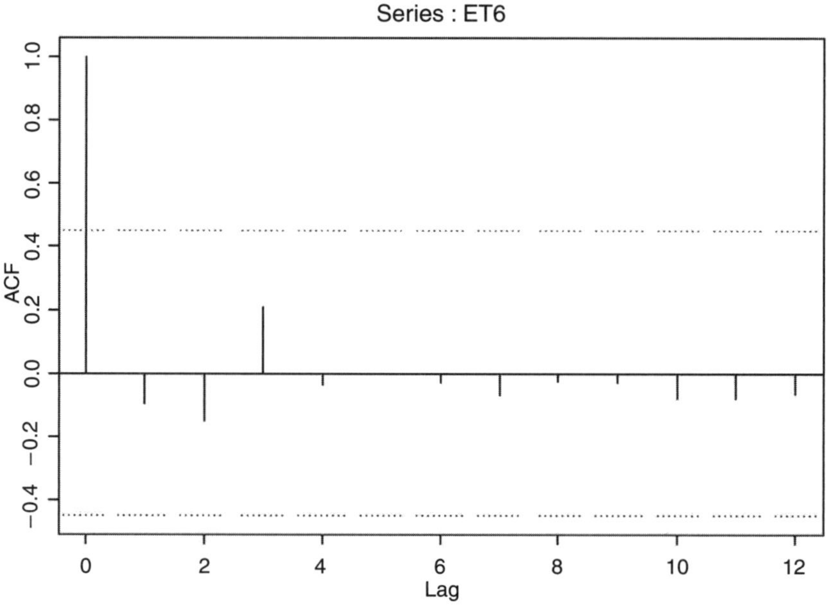

Figure 3.13 Autocorrelation plot for IT systems losses

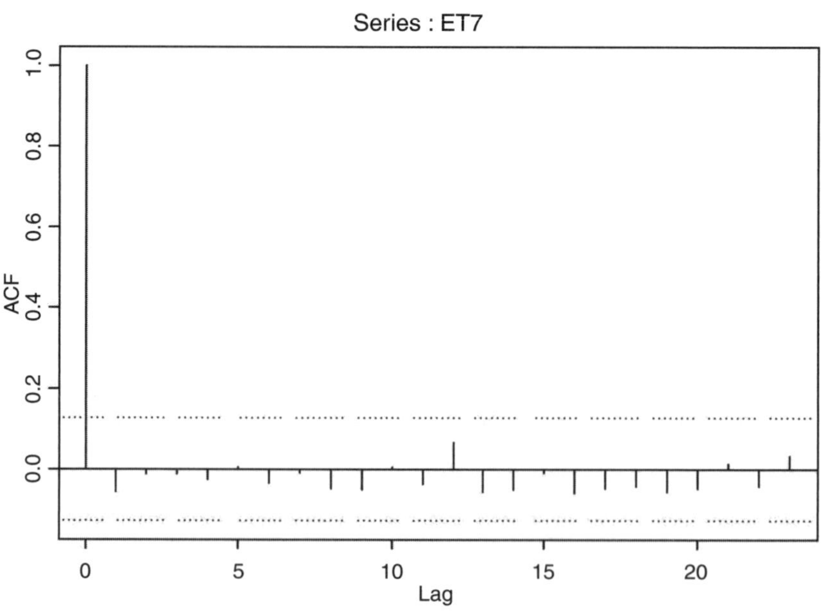

Figure 3.14 Autocorrelation plot for process management losses

Given that only a negligible number of autocorrelation estimates fall outside the confidence interval defined by the dotted lines, we assume there is no significant serial correlation.

3.15.3 Capital at Risk Estimates using Parametric Models

We first estimate the severity distribution using a classical parametrical model; that is, using only one distribution for the whole range of loss amounts. For every risk class, the severity is estimated with a distribution from among the probability distributions listed in Table 3.1. This best-fit procedure is based on the analytical and graphical method as in Section 3.4. Parameters of distributions are estimated on data in thousands of Euros.

In the following pages we show, for each risk class and for each distribution, the estimated parameters, SBC results, and goodness-of-fit test results. Q–q plots are reported for distributions showing good results for SBC and goodness-of-fit test results.

Looking at Table 3.5, at a glance, we can exclude the exponential and gamma distributions as these present significantly higher SBC values compared to the others. Based on the Kolmogoroff–Smirnov and Anderson–Darling test p-value results, we can exclude also the Pareto and loglogistic distributions; as we do not perform only a quantitative analysis, but look at graphical results and reasonableness. For this reason, we prefer not to discard too many distributions: plots for each of the remaining distributions are presented in Figures 3.15 to 3.18.

The analysis of q–q plots suggests as best distribution to use for data fitting is the Weibull. At first glance, the three remaining distributions appear alike, but looking at the plots, the lognormal provides a lower

Table 3.5 Distribution parameters and goodness-of-fit statistics for internal fraud

Distribution	Param. 1	Param. 2	SBC	KS Stat.	KS p-value	AD Stat.	AD p-value
lognormal	2.65471	2.25344	5781.7	0.01498	0.97131	0.34943	0.47424
exponential	0.00487	0.00000	6563.7	0.38193	0.00000	∞	0.00000
Pareto	0.76809	15.35708	5795.8	0.03625	0.12779	2.44385	0.00000
Weibull	0.27618	6.00644	5780.4	0.01264	0.99571	0.26026	0.71056
gamma	0.00000	2079.58642	5861.0	0.17138	0.00000	69.97951	0.00000
loglogistic	0.81250	18.68738	5791.0	0.02645	0.45469	1.31942	0.00201

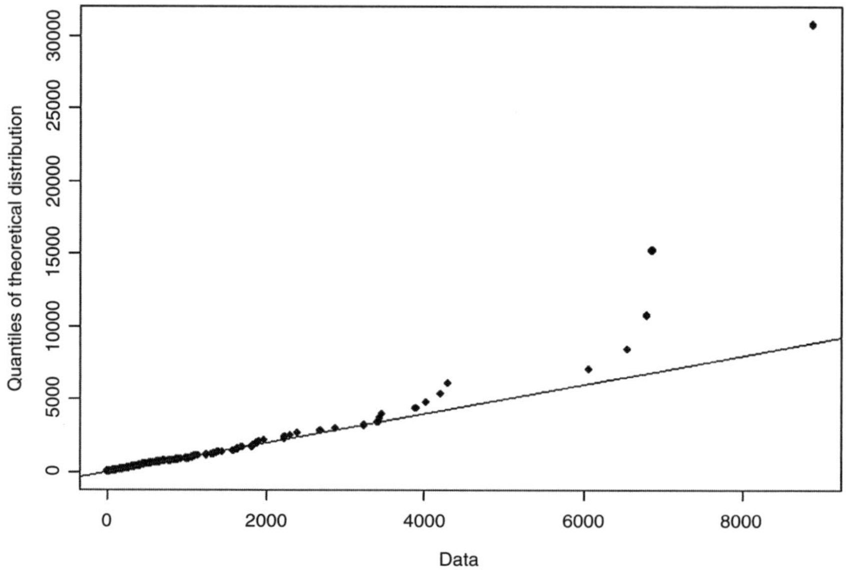

Figure 3.15 q–q plot of lognormal distribution for internal fraud

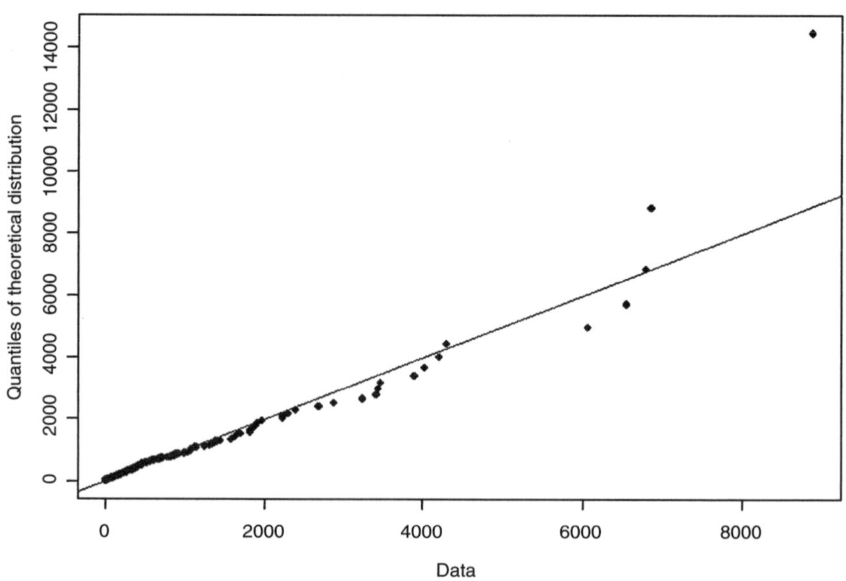

Figure 3.16 q–q plot of Weibull distribution for internal fraud

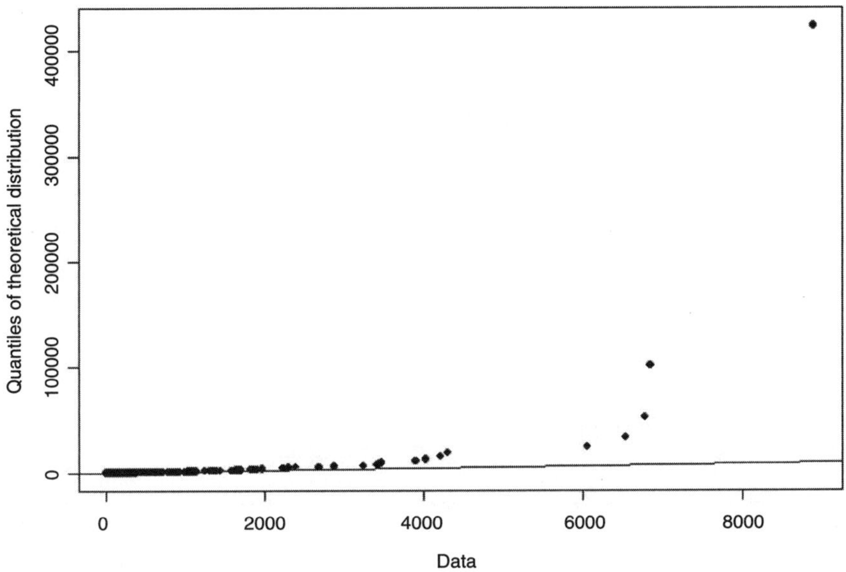

Figure 3.17 q–q plot of Pareto distribution for internal fraud

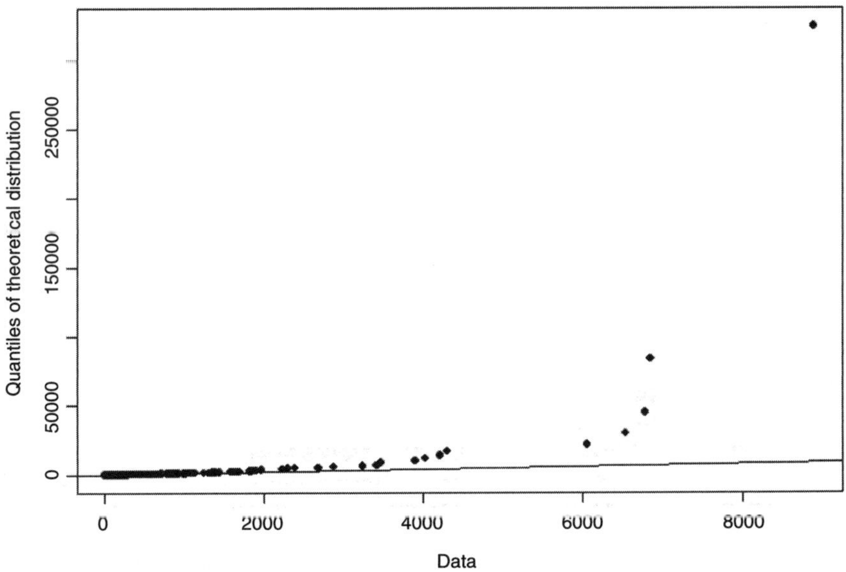

Figure 3.18 q–q plot of loglogistic distribution for internal fraud

Table 3.6 Distribution parameters and goodness-of-fit statistics for external fraud

Distribution	Param. 1	Param. 2	SBC	KS Stat.	KS *p*-value	AD Stat.	AD *p*-value
lognormal	1.20112	2.39470	1652.8	0.03564	0.77433	0.41474	0.33474
exponential	0.01046	0.00000	1866.4	0.37892	0.00000	122.52707	0.00000
Pareto	0.81628	7.09135	1656.3	0.04265	0.56123	0.80752	0.03672
Weibull	0.22638	0.42903	1652.1	0.03269	0.85447	0.35346	0.46432
gamma	0.00000	695.64634	1682.0	0.20629	0.00000	29.40548	0.00000
loglogistic	0.84148	7.43095	1655.6	0.04041	0.62950	0.64314	0.09344

overestimation of the highest quantiles. We reduce the set of distributions to be tested to the Weibull and the lognormal.

Looking at the SBC values for external fraud in Table 3.6, we can discard the exponential and gamma distributions. Considering the Anderson–Darling *p*-value results, we can also exclude the Pareto distribution for the external fraud class. Plots for the remaining distributions are in Figures 3.19 to 3.21.

The analysis of the q–q plots indicates as the best-fitting distribution the Weibull, a good fit for the high quantiles. As we don't want to overly

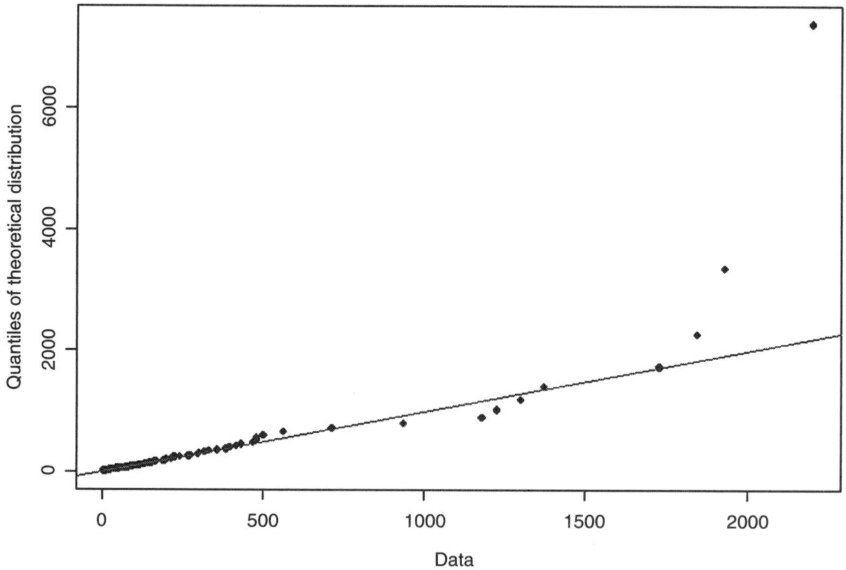

Figure 3.19 q–q plot of lognormal distribution for external fraud

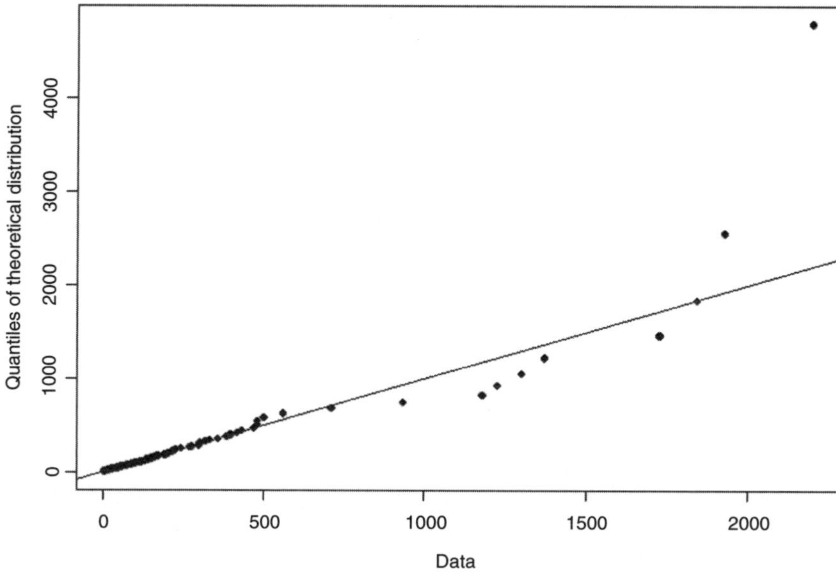

Figure 3.20 q–q plot of Weibull distribution for external fraud

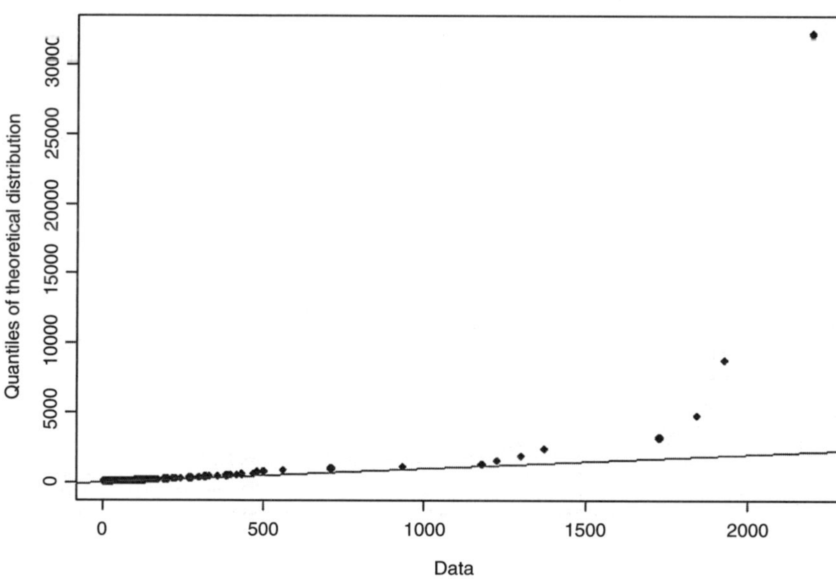

Figure 3.21 q–q plot of loglogistic distribution for external fraud

Table 3.7 Distribution parameters and goodness-of-fit statistics for employment

Distribution	Param. 1	Param. 2	SBC	KS Stat.	KS p-value	AD Stat.	AD p-value
lognormal	0.77354	2.50307	674.4	0.05885	0.70298	0.42447	0.31750
exponential	0.01184	0.00000	753.1	0.37508	0.00000	47.39011	0.00000
Pareto	0.77827	5.18160	676.3	0.06120	0.65636	0.59585	0.11979
Weibull	0.21949	0.28155	673.8	0.06000	0.68031	0.40167	0.35924
gamma	0.00000	540.32971	683.9	0.20496	0.00001	10.94072	0.00000
loglogistic	0.80808	5.34949	675.9	0.05842	0.71135	0.51400	0.19276

restrict the subset of distributions to be tested, we will also consider the lognormal distribution, as the results are reasonable.

In Table 3.7, referring to the relationship operational risk class. Results show that the exponential and gamma distributions should be excluded. Looking at the Anderson–Darling p-value results, the Pareto and loglogistic distributions also should be excluded, but considering the very positive Kolmogoroff–Smirnov test results, we still consider these two distributions in the q–q plot analysis. Plots for the remaining distributions are reported in Figures 3.22 to 3.25.

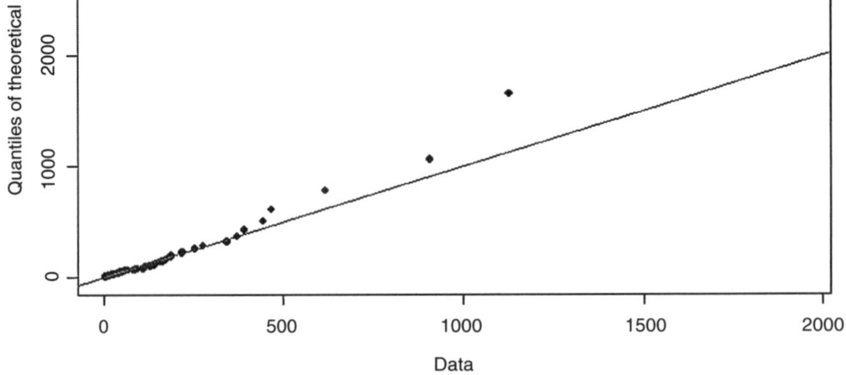

Figure 3.22 q–q plot of lognormal distribution for employment problems

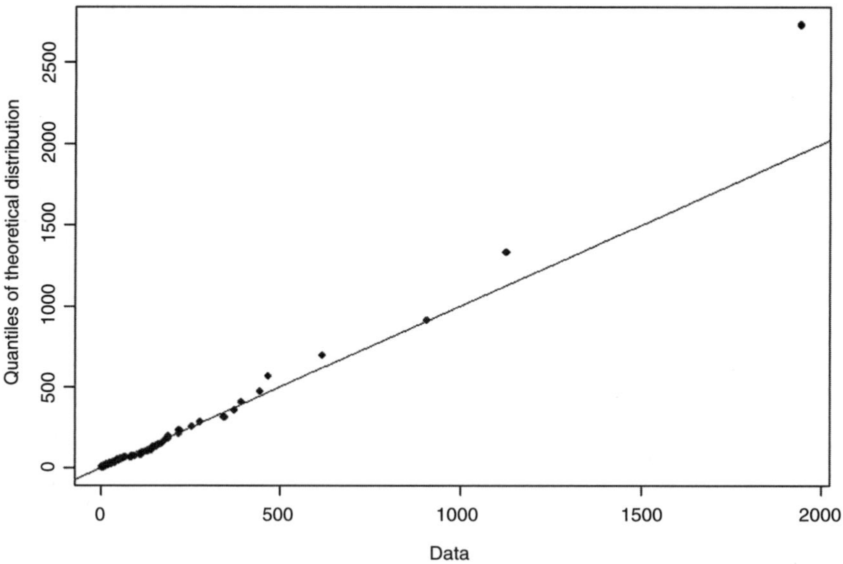

Figure 3.23 q–q plot of Weibull distribution for employment problems

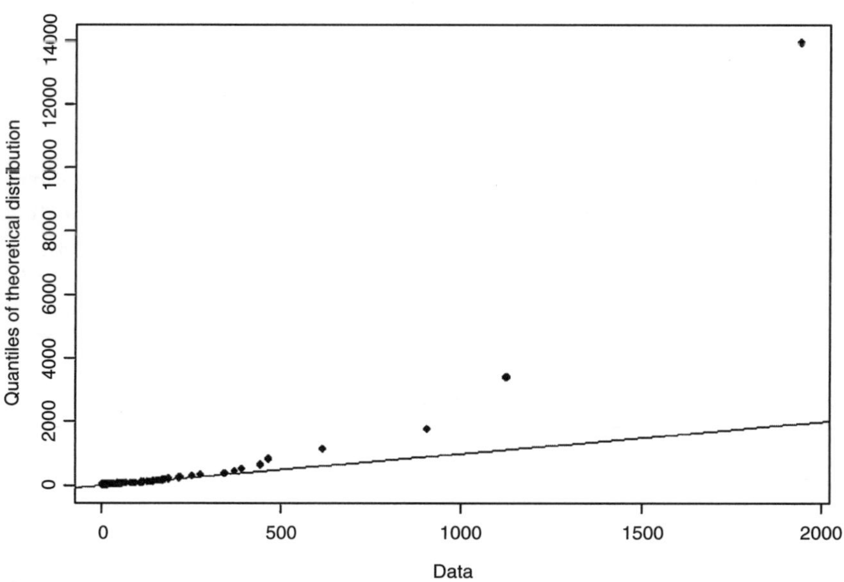

Figure 3.24 q–q plot of Pareto distribution for employment problems

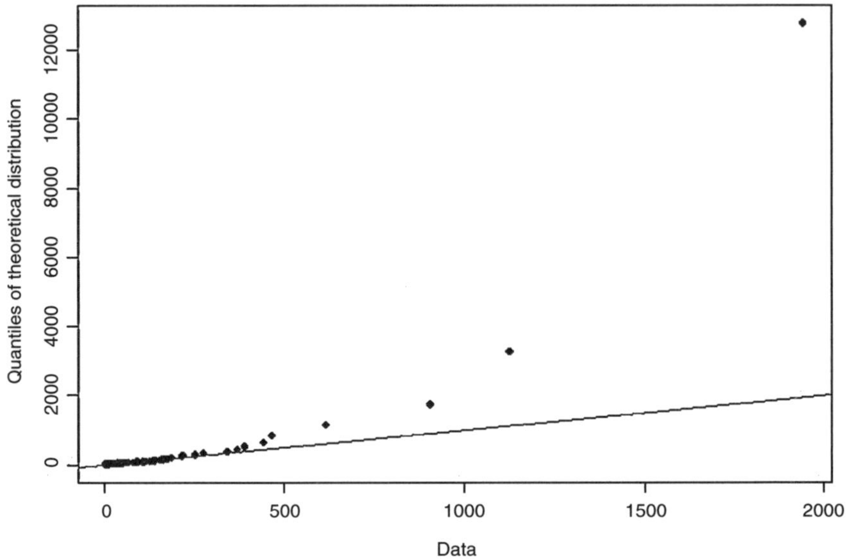

Figure 3.25 q–q plot of loglogistic distribution for employment problems

The Weibull distribution presents the best-fitting behavior. The loglogistic and Pareto distributions behave similarly, while the lognormal q–q plot, although not as well as the Weibull, presents reasonable results for the high quantile overestimation.

Table 3.8, referring to the clients, products operational risk class, highlights negative results for almost all the distributions: the lognormal and the Weibull also provide very poor Anderson–Darling test *p*-values. Plots for these two distributions are reported in Figures 3.26 and 3.27.

Table 3.8 Distribution parameters and goodness-of-fit statistics for clients

Distribution	Param. 1	Param. 2	SBC	KS Stat.	KS *p*-value	AD Stat.	AD *p*-value
lognormal	2.80241	2.22006	7064.4	0.02011	0.68271	0.76027	0.04802
exponential	0.00441	0.00000	8060.8	0.38771	0.00000	∞	0.00000
Pareto	0.78170	17.50157	7082.0	0.03823	0.04984	3.81968	0.00000
Weibull	0.28271	7.52574	7063.8	0.02313	0.50557	0.59358	0.12142
gamma	0.00000	3037.59720	7196.6	0.19792	0.00000	110.00462	0.00000
loglogistic	0.81952	21.00270	7075.5	0.03058	0.18731	2.17185	0.00001

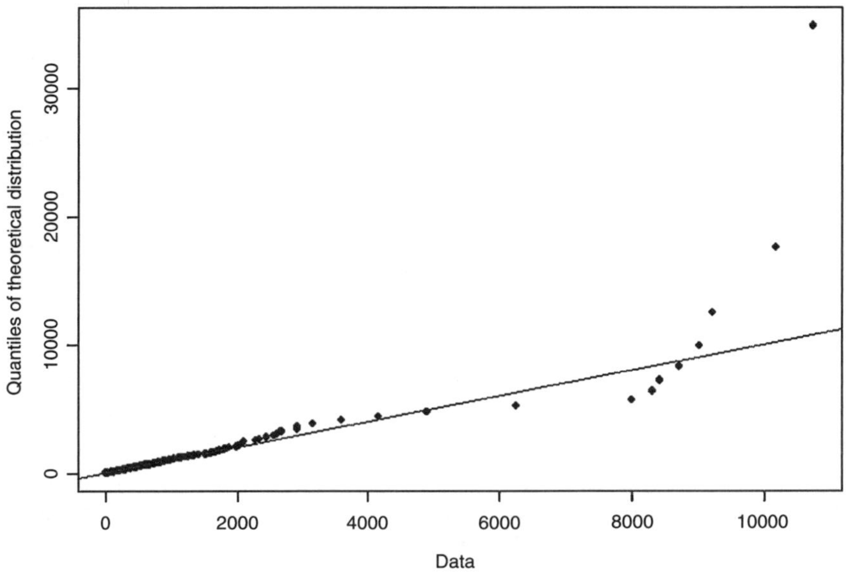

Figure 3.26 q–q plot of lognormal distribution for clients

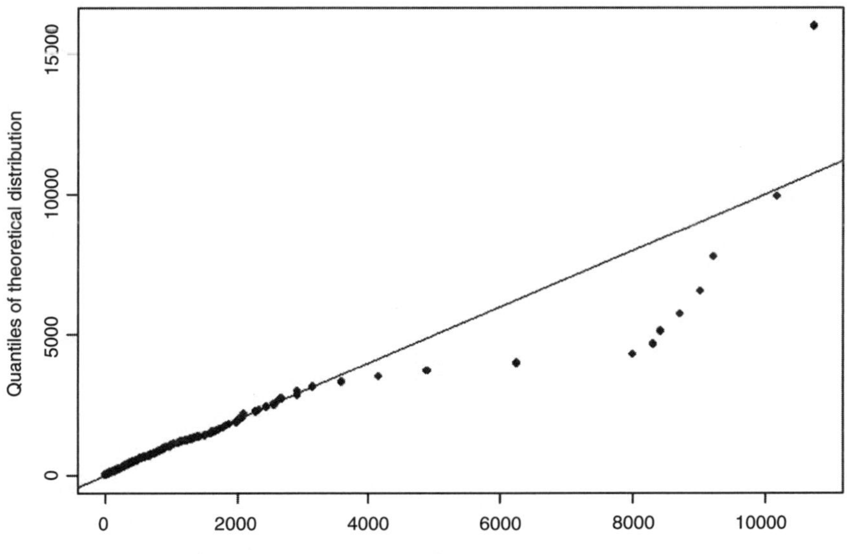

Figure 3.27 q–q plot of Weibull distribution for clients

Table 3.9 Distribution parameters and goodness-of-fit statistics for physical assets

Distribution	Param. 1	Param. 2	SBC	KS Stat.	KS *p*-value	AD Stat.	AD *p*-value
lognormal	5.51832	1.88642	84.6	0.09995	0.99924	0.18996	0.89940
exponential	0.00097	0.00000	87.8	0.33464	0.13372	2.81586	0.00100
Pareto	0.77161	155.01077	85.0	0.10655	0.99806	0.21981	0.83584
Weibull	0.49795	481.23458	84.5	0.10498	0.99843	0.18943	0.90026
gamma	0.25473	3184.74695	84.5	0.12240	0.98946	0.20374	0.87590
loglogistic	0.84705	231.19557	84.9	0.09570	0.99963	0.18620	0.90562

The q–q plots present different, albeit not great, behaviors: the Weibull seems preferable as it involves a lower overestimation in the highest quantiles than the lognormal.

Table 3.9, referring to the physical asset operational risk class, shows positive values, where we can exclude, from a strict quantitative point of view, only the exponential distribution. We are convinced that the positive values are due to the limited data available. Plots for the remaining distributions are shown in Figures 3.28 to 3.32.

The q–q plot suggests as the best distribution the Weibull: this time a very good fit for the extreme quantiles. Here the lognormal distribution

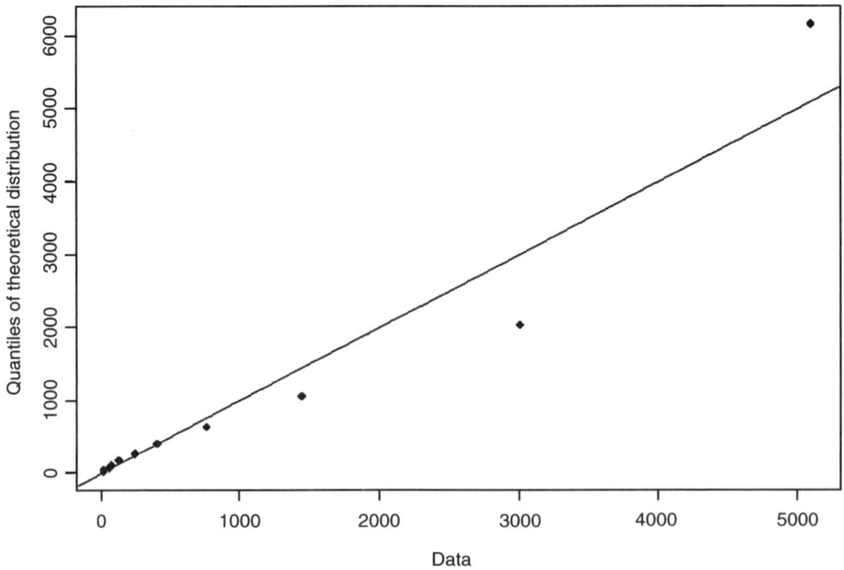

Figure 3.28 q–q plot of lognormal distribution for physical assets losses

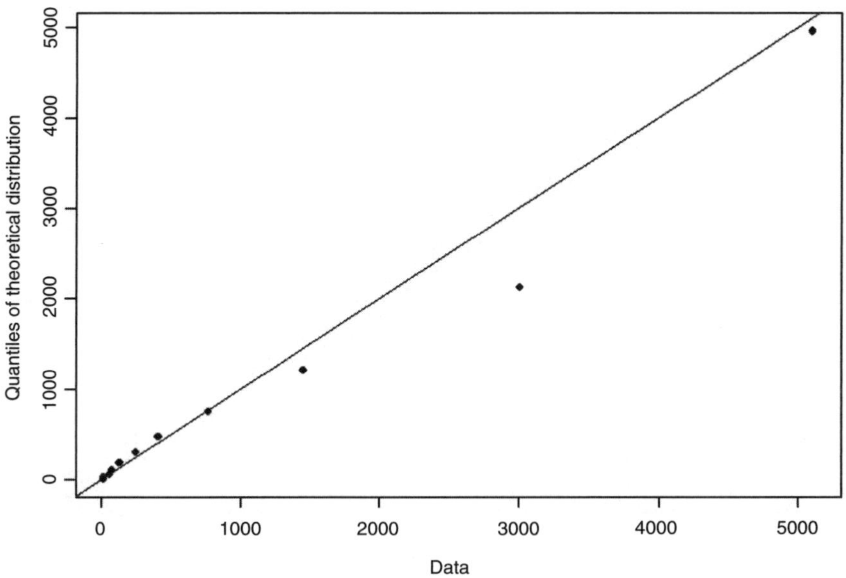

Figure 3.29 q–q plot of Weibull distribution for physical assets losses

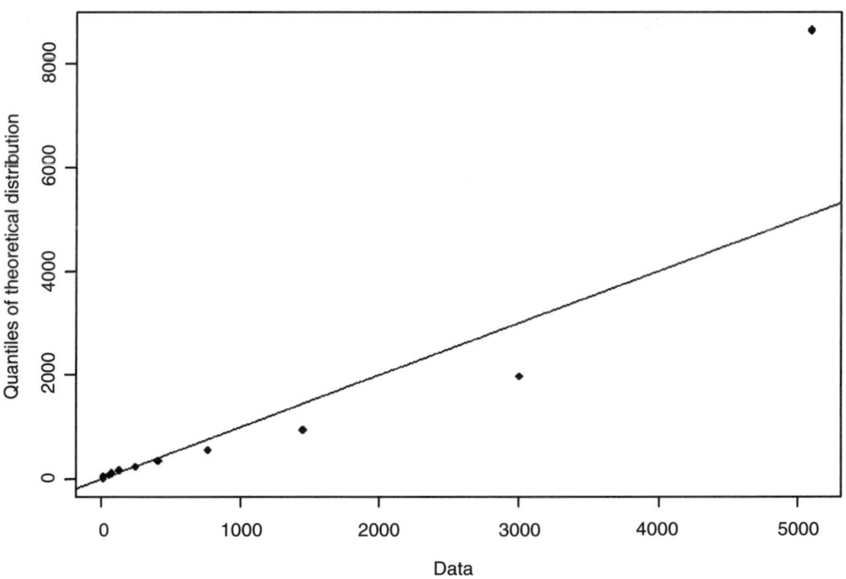

Figure 3.30 q–q plot of Pareto distribution for physical assets losses

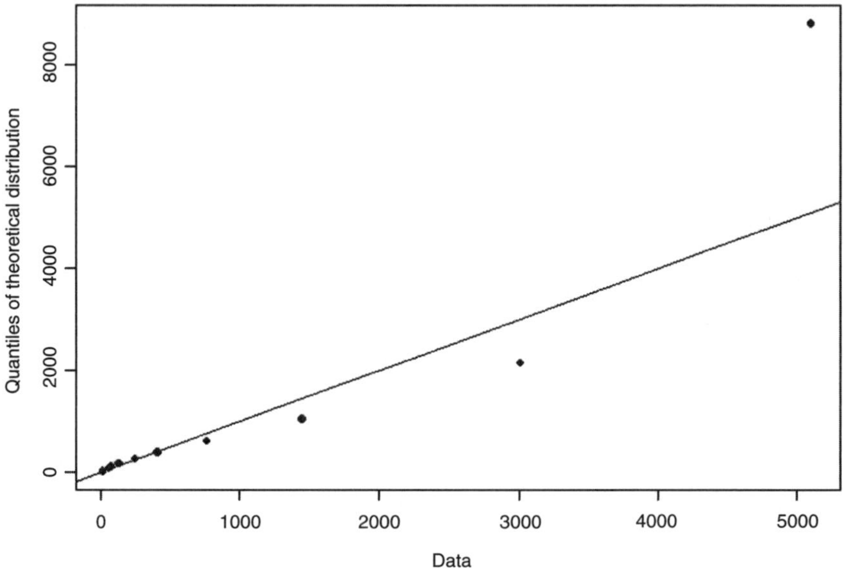

Figure 3.31 q–q plot of loglogistic distribution for physical assets losses

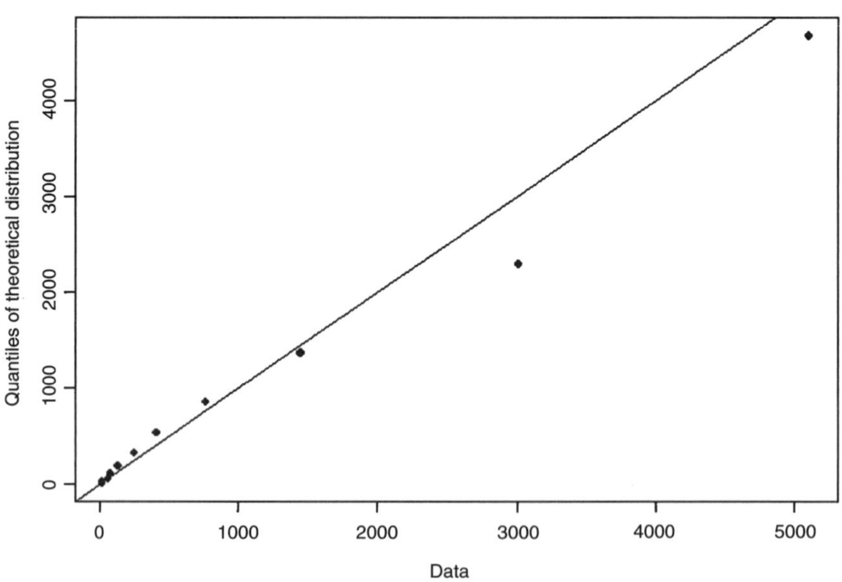

Figure 3.32 q–q plot of gamma distribution for physical assets losses

Table 3.10 Distribution parameters and goodness-of-fit statistics for IT systems

Distribution	Param. 1	Param. 2	SBC	KS Stat.	KS *p*-value	AD Stat.	AD *p*-value
lognormal	0.40575	2.88849	100.0	0.11563	0.93607	0.13173	0.98159
exponential	0.00705	0.00000	114.2	0.42612	0.00120	9.74836	0.00000
Pareto	0.67236	4.74675	100.21	0.11013	0.95581	0.14993	0.96316
Weibull	0.18370	0.09731	99.9	0.11752	0.92832	0.13202	0.98136
gamma	0.00000	816.78666	101.3	0.24335	0.17809	1.50022	0.00072
loglogistic	0.72225	5.18043	100.26	0.11353	0.94411	0.13974	0.97455

can be an alternative as it presents reasonable overestimation for the highest quantiles.

Looking at Table 3.10, due to the poor SBC value, we can exclude the exponential distribution and considering the Anderson–Darling test *p*-values, we can exclude the gamma distribution. Knowing that the positive values are caused by limited data available, we consider only distributions resulting with very high values: the Weibull, lognormal, and loglogistic. Plots for these distributions are reported in Figures 3.33 to 3.35.

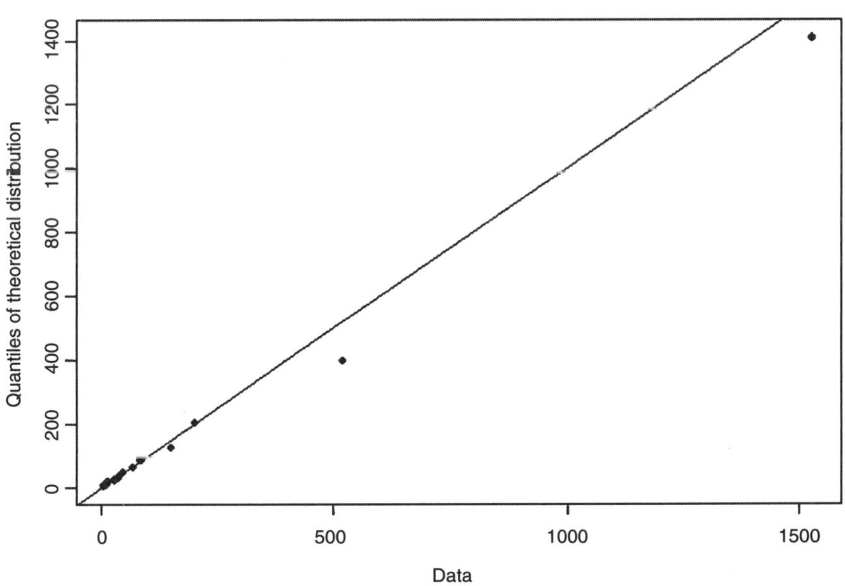

Figure 3.33 q–q plot of lognormal distribution for IT systems losses

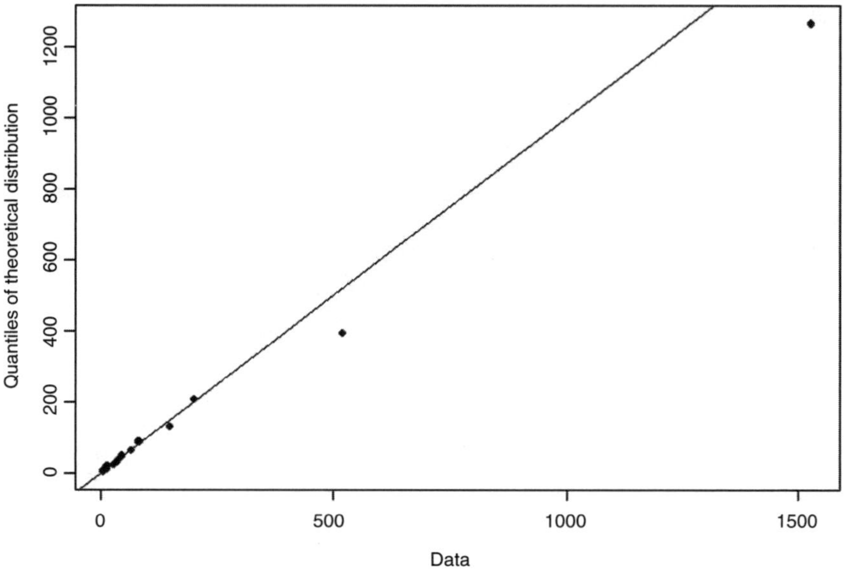

Figure 3.34 q–q plot of Weibull distribution for IT systems losses

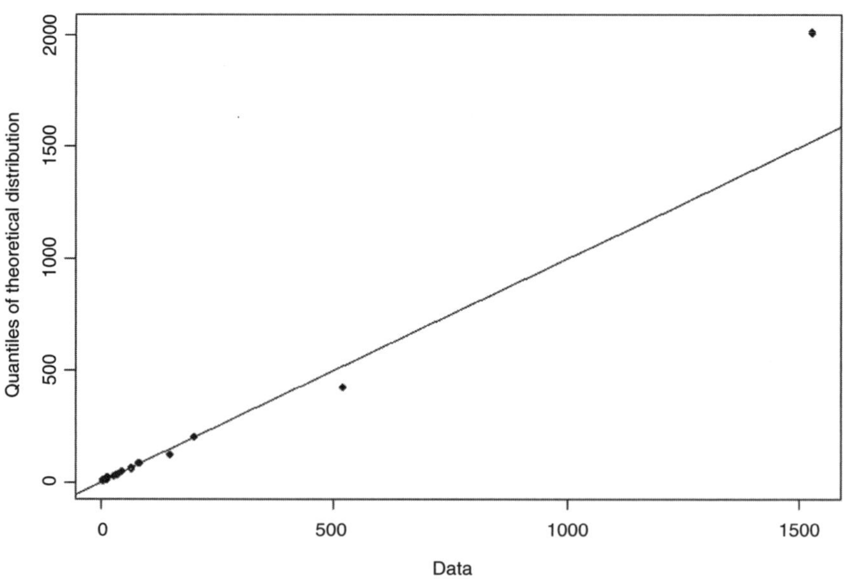

Figure 3.35 q–q plot of loglogistic distribution for IT systems losses

Table 3.11 Distribution parameters and goodness-of-fit statistics for process management

Distribution	Param. 1	Param. 2	SBC	KS Stat.	KS p-value	AD Stat.	AD p-value
lognormal	1.54422	2.37423	1196.2	0.05211	0.52876	0.84470	0.02973
exponential	0.00974	0.00000	1326.9	0.33999	0.00000	77.57010	0.00000
Pareto	0.76959	7.40918	1200.9	0.05848	0.38282	1.44276	0.00100
Weibull	0.25489	1.44512	1194.9	0.05145	0.54507	0.74085	0.05362
gamma	0.00000	800.55707	1210.4	0.17556	0.00000	17.06985	0.00000
loglogistic	0.79842	7.95172	1199.7	0.05528	0.45305	1.12766	0.00597

From the q–q plot analysis, the best distribution is the lognormal, even if producing a little underestimation of the highest quantiles, thus making it not necessarily the most conservative choice.

Table 3.11, which refers to process management risk class, shows poor Anderson–Darling test p-values for almost all distributions. Combining SBC values and p-values, we decide to limit our focus to the Weibull, lognormal, and loglogistic distributions. Plots for these distributions are in Figures 3.36 to 3.38.

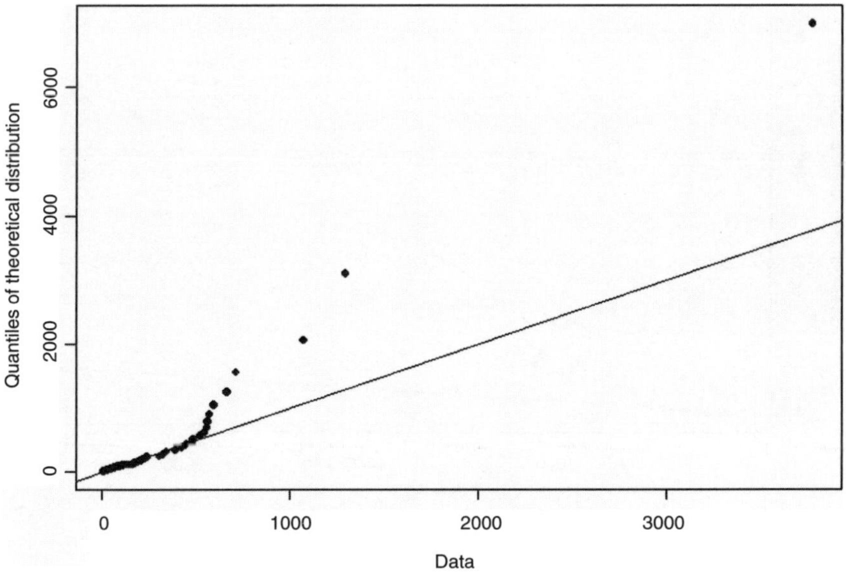

Figure 3.36 q–q plot of lognormal distribution for process management losses

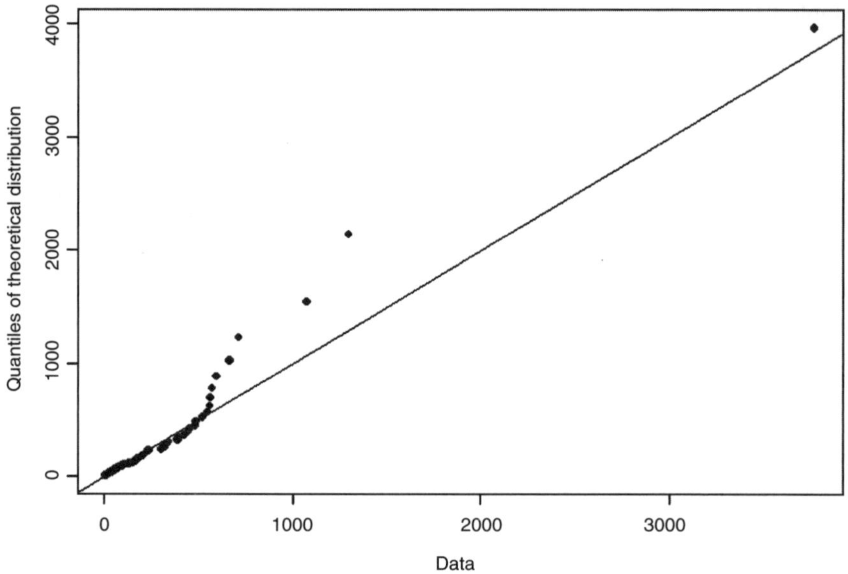

Figure 3.37 q–q plot of Weibull distribution for process management losses

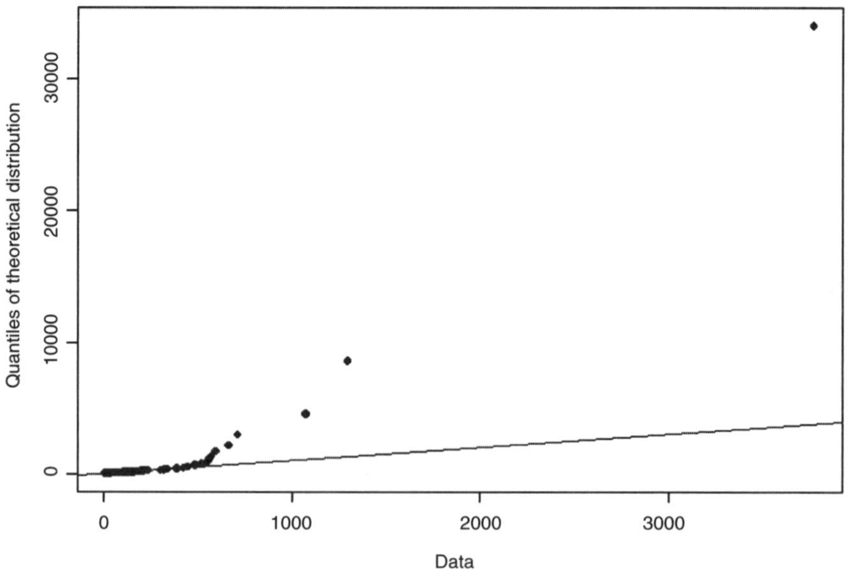

Figure 3.38 q–q plot of loglogistic distribution for process management losses

Table 3.12 Capital at risk results using parametric models (€'000)

Event type	Distribution	VaR	EL	UL
Internal fraud	Weibull	350 307	218 101	132 206
External fraud	Weibull	98 321	35 377	62 944
Employment	Weibull	58 774	13 089	45 686
Clients	Weibull	418 232	277 600	140 631
Physical assets	Weibull	60 925	9 914	51 010
IT systems	lognormal	232 013	2 317	229 695
Process management	Weibull	73 960	27 018	46 942
Total		1 292 532	583 417	709 114

All the q–q plots present a rather unsatisfactory behavior, however the Weibull may be considered the best in relative terms.

Looking at all the results, the Weibull distribution has the best fit for all event types apart from the IT systems class, where the lognormal presents a better accurate fit than other distributions. We are aware that in some cases this best fit is a poor one: this is why we do not apply simply this criterion to choose the distribution.

Frequency is estimated supposing that Algo OpData is a one year long time series. For every event type, the estimate of λ for the Poisson distribution is supposed to be the number of losses.

Having estimated severity and frequency distributions, the annual loss distribution and the capital at risk measures can be obtained through Monte Carlo simulation. Table 3.12 reports, for each event type, the selected distribution for severity, the Value at Risk (VaR) estimated as quantile 99.9%, the expected loss (EL) estimated as the median and the unexpected loss (UL) as the difference between VaR and EL. As described in Section 3.10, the operational capital at risk (OpVaR) can be estimated as UL assuming that sufficient specific provision is available *against* EL.

The overall capital at risk (Table 3.12), obtained summing each class, *is not sufficiently conservative*. We can see that the ratio between EL and VaR is circa 45%, very high compared to those expected (see references 3 and 28 on pages 193–194). These results may be caused by the thin tail of the Weibull distribution. More conservative and robust results can be obtained by using the lognormal distribution for each risk class (Table 3.13). Looking at the q–q plots, this provides a good fit on data and is characterized by a fatter tail than the Weibull.

Table 3.13 Capital at risk results using the lognormal distribution (€'000)

Event type	Distribution	VaR	EL	UL
Internal fraud	lognormal	1 071 449	258 916	812 533
External fraud	lognormal	308 936	39 743	269 194
Employment	lognormal	879 751	46 079	833 671
Clients	lognormal	722 489	211 963	510 527
Physical assets	lognormal	307 187	10 244	296 942
IT systems	lognormal	232 013	2 317	229 695
Process management	lognormal	302 359	32 327	270 031
Total		3 824 184	601 590	3 222 594

Using the lognormal, the ratio between EL and VaR falls at 16%, a more realistic level than the value obtained using the Weibull distribution.

This example shows that: in selecting the distribution, it is not possible to rely solely on goodness-of-fit results. When choosing the distribution, check reasonableness of the capital at risk figures. In the example, as operational capital at risk should be representative of an aggregated annual loss to be suffered, in average, only once in every 1000 years, it is not possible for the observed losses to be such a high confidence level VaR. We observe that the differences in capital at risk results obtained using different distributional hypotheses are significant. This is due to the fact that the part of the severity distribution affecting capital at risk figures is above the maximum observed loss. This problem is known as *extrapolation issue* (see reference 29 on page 194 for further details).

3.15.4 Capital at Risk Estimates using EVT

As observed in Section 3.15.3, using just one distribution to estimate all types of losses may not be adequate to model both body and tail of severity. We apply EVT techniques to model the tail of severity.

We set an appropriate body–tail threshold for each risk class. As described in Section 3.5, there are no consolidated analytical methods for this purpose and a standard approach is qualitative setting through graphical analysis. It may be useful to set an initial threshold value, for example, on the empirical quantile at level 90% and verify, through plots, if this is an appropriate value. There is an exception here for the physical assets and IT systems operational risk classes, where we apply a lower threshold where considering the usual small sample size, with 90% we don't obtain a sufficient number in excess to perform an

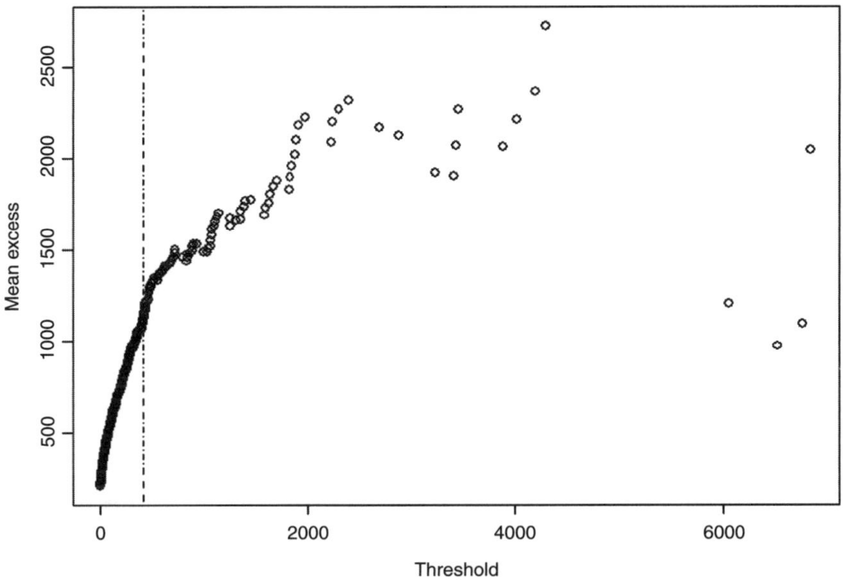

Figure 3.39 Mean excess function for internal fraud

accurate estimate. Analyze the empirical mean excess function plot for each risk class (see Figures 3.39 to 3.45). The vertical line represents the empirical 90% quantile.

Looking at empirical mean excess function plots, there is no evidence that the initial threshold should be changed. We change the threshold according to the mean excess function plots only when there is a clear and shared opinion on a better threshold level.

A further useful graphical analysis studies the variation of shape parameter ξ for a varying threshold. Theoretically, the shape parameter estimate tend to be stable as the threshold u increases. When the excess over threshold is very low, we get a high level of variance, and the estimate may not be stable. The threshold should be selected within values where the shape parameter estimate is stable. Plots of shape parameters for each operational risk classes are reported Figures 3.46 to 3.52).

The graphical analysis validates the identified threshold value: we are just concerned for the internal and external fraud classes where, looking at the shape parameter plots, the most evident threshold levels of stability seem to be localized for values lower than the 90% quantile.

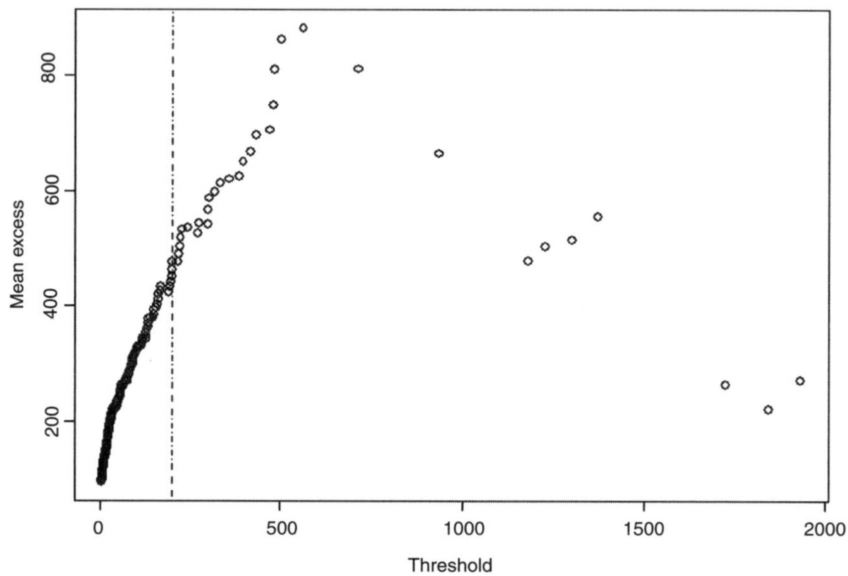

Figure 3.40 Mean excess function for external fraud

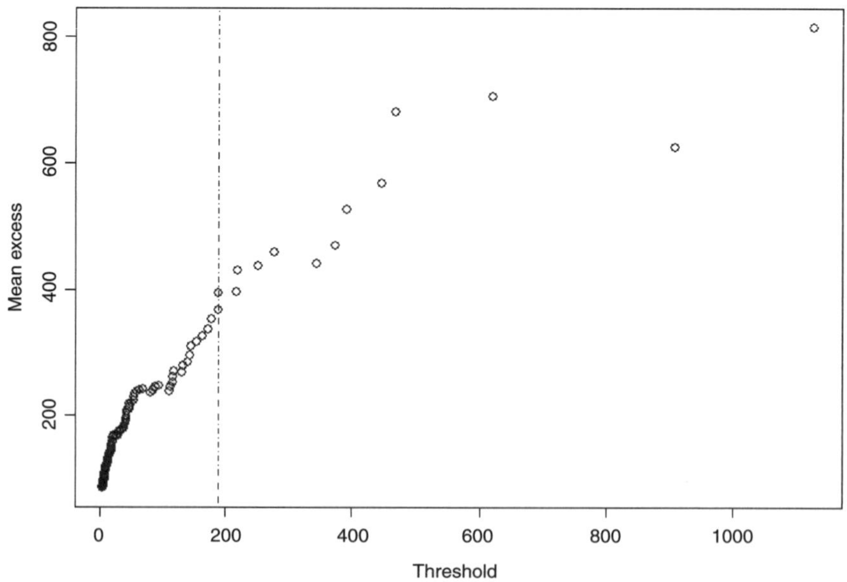

Figure 3.41 Mean excess function for employment problems

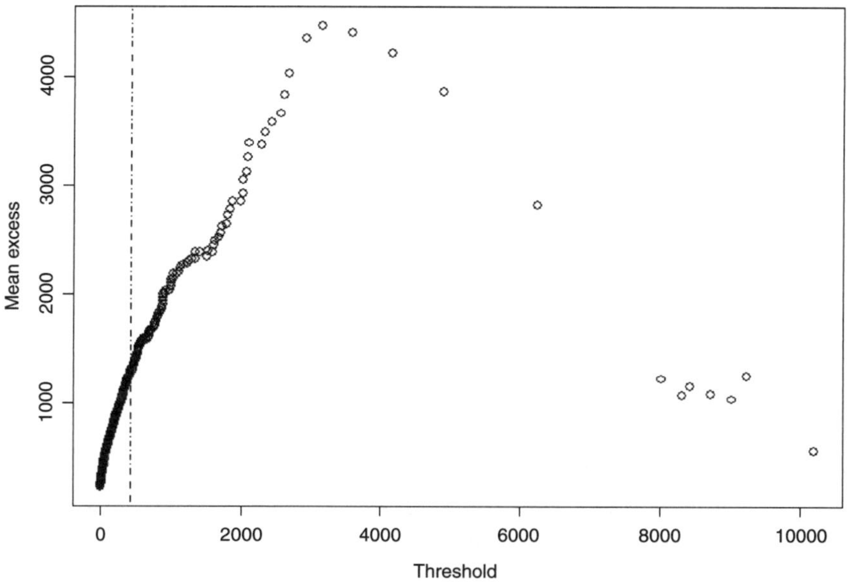

Figure 3.42 Mean excess function for clients claims

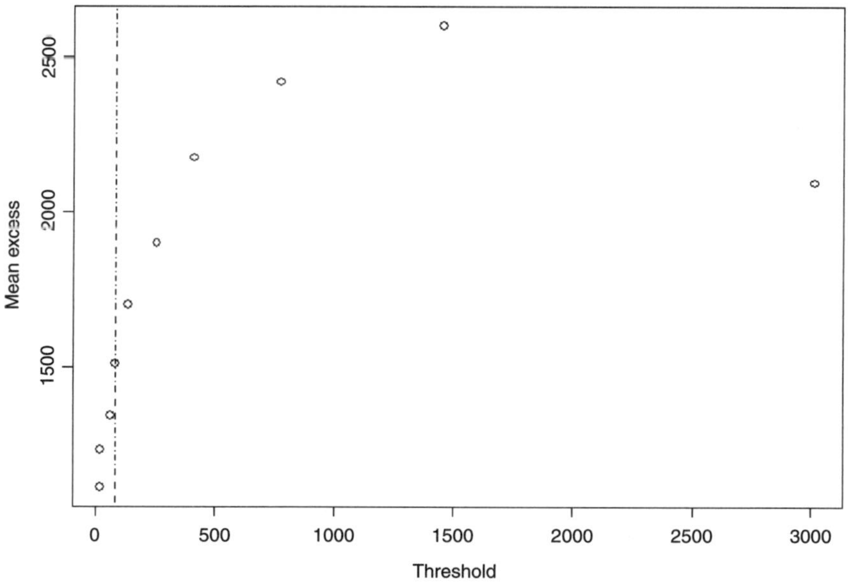

Figure 3.43 Mean excess function for physical assets losses

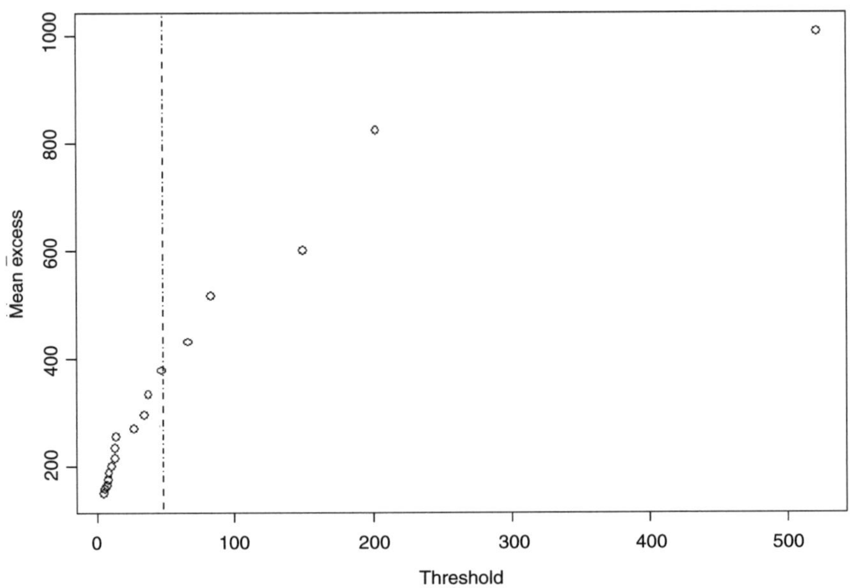

Figure 3.44 Mean excess function for IT systems losses

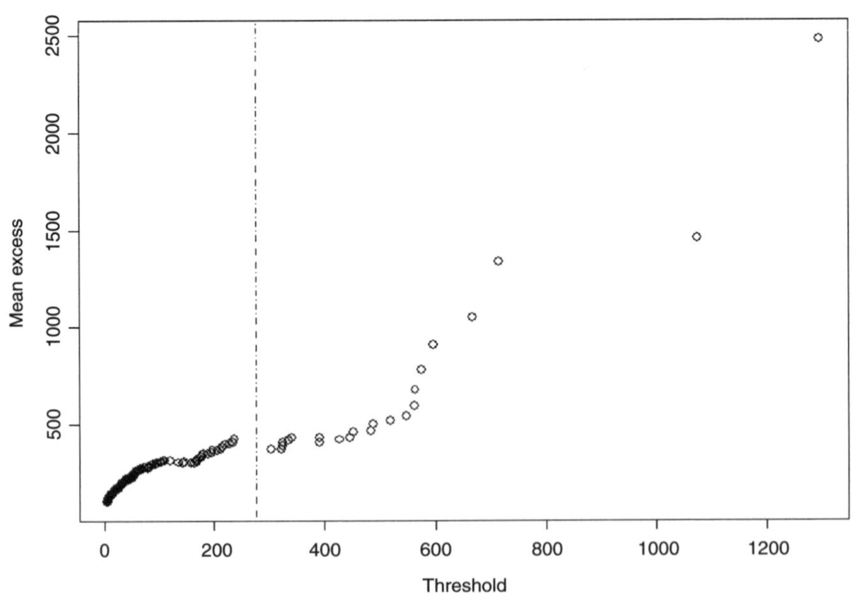

Figure 3.45 Mean excess function for process management losses

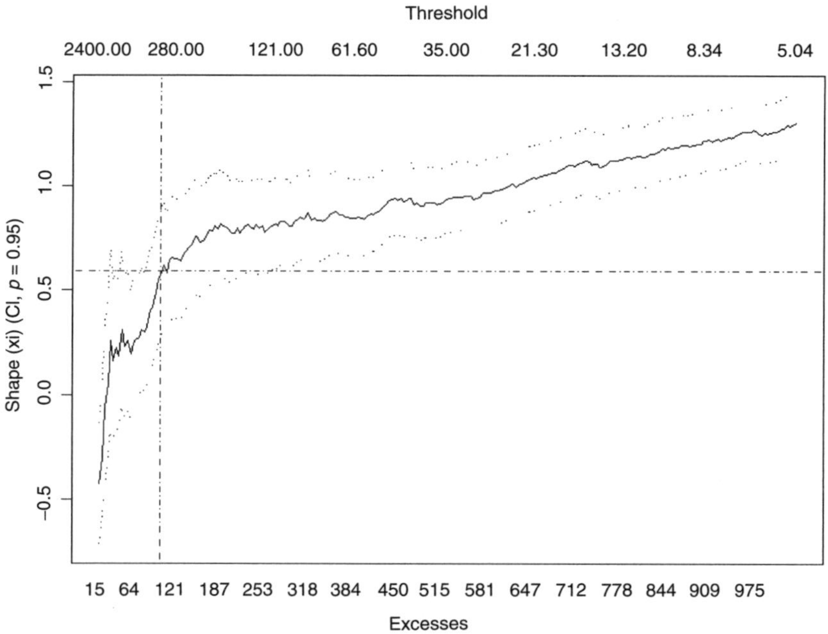

Figure 3.46 Shape parameter estimation for internal fraud

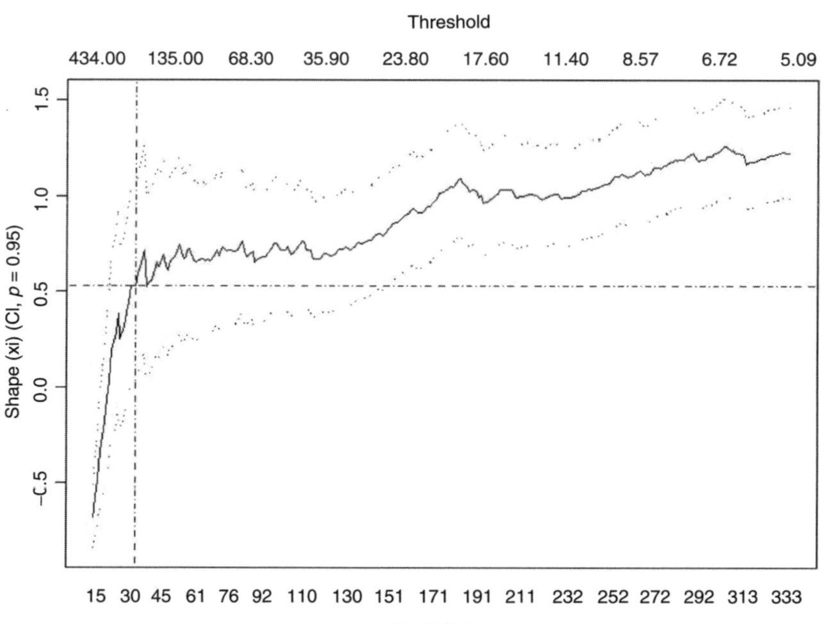

Figure 3.47 Shape parameter estimation for external fraud

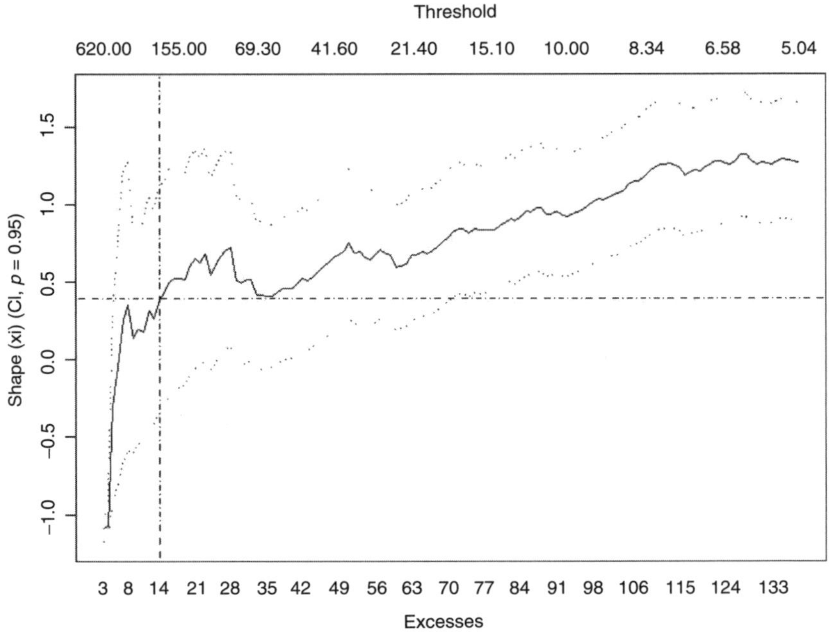

Figure 3.48 Shape parameter estimation for employment problems

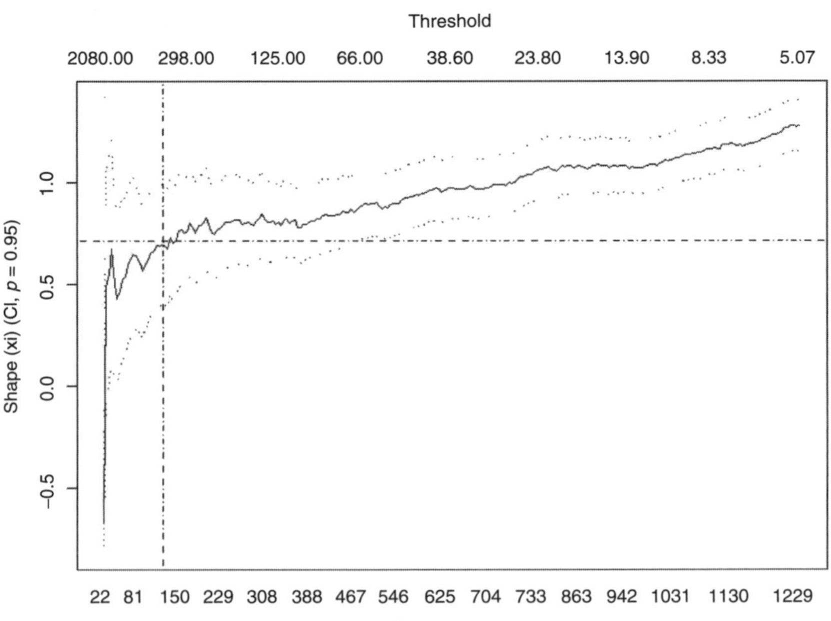

Figure 3.49 Shape parameter estimation for clients claims

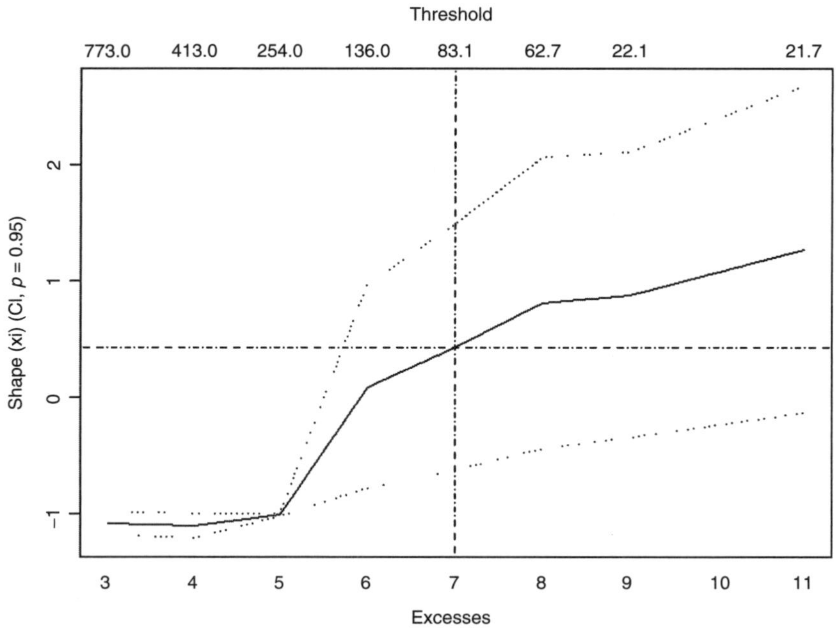

Figure 3.50 Shape parameter estimation for physical assets losses

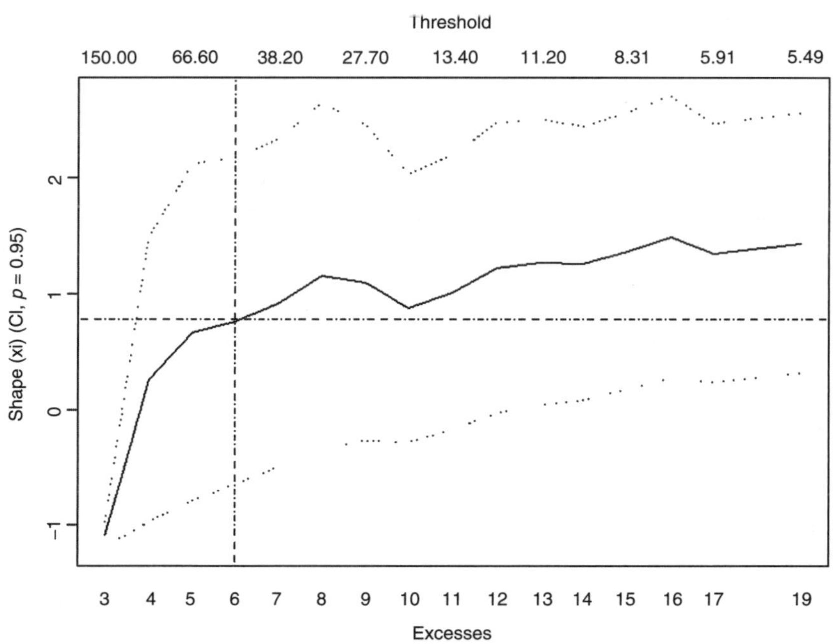

Figure 3.51 Shape parameter estimation for IT systems losses

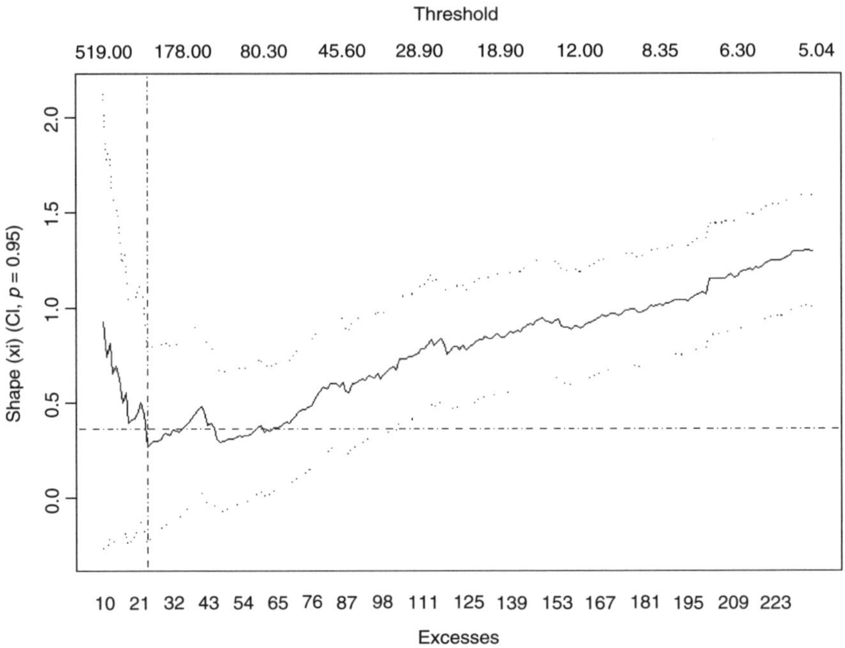

Figure 3.52 Shape parameter estimation for process management losses

In any case for the purposes of this exercise, we will maintain the set threshold.

The GPD parameter estimates and goodness-of-fit test results for every risk class are reported in Table 3.14. The q–q plots are presented in Figures 3.53 to 3.59. Goodness-of-fit test results of GPD estimated

Table 3.14 GPD parameters estimates

Event type	Threshold	ξ	β	KS Stat.	KS p-value	AD Stat.	AD p-value
Internal fraud	407	0.59322	547.5258	0.08464	0.42231	1.36373	0.00157
External fraud	201	0.53305	256.2966	0.11076	0.75739	0.52215	0.18400
Employment	189	0.39187	236.2489	0.09442	0.99835	0.24442	0.76273
Clients	425	0.71199	502.3257	0.04451	0.95469	0.34514	0.48504
Physical assets	83	0.43127	954.3001	0.15313	0.98689	0.20780	0.86643
IT systems	48	0.78006	149.5491	0.13855	0.99869	0.17045	0.93258
Process management	277	0.36478	235.9846	0.12774	0.78262	0.63731	0.09660

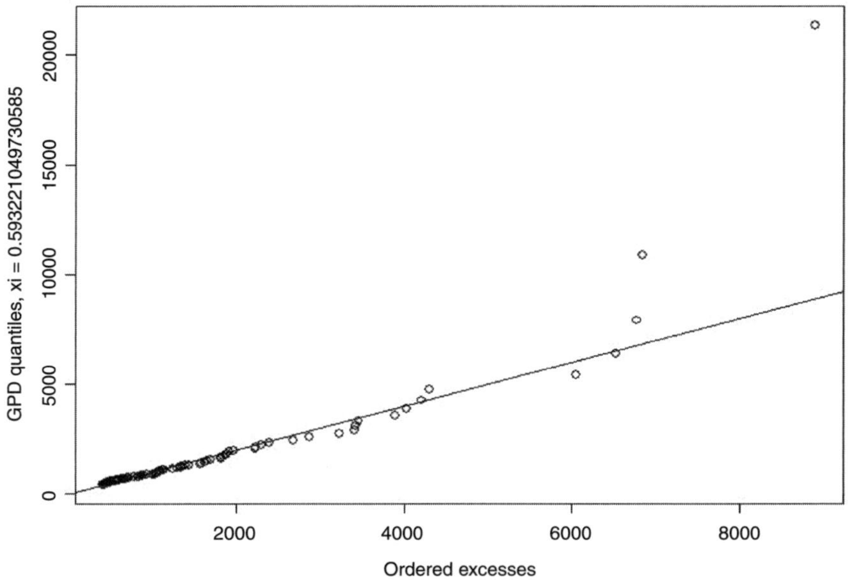

Figure 3.53 q–q plot of GPD for internal fraud

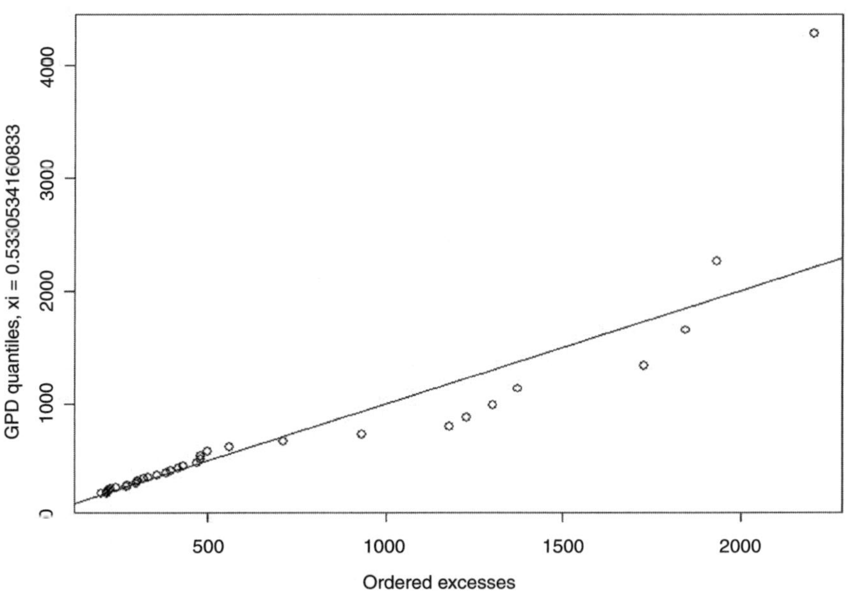

Figure 3.54 q–q plot of GPD for external fraud

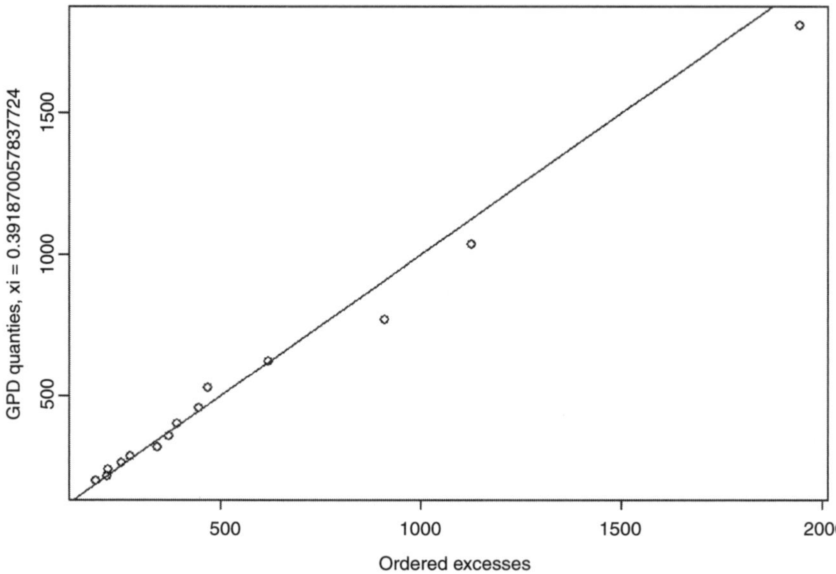

Figure 3.55 q–q plot of GPD for employment problems

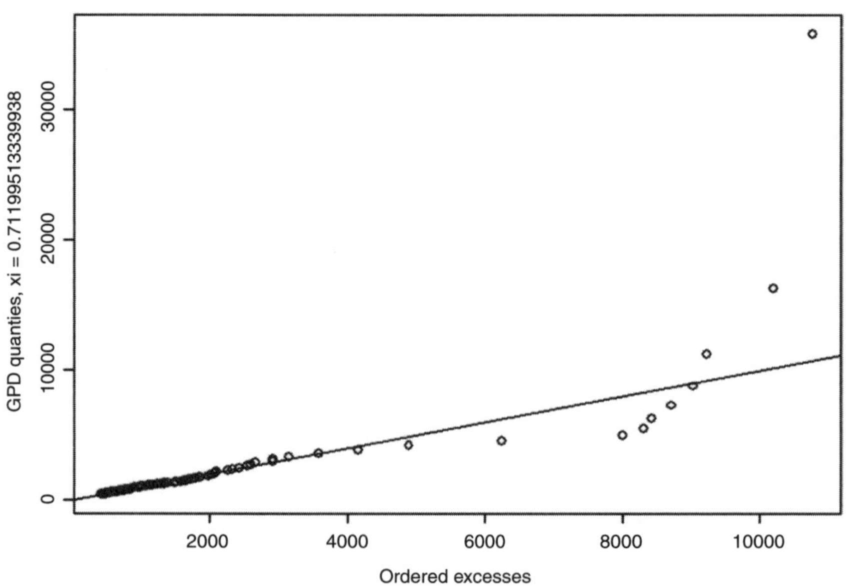

Figure 3.56 q–q plot of GPD for clients claims

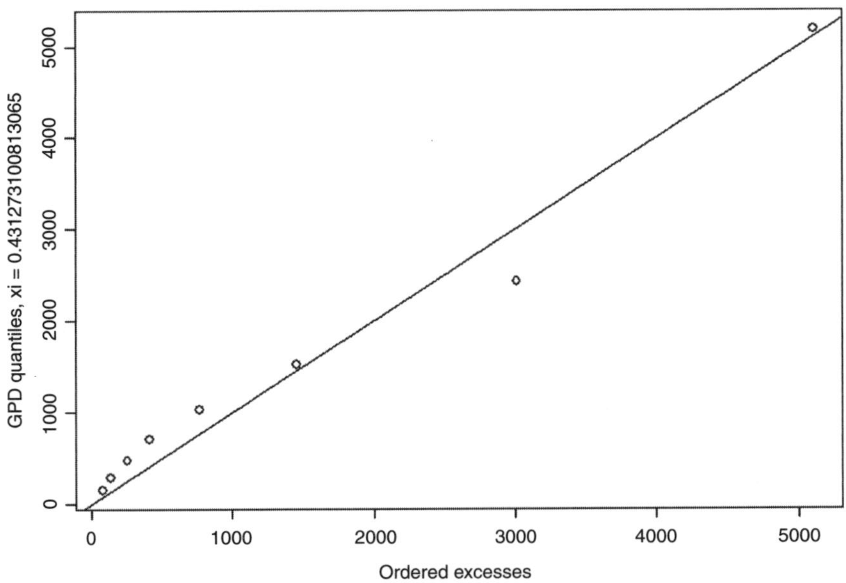

Figure 3.57 q–q plot of GPD for physical assets problems

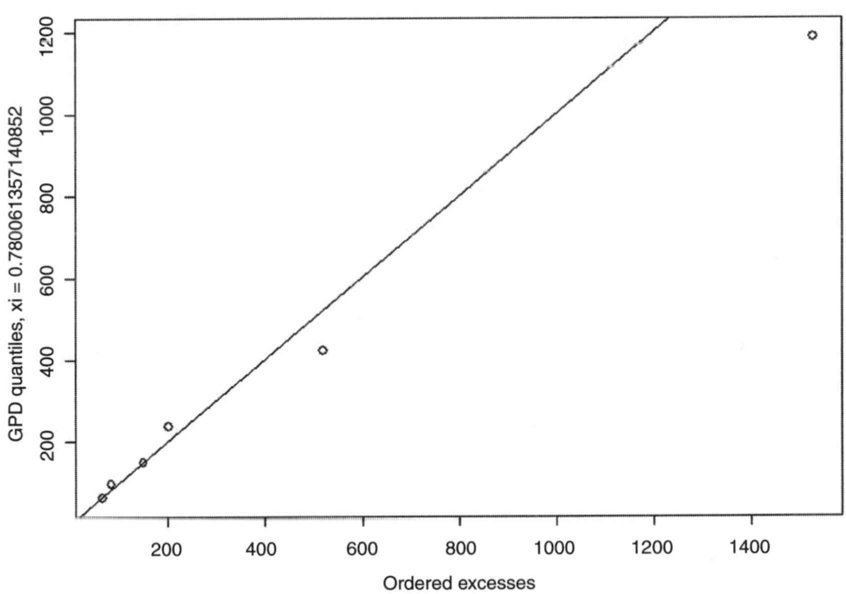

Figure 3.58 q–q plot of GPD for IT systems losses

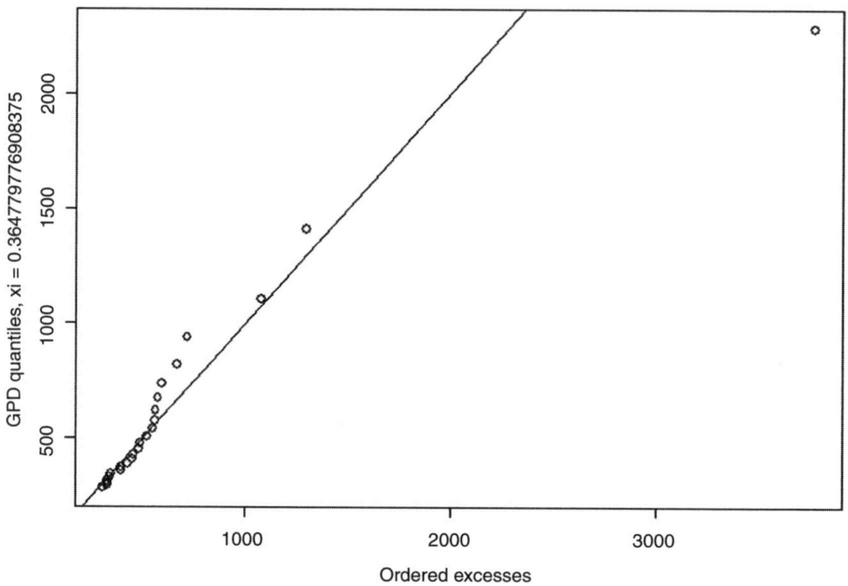

Figure 3.59 q–q plot of GPD for process management losses

on tail data show a relevant improvement compared to the ones obtained before.

Comparing the q–q plots of the GPD with those shown previously, we see that in some cases (employment risk class) the fitting is more precise while in other cases the improvement is not evident. We think this is principally due to the structure. This is obtained by scaling *the original data including mostly large losses*. When applying the internal loss dataset, the improvement in the quality of fitting obtained by applying EVT techniques is more evident.

Once the parameters are estimated, the capital at risk is calculated applying EVT, using GPD to estimate the tail severity. The body of the severity distribution can be estimated applying a lognormal distribution. The results are reported in Table 3.15.

With EVT the ratio between EL and VaR is around 10.8%, lower than those obtained using the Weibull or lognormal. The capital estimation is then more conservative, the ratio EL/VaR is also consistent with other estimations reported in the literature (see references 3 and 28). When we use the internal loss dataset, we obtain significant improvement implementing EVT techniques.

Table 3.15 Capital at risk results using EVT (€'000)

Event type	VaR	EL	UL
Internal fraud	1 114 640	230 105	884 535
External fraud	152 304	26 747	125 557
Employment	34 559	8 562	25 997
Clients	3 309 104	236 385	3 072 719
Physical assets	124 201	16 546	107 655
IT systems	177 916	2 361	175 556
Process management	39 271	13 099	26 171
Total	4 951 993	533 803	4 418 190

3.15.5 Capital at Risk Estimates using the *g-and-h* Distribution

Here we present, the capital at risk figures obtained by estimating the severity using the *g-and-h* distribution. As mentioned in Section 3.6, in this case, the severity distribution is not truncated from above but has shifted. Parameter estimates of the severity distribution for each risk class are presented in Table 3.16.

To assess goodness of fit given by the *g-and-h* for each risk class, q–q plots are analyzed (see Figures 3.60 to 3.66).

Studying the q–q plots we noted that *g-and-h* distribution gives a good fit for the body of data but the tail gets overestimated. Table 3.17 reports the capital at risk results.

The capital estimation using the *g-and-h* is lower than for EVT or the lognormal as the ratio EL/VaR is higher (21.1%). Even if the q–q plots indicates an overestimation for extreme points, the capital figures do not seem to be adequately conservative using this distributional hypothesis. In our opinion, further studies on the *g-and-h* should be performed to check whether this distribution may be used to model operational losses

Table 3.16 *g-and-h* parameter estimates

Event type	A	B	g	h
Internal fraud	31.6385160	63.2924210	2.0003840	0.0022391
External fraud	16.4865275	32.0730759	2.0009181	0.0137908
Employment	14.9584830	30.3079274	2.0960616	0.0120687
Clients	34.1728501	67.9727935	1.9685451	−0.0007359
Physical assets	244.6322920	523.086182	2.1618072	−0.0037933
IT systems	17.8271684	38.3859575	2.3363951	0.0437545
Process management	19.1929199	39.7538487	2.0675810	−0.0002511

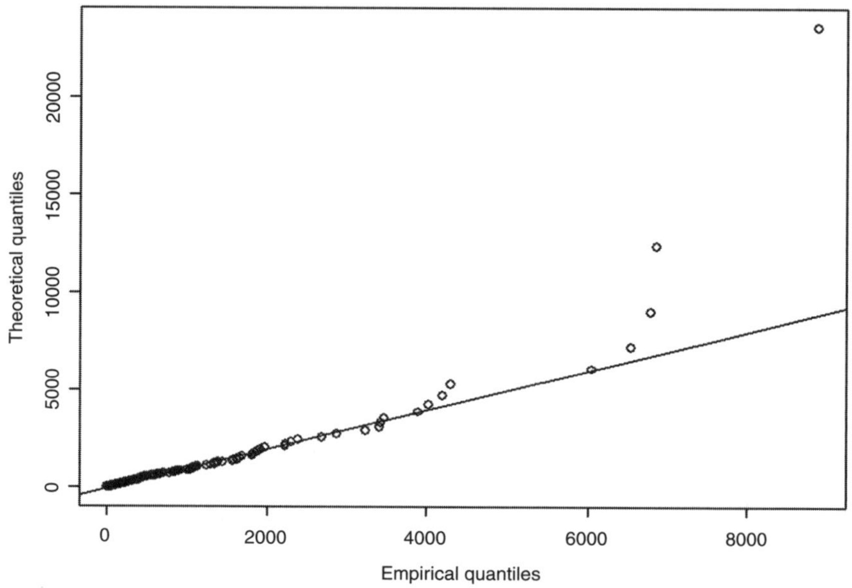

Figure 3.60 q–q plot of *g-and-h* distribution for internal fraud

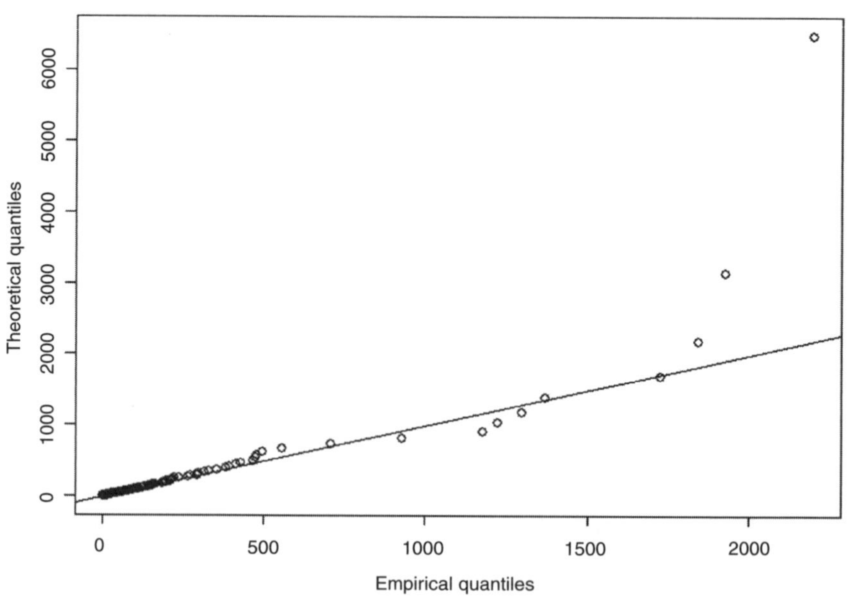

Figure 3.61 q–q plot of *g-and-h* distribution for external fraud

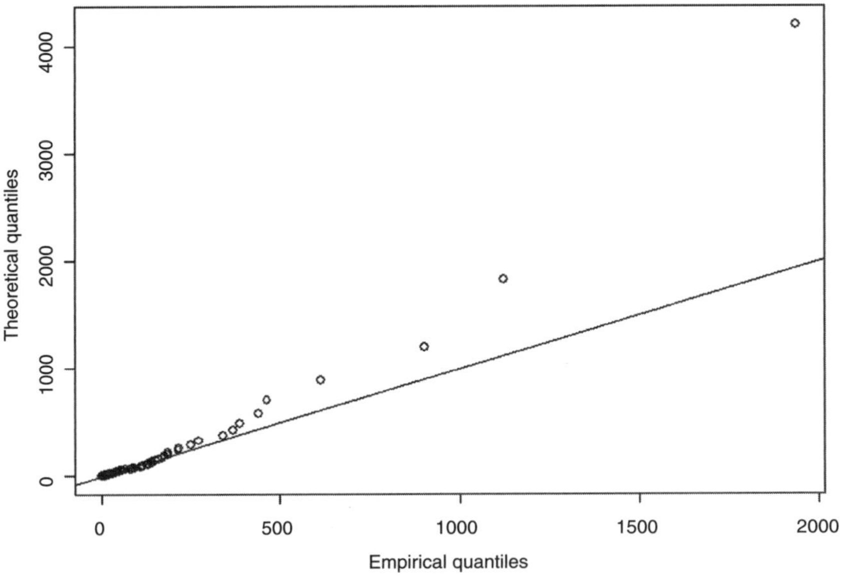

Figure 3.62 q–q plot of *g-and-h* distribution for employment problems

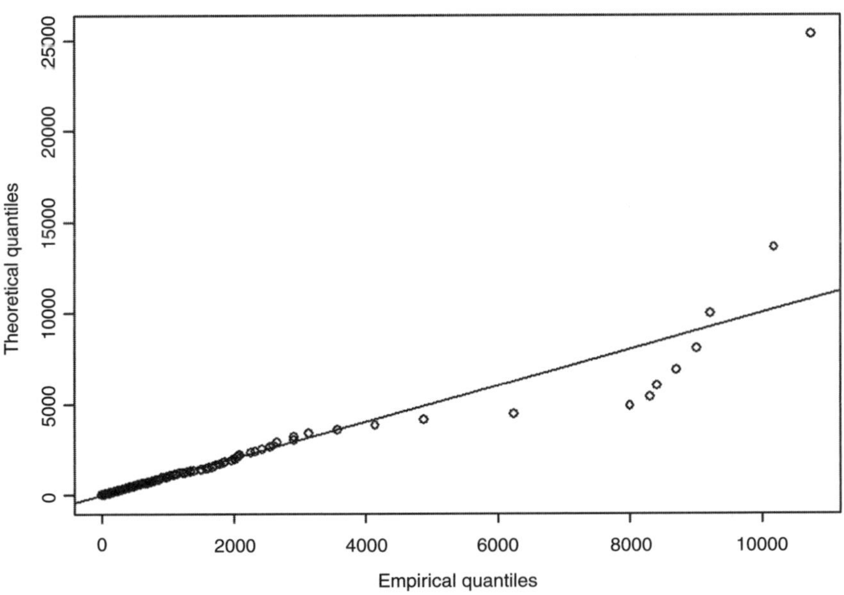

Figure 3.63 q–q plot of *g-and-h* distribution for clients claims

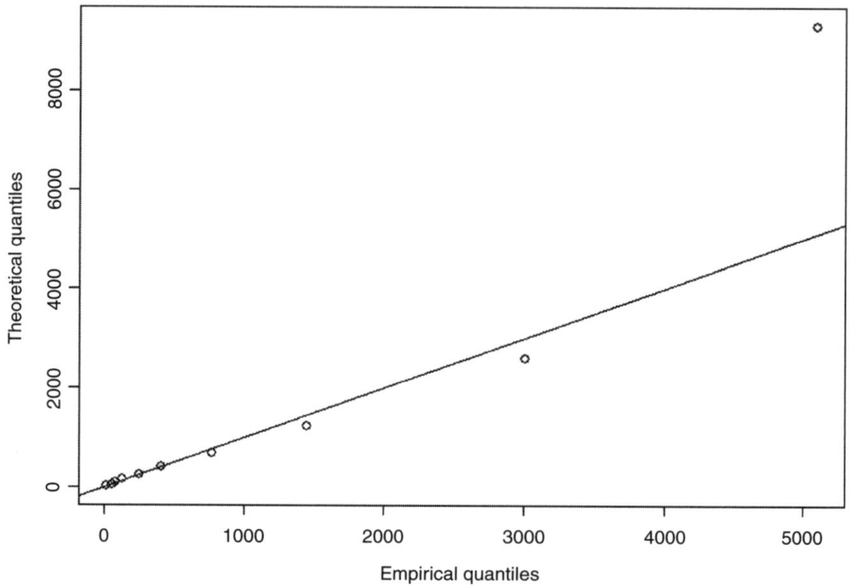

Figure 3.64 q–q plot of *g-and-h* distribution for physical assets losses

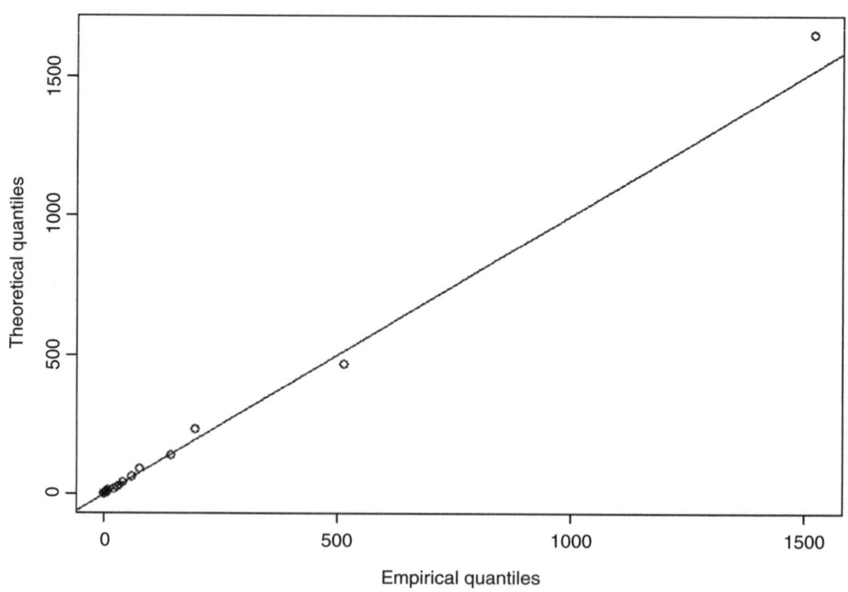

Figure 3.65 q–q plot of *g-and-h* distribution for IT systems losses

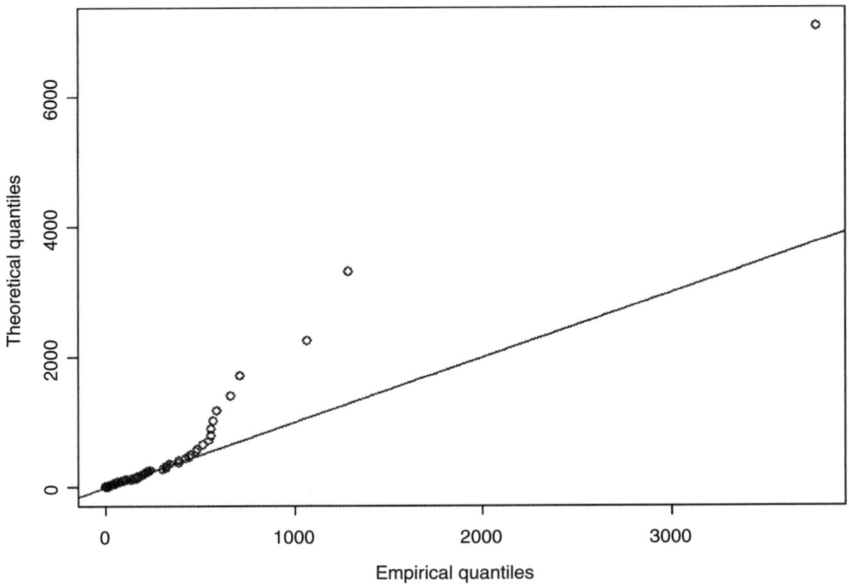

Figure 3.66 q–q plot of *g-and-h* distribution for process management losses

(at least for certain risk classes). We believe a robust LDA method should combine parametric, EVT and *g-and-h* techniques.

3.15.6 Capital at Risk Estimates Considering Correlation

Diversification effects could have a relevant impact in operational risk modeling; in fact, operational risk classes might be, at least partially, uncorrelated. It is highly unlikely, and it is hardly supported by any

Table 3.17 Capital at risk results using the *g-and-h* distribution (€'000)

Event type	VaR	EL	UL
Internal fraud	696 386	239 834	456 551
External fraud	204 277	39 592	164 685
Employment	164 027	16 358	147 669
Clients	753 520	296 801	456 719
Physical assets	803 449	13 502	789 947
IT systems	200 635	2 663	197 973
Process management	231 882	35 397	196 484
Total	3 054 176	644 148	2 410 027

Table 3.18 Pearson's linear correlation matrix – Algo OpData

	ET1	ET2	ET3	ET4	ET5	ET6	ET7
ET1	1.000	0.230	0.097	−0.117	0.036	−0.331	0.051
ET2	0.230	1.000	−0.178	0.530	−0.137	−0.121	0.018
ET3	0.097	−0.178	1.000	−0.066	−0.389	0.132	−0.017
ET4	−0.117	0.530	−0.066	1.000	0.013	0.157	0.050
ET5	0.036	−0.137	−0.389	0.013	1.000	−0.168	−0.013
ET6	−0.331	−0.121	0.132	0.157	−0.168	1.000	−0.037
ET7	0.061	0.018	−0.117	0.050	−0.013	−0.037	1.000

empirical evidence, that the most severe operational risk losses will occur systematically during the same period.

Analyzing the correlation among risk classes, we use the dataset of operational public losses (Algo OpData), covering a long timeframe. Loss data with settlement dates falling in the period 1993 and 2006 and with amounts larger than one million Euros are considered. The analysis we performed shows the correlation results between the Basel event type classes considering loss data aggregated on a yearly basis. Pearson's linear and Kendall's rank correlation coefficients between each pair of risk classes are evaluated and reported in the Tables 3.18 and 3.19, respectively.

As we can see the correlation coefficients are very low and many values are negative: these results support the use of diversification from an empirical point of view.

Table 3.20 presents years of occurrence for maximum aggregated losses, maximum frequencies, and maximum single loss amongst risk classes: one notes that the years of occurrence mainly differ among risk classes.

Table 3.19 Kendall's rank correlation matrix – Algo OpData

	ET1	ET2	ET3	ET4	ET5	ET6	ET7
ET1	1.000	0.253	0.077	−0.033	0.077	−0.011	−0.099
ET2	0.253	1.000	−0.055	−0.033	0.011	0.033	−0.055
ET3	0.077	−0.055	1.000	0.099	−0.253	0.363	−0.055
ET4	−0.033	−0.033	0.099	1.000	−0.165	0.363	0.055
ET5	0.077	0.011	−0.253	−0.165	1.000	−0.264	0.077
ET6	−0.011	0.033	0.363	0.363	−0.264	1.000	0.077
ET7	−0.099	−0.055	−0.055	0.055	0.077	0.077	1.000

Table 3.20 Years with maximum aggregated losses, maximum frequencies, and maximum single loss among risk classes – Algo OpData

	ET1	ET2	ET3	ET4	ET5	ET6	ET7
Year with maximum annual losses	1995	2005	1998	2005	2003	1994	1999
Year with maximum annual frequencies	2003	2002	1999	2005	2002	2001	1999
Year with maximum single loss	1997	2005	1996	2005	2003	1994	1999

As we described in Section 3.10, the overall Value at Risk depends on both the loss distribution of each risk class and the correlation structure among all classes, specified by the copula function. In the example we consider the loss distributions estimated with EVT (see Section 3.15.4) and we apply the copula function to determine the overall loss distribution and the capital at risk. Results are calculated using Gaussian, Student-t, and Gumbel copulae to compare the sensitivity obtained with different copula functions. Parameters are estimated as described in Section 3.10. Table 3.17 reports the capital at risk figures and the diversification effects obtained by applying Gaussian, Student-t, and Gumbel copulae. The correlation matrix for the Gaussian and Student-t copulae is estimated from the Kendall's correlation matrix (see Table 3.19). For the Student-t copula the degrees of freedom are 5.407776 and for the Gumbel copula the correlation coefficient is 0.021978.

The diversification effect is relevant for every copula, varying from 16.88% for the Student-t copula to 18.94% for the Gaussian copula. We are aware that regulators may have a problem validating such high percentages. However, we believe, for correlation, it is not possible to impose a cap as we do for insurance recoveries also because a different granularity of the model (i.e. a different number of risk classes) should lead to a different diversification effect.

Table 3.21 Capital at risk results using different correlation hypotheses

Correlation hypothesis	VaR	EL	UL	Diversification
Perfect dependence	4 951 993	533 803	4 418 190	0%
Gaussian copula	4 014 111	550 767	3 463 344	18.94%
Student-t copula	4 116 238	549 959	3 566 279	16.88%
Gumbel copula	4 035 718	549 876	3 485 842	18.50%

Once we have analyzed the correlation coefficients, we use a method to describe the true dependence structure between different operational risk.

3.16 REGULATORY CAPITAL REQUIREMENT

According to the regulatory requirements (see references 1 and 2), the capital charge for operational risk can be calculated by banks using three alternative methods:

- the basic indicator approach (BIA);
- the standardized approach (TSA);
- the advanced measurement approach (AMA).

The first two methods are functions of gross income,[28] while the advanced method is based on internal models, satisfying qualitative and quantitative requirements. These internal models are usually implemented through a loss distribution approach, a scenario-based approach or some LDA–SBA combined method. Clearly, the more complex the approach, the more requirements are prescribed.

According to the new accord, each method can be applied on a partial use basis: for example, a financial institution classified as AMA could apply the internal model only on parts, calculating the rest through TSA and/or BIA.

For a group holding bank, there will be two kinds of capital requirements:

- the consolidated capital requirement;
- the individual capital requirement.

3.16.1 The Consolidated Capital Requirement

Consider an international banking group controlled by n companies (or legal entities or subsidiaries). Group companies can be classified into three different types based on different risk profiles and compliance levels with regulatory requirements:

- BIA-compliant legal entities;
- TSA-compliant legal entities;
- AMA-compliant legal entities.

[28] BIA is 15% of gross income, while TSA applies different weights (12%, 15%, 18%) to the Basel business lines.

For the set of AMA-compliant companies, just one AMA calculation will be necessary. This AMA capital at risk covers the perimeter of AMA-compliant legal entities. Non-AMA-compliant companies must calculate their capital using the TSA or BIA method. The TSA and BIA used for Group capital calculation purposes are based on gross income net intragroup contributions: the Group capital at risk will be the sum of the AMA capital of AMA-compliant companies and the net TSA or net BIA capital of the non-AMA-compliant companies.

For example, suppose the Group controls of the companies A, B, C, D, E, and F. A, B, and C are AMA-compliant and D, E, and F are non-AMA-compliant. In particular, D and E use TSA while F can only apply BIA. Companies A, B, and C calculate the AMA capital, while D and E calculate their TSA capitals and F uses BIA. The Group capital at risk is:

$$K_{\text{Group}}(A \cup B \cup C \cup D \cup E \cup F) = K_{\text{AMA}}(A \cup B \cup C) + K^*_{\text{TSA}}(D) + K^*_{\text{TSA}}(E) + K^*_{\text{BIA}}(F), \tag{3.152}$$

where

$K_{\text{Group}}(A \cup B \cup C \cup D \cup E \cup F)$ is the Group capital at risk;

$K_{\text{AMA}}(A \cup B \cup C)$ is the AMA capital for AMA-compliant companies;

$K^*_{\text{TSA}}(D) + K^*_{\text{TSA}}(E) + K^*_{\text{BIA}}(F)$ is the sum of capital for non-AMA-compliant companies calculated using net TSA or net BIA.

3.16.2 The Individual Capital Requirement

Considering the company classification (AMA-compliant, TSA-compliant, and BIA-compliant):

- BIA-compliant companies will hold capital based on the BIA calculation;
- TSA-compliant companies will hold capital based on TSA calculation;
- AMA-compliant companies will hold a portion of the Group AMA capital according to their risk profiles.

The simplest criterion for splitting AMA capital is the proportion of capital at risk calculated through TSA (K_{TSA}).

For example, for the previous case allocated capital will then become:

$$K_{\text{Allocated}}A = [K_{\text{TSA}}(A)/(K_{\text{TSA}}(A) + K_{\text{TSA}}(B) + K_{\text{TSA}}(C))] \times K_{\text{AMA}}(A \cup B \cup C) \quad (3.153)$$

$$K_{\text{Allocated}}(B) = [K_{\text{TSA}}(B)/(K_{\text{TSA}}(A) + K_{\text{TSA}}(B) + K_{\text{TSA}}(C))] \times K_{\text{AMA}}(A \cup B \cup C) \quad (3.154)$$

$$K_{\text{Allocated}}(C) = [K_{\text{TSA}}(C)/(K_{\text{TSA}}(A) + K_{\text{TSA}}(B) + K_{\text{TSA}}(C))] \times K_{\text{AMA}}(A \cup B \cup C) \quad (3.155)$$

$$K_{\text{Allocated}}(D) = K_{\text{TSA}}(D) \quad (3.156)$$

$$K_{\text{Allocated}}(E) = K_{\text{TSA}}(E) \quad (3.157)$$

$$K_{\text{Allocated}}(F) = K_{\text{BIA}}(F) \quad (3.158)$$

The Allocation Mechanism

Allocating the proportion of AMA capital at risk on the basis of TSA has some advantages:

- TSA is a measure defined by regulators, hence it is commonly accepted;
- the calculation is very simple and can be explained intuitively without any statistical knowledge;
- the capital proportion is linked to the size of the company.

The TSA method does not present the real operational risk profile:

- the company is penalized simply because it is doing a better job. In fact, in this case, increasing the gross income means increasing the capital at risk;
- if a company experiences many large losses, increasing the AMA capital at risk, this variation impacts on all AMA-compliant legal entities without any distinction;
- if some company is able to reduce its operational risk, it does not see an effect in terms of a capital at risk decrease. TSA does not provide an incentive for the legal entity to correctly hedge its operational risk.

Such problems clearly shows that TSA-based allocation can be only a first proxy for operational risk capital allocation. The bank could initially use TSA-based allocation, but it then shall define more risk-sensitive methodologies.

If we apply the internal model to each controlled company, using only its data, do we get a consistent and sufficiently robust figure, the simplest solution is to allocate the AMA group capital at risk on the basis of the OpVaR of every company.

For the previous example, the allocated capital will be:

$$K_{\text{Allocated}}(A) = [K_{\text{AMA}}(A)/(K_{\text{AMA}}(A) + K_{\text{AMA}}(B) + K_{\text{AMA}}(C))] \times K_{\text{AMA}}(A \cup B \cup C) \quad (3.159)$$

$$K_{\text{Allocated}}(B) = [K_{\text{AMA}}(B)/(K_{\text{AMA}}(A) + K_{\text{AMA}}(B) + K_{\text{AMA}}(C))] \times K_{\text{AMA}}(A \cup B \cup C) \quad (3.160)$$

$$K_{\text{Allocated}}(C) = [K_{\text{AMA}}(C)/(K_{\text{AMA}}(A) + K_{\text{AMA}}(B) + K_{\text{AMA}}(C))] \times K_{\text{AMA}}(A \cup B \cup C) \quad (3.161)$$

where $K_{\text{AMA}}(A)$, $K_{\text{AMA}}(B)$, and $K_{\text{AMA}}(C)$ represent the operational value at risk calculated on legal entities A, B, and C through the internal model.

As an alternative, we could use methods based on expected shortfall. This is a useful allocation mechanism because it has the additive property (for details see reference 30 on page 194).

If this is usually possible with SBA models, we could have some problems with LDA models: we propose a prudential method: to allocate the group AMA capital at risk on the basis of weighted average between the standalone OpVaR and the TSA.

If we give the weight α to the standalone OpVaR and the weight β to the TSA ($\alpha + \beta = 1$), for the same example we get:

$$K_{\text{Allocated}}(A) = [K_W(A)/(K_W(A) + K_W(B) + K_W(C))] \times K_{\text{AMA}}(A \cup B \cup C) \quad (3.162)$$

$$K_{\text{Allocated}}(B) = [K_W(B)/(K_W(A) + K_W(B) + K_W(C))] \times K_{\text{AMA}}(A \cup B \cup C) \quad (3.163)$$

$$K_{\text{Allocated}}(C) = [K_W(C)/(K_W(A) + K_W(B) + K_W(C))] \times K_{\text{AMA}}(A \cup B \cup C) \quad (3.164)$$

and for the legal entity A:

$$K_W(A) = \alpha \times K_{\text{AMA}}(A) + \beta \times K^*_{\text{TSA}}(A) \quad (3.165)$$

This way, if we are not confident of the standalone OpVar results, we give higher weight to the TSA at the same time introducing a risk-sensitive component.

3.17 ECONOMIC CAPITAL REQUIREMENT

According to Pillar II (see reference 2), the capital requirements for different risk types (e.g. market, credit, operational, etc.) should not be considered as regulatory only, but they should be used for internal economic risk capital as well. The regulatory capital charge, just regulatory, but used for risk management purposes. The regulatory capital charge, as in Pillar I, considers market risk, credit risk, and operational risk and the overall capital requirement is obtained by summing the figures for every risk, under the hypothesis of perfect dependence. Economic capital should consider the complete list of risks to which the bank is exposed.

The total risk of the bank should be calculated considering the diversification effect among different types of risk. We do not want to analyze here the risk integration process,[29] but we look at the operational risk aspects.

For economic capital, the holding time is one year; the same as the regulatory requirement. On the other hand, usually there could be differences in confidence level. This is linked to bank rating: for example, the probability of default given by the rating AA-, according to Standard & Poors, is 0.03%. The consistent confidence level would then be 99.97%. Generally, confidence level for the economic capital requirement is somewhere between 99.95% and 99.98%, which differs from the regulatory one at least for operational risk.

The risk integration can be performed applying:

- a variance/covariance framework (à la Markowitz);
- copula function-based methods.

The copula-function-based method is the same approach used to aggregate the different operational risk classes. In this case, in place of operational risk classes we consider the risk types provided for each risk type, the annual loss distribution is available. Operational risk should

[29] For details on the risk integration process see reference 31 on page 194.

provide the overall annual loss distribution. The copula method is often applied risk integration and it is suitable when considering heavy-tailed (or non-normal) distributions.

The variance–covariance method is simpler. The overall capital at risk is obtained from the equation:

$$VaR(\alpha) = \sqrt{\sum_{i,j} \rho_{i,j} VaR_i(\alpha) VaR_j(\alpha)} \tag{3.166}$$

where $VaR_i(\alpha) = \omega_i \cdot \sigma_i \cdot F^{-1}(\alpha)$ is the standalone capital requirement for risk i, ω_i is the exposure, σ_i the volatility and $F^{-1}(\alpha)$ is the quantile α of the standardized normal distribution. ρ is the linear correlation coefficient between each risk pair.

This technique implies that all distributions are normal, which is not the case when some risks (e.g. operational risk) have heavy-tailed distributions. The linear correlations do not capture the whole dependence structure excluding the case of elliptical multivariate distributions (e.g. Gaussian). In the case of heavy-tailed distributions, we may have a biased estimation of the diversification benefits.

For the variance–covariance method, the input for operational risk is the operational VaR figure. As the regulatory one is calculated with confidence level 99.9%, we shall adjust this figure for economic capital calculation.

We can calculate with a higher confidence level. This results in a scaling factor to obtain the economic one starting from the regulatory capital. Provided that we are considering a very high confidence level, we calculate a quantile of the overall annual loss distribution with high probability (i.e. 99.95%–99.98%) is near to 1. Considering the distribution is obtained through Monte Carlo simulation, calculating directly this higher confidence level OpVaR means increasing the volatility of the estimation given the numerical sampling error. We should increase the number of simulated annual losses to over 10 million, involving a very time-consuming calculation.[30] The easiest solution is to apply the closed form approximation (see Section 3.11) for the OpVaR (i.e. the one event approximation). If we model the tail of the severity distribution

[30] Running more than 10 million simulations is not just time consuming. Over this threshold, a computer used for the calculation may have problems given structural numerical limits. In this case, more complex architectures should be set up, for example through a parallel calculation using more CPUs.

through a GPD, we get:

$$OpVaR(\alpha) = u + \frac{\beta}{\xi}\left[\left(\frac{\lambda_{\text{tail}}}{1-\alpha}\right)^{\xi} - 1\right], \quad \text{where } \alpha \to 1 \tag{3.167}$$

OpVaR can be further approximated when:

$$\frac{\beta}{\xi}\left[\left(\frac{\lambda_{\text{tail}}}{1-\alpha}\right)^{\xi} - 1\right] \gg u \tag{3.168}$$

and:

$$\left(\frac{\lambda_{\text{tail}}}{1-\alpha}\right)^{\xi} \gg 1 \tag{3.169}$$

In this case, we obtain:

$$OpVaR(\alpha) = \frac{\beta}{\xi}\left(\frac{\lambda_{\text{tail}}}{1-\alpha}\right)^{\xi} \tag{3.170}$$

Hence, the ratio between two OpVaRs with different confidence levels α_1 and α_2 can be:

$$\frac{OpVaR(\alpha_2)}{OpVaR(\alpha_1)} = \left(\frac{1-\alpha_1}{1-\alpha_2}\right)^{\xi} \tag{3.171}$$

Taking $\alpha_1 = 99.9\%$ to be the regulatory confidence level, if α_2 is the economic one, for $\alpha_2 = 99.95\%$ we have:

$$\frac{OpVaR(99.95\%)}{OpVaR(99.9\%)} = 2^{\xi} \tag{3.172}$$

for $\alpha_2 = 99.97\%$:

$$\frac{OpVaR(99.97\%)}{OpVaR(99.9\%)} = \left(\frac{10}{3}\right)^{\xi} \tag{3.173}$$

and for $\alpha_2 = 99.98\%$:

$$\frac{OpVaR(99.98\%)}{OpVaR(99.9\%)} = 5^{\xi} \tag{3.174}$$

In the plots shown in Figures 3.67, 3.68, and 3.69, we can get the values of the scaling factors in the function of shape parameter ξ.

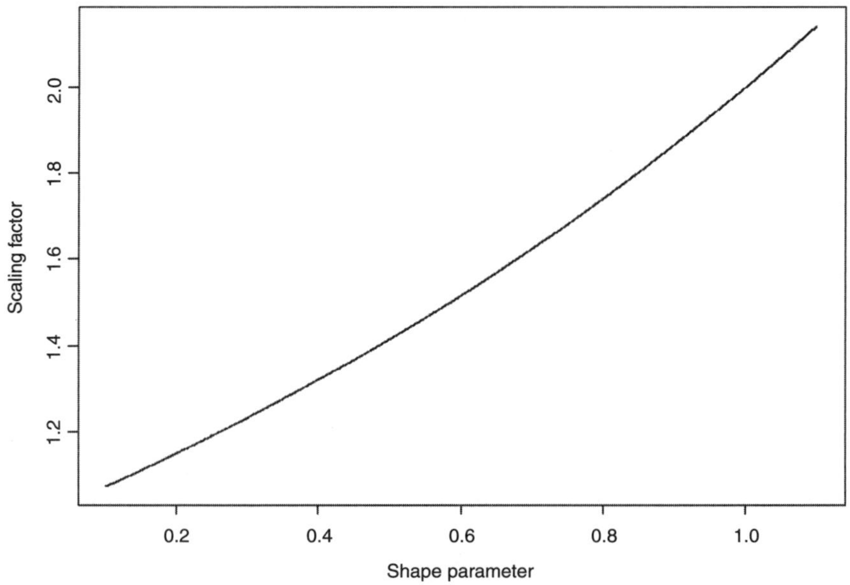

Figure 3.67 Scaling factor for confidence level 99.95%

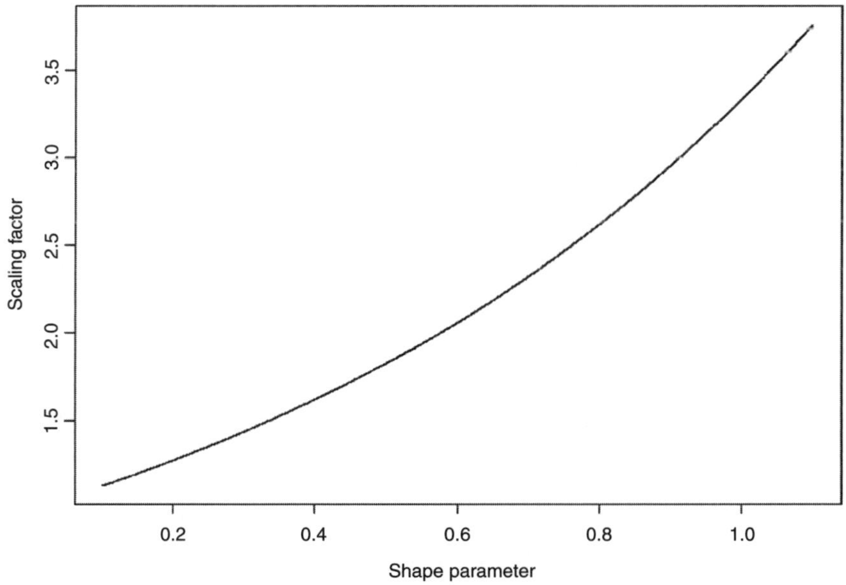

Figure 3.68 Scaling factor for confidence level 99.97%

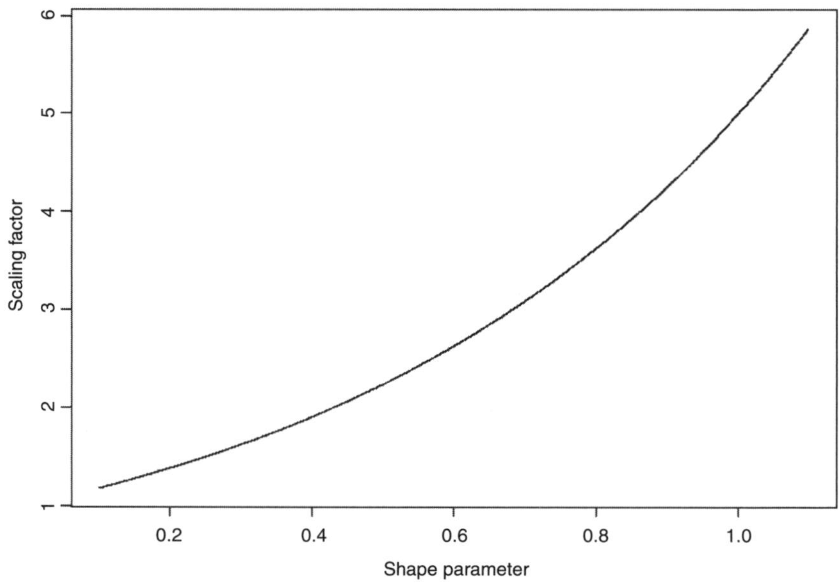

Figure 3.69 Scaling factor for confidence level 99.98%

For the shape parameter ξ, we could consider the maximum value we obtained (see Section 3.15.4); that is $\xi = 0.78$. We would get:

$$\frac{OpVaR(99.95\%)}{OpVaR(99.9\%)} = 1.717 \tag{3.175}$$

$$\frac{OpVaR(99.97\%)}{OpVaR(99.9\%)} = 2.558 \tag{3.176}$$

$$\frac{OpVaR(99.98\%)}{OpVaR(99.9\%)} = 3.509 \tag{3.177}$$

These values are too conservative, so we look at the plot of the shape parameter as a function of the threshold.

If we analyze the plot in Figure 3.70, we observe the shape parameter estimate decreases with the threshold until around 0.4. It then displays a kind of stable behavior before falling. As for economic capital, we are analyzing the very extreme part of the tail, we should consider the highest threshold where the shape parameter is stable. We could set the threshold at one million (1000 in the shape parameter plot), providing a

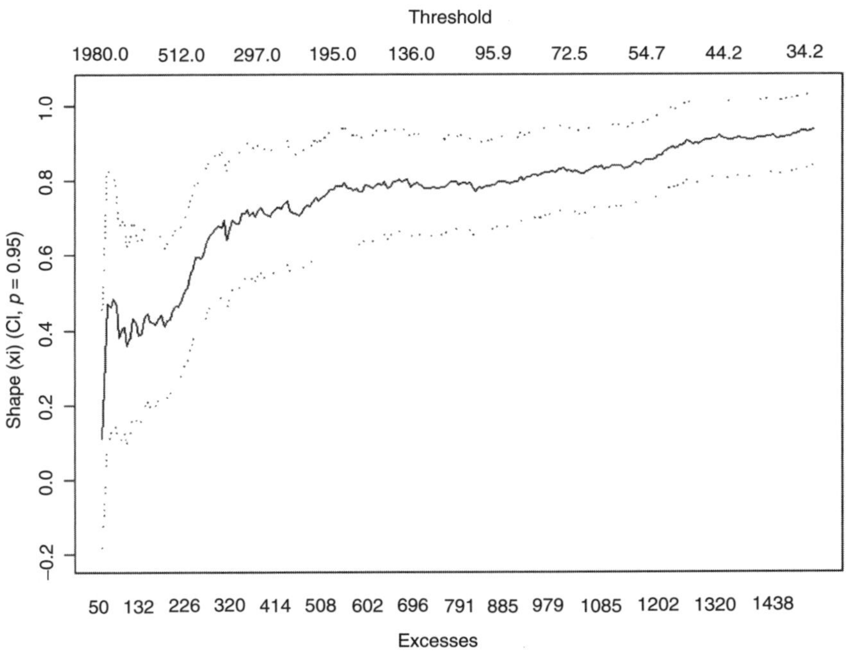

Figure 3.70 Shape parameter estimation

shape parameter around 0.4, then our scaling facors would be:

$$\frac{OpVaR(99.95\%)}{OpVaR(99.9\%)} = 1.320 \tag{3.178}$$

$$\frac{OpVaR(99.97\%)}{OpVaR(99.9\%)} = 1.619 \tag{3.179}$$

$$\frac{OpVaR(99.98\%)}{OpVaR(99.9\%)} = 1.904 \tag{3.180}$$

The values now could be used to scale OpVar from the regulatory confidence level.

3.18 INTEGRATION OF OPERATIONAL RISK IN THE BUDGETING PROCESS

Once the Basel 2 regulation comes into force, the operational risk values will be considered in the budgeting process. This will set targets or forecasts for forthcoming years: we consider a bank or financial institution with a simplified structure: one holding company and n subsidiaries. The budgeting process can be articulated into two different steps to be performed at different times:

1. Top down: the holding company sets the initial targets and indicates them to each controlled subsidiary.
2. Bottom up: each subsidiary discusses the targets with the holding company and then the final values are set.

Targets are also set for performance indicators adjusted for risk such as, for example, EVA (economic value added) and RARORAC (Risk Adjusted Return on Risk Adjusted Capital). The fulfillment of these targets may be linked to incentive systems for employees, so the target figures are taken into account by management. The calculation of these performance indicators includes the risk figures and so the operational capital at risk is also considered. From this point of view (and also considering the economic capital), measuring the operational risk.

Operational capital figures for budgeting purposes shall be projected for the required budgeting years. In our opinion, one out of two different approaches could be considered:

- projected figures are simple forecasts based on the variation of some exposure indicator;
- projected figures are fixed as targets to stimulate operational risk management and risk profile improvement.

This first approach may be necessary because, for operational risk, it is more difficult to adjust the risk profile than for market risk and credit risk: for market risk we could adjust the portfolio, closing some positions; for credit risk, we can modify exposure; for operational risk it is difficult to make any adjustments that would reduce the exposure, besides when insurance is available.

The second approach requires an operational risk function that is able to manage the risk. The subsidiaries should also understand how to reduce the exposure: for example, we could verify how the capital at risk is modified changing the annual number of losses.

4

Analyzing insurance policies

4.1 INSURANCE MANAGEMENT AND RISK TRANSFER

Banks risk decisions were mostly based on a financial institution's risk appetite, the amount it was willing to bear, or considered appropriate given its business activities. When the set risk appetite was exceeded, companies would intervene, changing procedures, improving controls, or even with exit strategies. Other interventions would aim at reducing the impact if an operational event occurred (see Figure 4.1).

If the residual risk was too high, transfer to a third party using insurance could be considered, the remaining risk then retained.

When we started to get involved in the Group's insurance management process, we added internal and external loss databases, first scenario analyses and operational risk modelling to calculate the impact of insurance decisions. While in the past the experience of business experts and insurance brokers guided renewal decisions (together with the risk appetite), operational risk managers added a quantitive element to the decision process. Our support is combined with the experience of other departments: the insurance decisions are now the results of a process involving many organisational functions.

Operational risk analyses helped render the Group's insurance policies more efficient, providing some significant cost savings without altering the risk exposure. It is now commonly accepted that insurance is bought with higher deductibles (and higher limits), that insurance should ideally be activated rarely and should be considered a cost item that has to be managed actively and should not expected to a return every year in terms of premium/reimbursements.

We looked at a number of insurance components:

1. Risk type. Operational risks are analyzed and mitigated. When the residual risk is still too high, we evaluated the possibility to transfer the risk. When performing scenario analyses, insurance coverage is discussed.

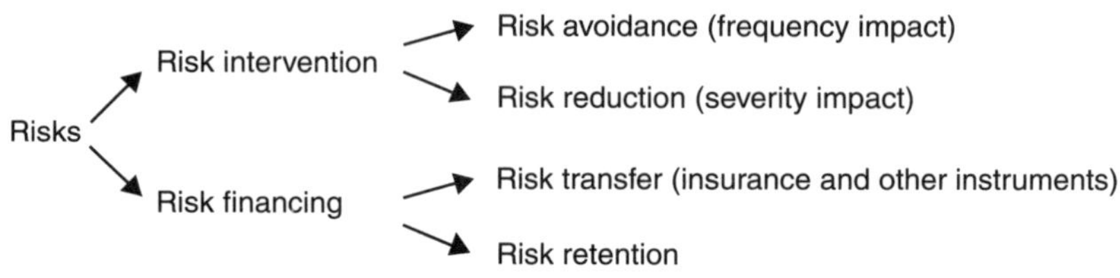

Figure 4.1 Decision scheme

2. Amount. Rather than policy limits based on experience, the operational risk function can now estimate the probabilities that a given limit is exceeded by actual losses.
3. Deductible. Analysis of the bank's internal losses is used to set the deductible level. We are convinced that a correct deductible excludes frequent, routine losses from the insurance coverage: high-frequency losses are predictable for the insurance company that will then charge it back, plus charges for costs, margins, and taxes.
4. Premium. Insurance companies take into account also other factors like the premium/loss development of the banking or sector, the insurance, and reinsurance markets. It is possible that an insurance company might ask a different premium than the theoretical one. If we want to increase a deductible, we now apply our operational risk model to estimate the corresponding price.

We believe UniCredit Group became a more conscious and informed insurance buyer over the years thanks to the contributions of the operational risk department.

4.2 QUALIFYING CRITERIA IN THE BASEL 2 CAPITAL FRAMEWORK

The new Basel Capital Accord and the European Capital Adequacy Directive state that if risk mitigation can be proved, supervisors may allow a reduction of up to 20% of the minimum capital requirement. This possibility is permitted only to financial institutions that will apply the *Advanced Measurement Approach*.

We list below the elements insurance policies must possess to qualify for capital, indicating the challenges, given the current insurance market, a bank faces in complying with the Basel 2 requirements.

Major constraints and challenges are described and commented and some solutions are proposed.

4.2.1 Rating of the Insurance Company

CAD: ... *the provider has a minimum claims paying ability rating by an eligible ECAI*[1] *which has been determined by the competent authority to be associated with credit quality step 3 or above under the rules for the risk weighting of exposures to credit institutions under Articles 78 to 83.*

- In a precedent version of this text, the Directive indicated that the insurer should have a minimum rating of A or similar for its *claims paying ability* or, stated differently, for its capacity of respecting its contractual obligations from its insurance portfolio. The final version states that the rating should be issued by an authorized ECAI and it should be equal to the 'credit quality step 3' as in the weight attribution for credit risk exposure. Although these are linked to a certain extent, the 'claims paying ability' rating is a different assessment from a credit risk rating. The first is predominantly a technical opinion on the insurer's insurance portfolio and its (re)insurance management (the ability to effectively pay eventual claims). The second is a more general opinion on the creditworthiness of the provider and its ability to meet obligations, capital, and its debt structure.
- Nothing is prescribed when an insurer's rating changes or is put on a negative outlook during the contract's validity.
- If there are several insurers, with different ratings, we guess that the calculation of the mitigation impact takes only the share of the insurance cover that is underwritten by insurers with a sufficient rating. Again, this is not specified.
- In some countries where we operate, there is no provider with a sufficient rating; in others there are very few. If domestic with a local insurance company is ceded (almost) completely to an international reinsurer with rating A, then the risk has been covered de facto by an insurer with adequate rating.

Suggestions on Ratings

Banks need clarifying with supervisors the exact nature of the required rating of the insurance providers and how to deal with rating variations.

[1] External Credit Assessment Institution, credit rating agency.

For the case of absence of qualifying providers in some countries, the individual contracts should explicitly refer to the reinsurance contracts in place. This ought to include a kind of *drop-down* clause ensuring cover when the local insurer fails, so removing any credit risk worries if the domestic insurer is not rated.

4.2.2 Duration and Residual Term of the Insurance Contract

> CAD: *The insurance policy must have an initial term of at least one year. For policies with a residual term shorter than one year, the bank must make appropriate haircuts reflecting the declining residual term of the policy. Haircuts could be up to a full 100% for policies with a residual term of 90 days or less.*

The Directive requires banks to consider a decreasing impact in time of the policy, to no impact at all starting from 90 days before the contract's expiry. This is to reflect uncertainty in the cover renewal near expiration date. Unfortunately, most existing contracts have a one-year duration and then renewed, with a cancellation term of 30 days; many often cease to exist at expiration, without notice period.

- Insurance contracts are normally renewed every year, with minor changes in conditions, so that most of contracts and cover are not really under discussion or at risk of non-renewal. For banks with a formalized insurance policy renewal procedure, this could be less problematic.
- If banks calculate the decreasing impact it results into higher capital at risk near expiration. Changing the policies' renewal dates, banks could arbitrate to a certain extent and have higher or lower capital impacts.

  Example: if all insurance renewals are shifted to the end of the year, capital at risk at 31st December, with policies renewed precisely then, will benefit from a 100% mitigation effect. Capital reduction will be lower if policies are renewed instead in June.

Figure 4.2 shows how an insurance renewal date impacts on capital at risk over time.

Suggestions on Duration and Renewals

In order to limit these haircuts, we suggest to subscribe to multiannual policies with annual pricing reviews, and formalize their renewal one

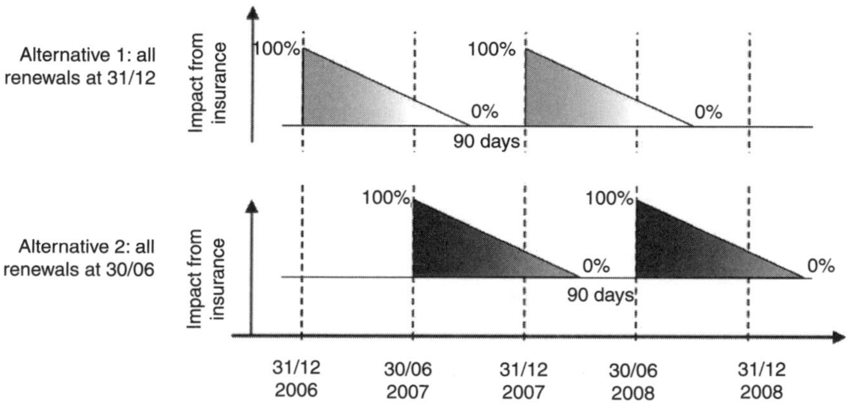

Figure 4.2 Degree of mitigation from insurance over time, according to CAD rules

year in advance. While this might be feasible for some policies like property insurance, it might be difficult for other risk types such as directors' and officers' liability (D&O cover) or for asset management, where one-year contracts are the market standard.

4.2.3 Policy Termination Requisites

> CAD: *The insurance policy has a minimum notice period for cancellation of the contract of 90 days.*

The regulation limits reducing uncertainty on insurance policy renewals. A 90-day notice period is consistent with the mentioned requirements. The cancellation period here is the insurer termination condition. Many contracts have a cancellation period of 30 days, while contracts without cancellation terms are also common: as the cover ceases at expiration, the renewal is thus considered a brand new contract in every sense.

Suggestions on Termination

We found the best solution a contract structure like the one described. If this is not available in the market, banks should at least seek insurance contracts with automatic renewals and a cancellation period longer than 90 days.

4.2.4 Claims Reimbursement Uncertainty and Ineffective Coverage

> CAD: *The methodology for recognising insurance shall capture the following elements through discounts or haircuts in the amount of insurance recognition*:
>
> a. *The residual term of a policy, where less than one year, as noted above;*
> b. *A policy's cancellation terms, where less than one year;*
> c. *The uncertainty of payment as well as mismatches in coverage of insurance policies.*

We looked at clauses (a) and (b). Clause (c) is the risk that a contract is not effective due for example to unclear policy amendments, interpretation of the policy's wording, delays in premium payments, misrepresentation or lack of disclosure, etc. It is often difficult to demonstrate the effectiveness of cover, as the insured event is often infrequent or was never experienced directly.

Suggestions on Contract Uncertainty

Banks shall prove to supervisors that policy coverage and payment certainty are addressed properly:

- checking that definitions and general policy wordings have been discussed with insurers, and if possible also with supervisors;
- making sure there are no cancellation or weakening clauses voiding the contract in case of incomplete or involuntary erroneous risk description;
- agreeing and documenting the claims handling procedure, defining procedures and timing, and if possible identifying a privileged 'fast track' procedure. This could be a contractual agreement to provide an immediate cash advance for certain event types, before the overall claim procedure is completed.

4.2.5 Conclusions

According to some estimates, less than 10% of operational risk exposure has been covered by traditional insurance.

Insurance companies and regulators could smooth some of the obstacles existing in the current insurance market.

Banks should also explore alternative strategies and instruments mitigating or transferring operational risks.

4.3 A PRACTICAL APPLICATION TO TRADITIONAL INSURANCE

We consider now the various types of operational risk insurance commonly used by financial institutions and how these protect against the risk types defined in the Basel 2 accord.

4.3.1 Insurance Policies to Cover Financial Institutions' Operational Risks

Various insurances, commonly available in the market are illustrated in Figure 4.3, where we report also their effectiveness versus the bank's risk exposure.

Bankers' Blanket Bond (BBB)

This policy is offered to financial institutions to protect against a range of risks involving material and direct damage. It usually includes the following sections:

- fraud by employees (internal fraud);
- loss of valuables (robbery, theft, etc.);
- losses during transport;
- falsification of securities and documents;
- falsification of banknotes;

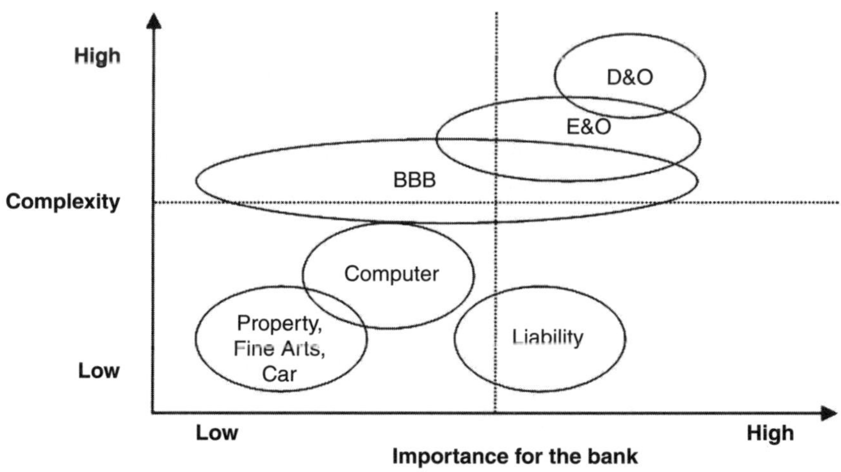

Figure 4.3 Relative importance of insurance coverage

- legal expenses relative to events covered in other sections;
- damage to premises and their content;
- fire;
- fraud through IT systems (electronic/computer crime);
- damage to and theft of safe deposit box contents.

We dedicate particular attention to the contractual definition of 'employee', ensuring the correct persons are listed in the cover, including or excluding, for example, temporary employees, students, etc.

Professional Liability Insurance or Errors and Omissions Cover (E&O)

This covers damage caused to third parties due to errors or delays in the ordinary business activities, such as error, omission, negligence, imprudence, lack of skill, or even nonobservance of regulations by employees. The costs of sorting out the mistakes or problems, in order also to limit further damage and claims, can be included in the policy.

Typical exclusions are fraud or willful malice by employees, insider trading, money laundering, and misleading sales practice. Other exclusions may be fiscal fines, penalties, or punitive damages of clients caused by errors or omissions.

Liability Insurance for Directors and Officers (D&O)

This protects against claims by third parties for liability of the company directors and officers. The losses incurred by third parties can only be economic losses and exclude personal injuries or material damage. The liability could derive from acts committed by the directors and officers, individually or collectively, in the fulfillment of their functions, duties, or tasks on behalf of the bank, violating obligations deriving from the law, or the deed of incorporation, or the by-laws of incorporation, or the resolutions of general or board meetings, or any regulation issued by the public administration or government authorities.

General Liability Insurance

This covers the liability of the bank for noneconomical damage (material loss, personal injuries) caused to third parties related to activities and properties of the financial institution or for accidents suffered by employees. The latter can also be insured on a specific workers' compensation program.

Property and Fine Arts Insurance

Policies protecting the bank's properties can be a list of covered risks or as an all-risk insurance. In the first case, risks included are fire, theft, vandalism, flooding, riots, earthquake, etc.

The bank's premises can be insured whether these are owned outright or rented estates. The contents of a building – furniture, fittings, and equipment – can also be included and insured against the same risks.

Specific fine arts insurance is also commonly available, for collections in the bank's offices and branches. This is normally included in an all-risk policy contract.

Computers/Information Technology Insurance

Issued on an all-risk basis, this protects the bank's information technology systems. Mainframes, networks, licensed software, technical systems supporting the IT systems (power continuity systems, air conditioning, etc.), security systems, fire alarms, desktop equipment, central telephone units, etc. can all be insured.

4.3.2 Operational Event Types and Available Insurance Coverage

To qualify for capital recognition, banks should document the impact of insurance policies on operational risk exposure. It is necessary to link a typical insurance policy to the bank's risk types. Risks and relevant coverage are reported in Table 4.1.

Existing insurance policies should be associated to Basel 2 event types, paying special attention to the conditions of the contracts. Based on our analysis, we will indicate, for every Basel 2 operational risk type, the related insurance policies available in the market.

Internal Fraud: BBB Insurance

BBB cover typically offers protection against losses caused by employees' fraud and theft. The bank should verify whether unauthorized trading activities, carried out without the aim of obtaining direct and personal benefits, are included in the contract.

Table 4.1 Risk types

Risk type	Examples
1. Internal fraud	Unauthorized activity Theft and fraud
2. External fraud	Theft and fraud (no bank employee is involved) Systems security
3. Employment relationships and workplace safety	Employee relations Safe environment Diversity and discrimination
4. Clients, products, business practices	Suitability, disclosure, and fiduciary Improper business or market practices Product flaws Selection, sponsorship, and exposure Advisory activities
5. Damage to physical assets	Fire, natural catastrophe, etc.
6. IT systems	Service interruptions, errors
7. Execution, delivery, and process management	Transaction capture, execution, and maintenance Monitoring and reporting Customer intake and documentation Customer/client account management Trade counterparties Vendors and suppliers

External Fraud: BBB Insurance

In the case of external fraud, our experience is that BBB will offer the broadest protection in instances of cash theft, robbery, falsification of documents and banknotes, and other fraud by third parties. As specific conditions typically apply to each individual BBB section, banks ought to check whether different possible event types are indicated in the contract. Fraud through information systems, trading on line, or internet banking could also be part of the BBB cover, or it may be insured separately as specific computer crime insurance.

Employment Relationships and Workplace Safety: General Liability Insurance, Accident/Workers' Compensation, D&O

Insurance hedging these event types are commonly available. In the working premises, banks can sign a personal accident policy, a workers' compensation program, and general liability insurance for accidents. In cases of disputes between employee and employer, insurance is also available, for example for accusations of discrimination or mobbing.

This can be covered by an employers' practice liability, often available as an extension of the D&O insurance.

Clients, Products, Business Practices: E&O Cover

In our experience, there are certain operational event types where appropriate insurance coverage is not available. Single events caused by errors, omissions, or negligence could be covered by an errors and omissions insurance contract.

Damage to Physical Assets: Property Insurance, BBB, IT

Most insurance policies cover the financial institution's assets against damage: property insurance, sections of the BBB insurance, information technology cover, fine arts, etc. We deem an *all-risk* insurance policy has the highest probability of covering these event types, as long as the insured limits are correct and the exceptions to the coverage are few and well described.

Information Systems: IT Cover

Some of the events in this risk category can be insured with specific IT insurance, for example losses caused by business interruption. Other events are difficult to hedge with insurance, for example a telecommunication outage.

Execution, Delivery, and Process Management: E&O, D&O

As for the clients, products, and business practices event type, E&O insurance will potentially cover these operational risks, as long as the event is caused by errors, omissions, or negligence. In some cases, Directors' & Officers' insurance will cover it, for example when the event is not strictly related to direct professional activities or when it is a consequence of management inadequacy (responsibility of supervision).

Table 4.2 summarizes the relations between risk categories and insurances types. The separation between risk categories is sometimes quite different from the traditional insurance policy categories. In our experience, there isn't just one type of insurance to correspond with one type of risk, and vice versa. Furthermore, when an insurance policy is

Table 4.2 Links between risk categories and insurance policies

Part of the event types:	. . . can be insured with:
1. Internal fraud	BBB
2. External fraud	BBB, Computer crime
3. Employment relationships and workplace safety	General liability insurance, Accident/workers compensation, D&O
4. Clients, products, business practices	E&O
5. Damage to physical assets	BBB, Property, IT, Fine Arts, . . .
6. IT systems	IT
7. Execution, delivery, and process management	E&O, D&O

indicated alongside an event type, not all events of that risk type will be necessarily covered by the insurance policy.

We found that insurance policies that fully hedge *operational risk as defined by the regulators* are not readily available. Models calculating insurance mitigation will have to consider a multitude of policies and conditions.

5 Managing reputational risk

5.1 INTRODUCING REPUTATIONAL RISK

The modeling of reputational and operational risks is strictly related; operational losses usually have a reputational impact, managerial decisions affecting reputational risk will trudge reputational exposure. Financial institutions control and manage the two in pretty much a combined manner.

Before moving on to the modeling, let's linger on the definition of reputational risk. This isn't included in the new Basel accord, except as a possible additional risk included in the second pillar. There isn't an official definition of reputational risk universally accepted by regulators or the financial industry. Though some regulatory authorities have come up with a definition, this is not yet commonly shared by all supervisors. It is also possible to find on individual companies' financial statements a proprietary definition of reputational risk. In order to model it correctly, we will need to define it. Reputational risk is thc risk of damaging the institution's trustworthiness in the marketplace. This is the key element of reputational risk: the impact of a specific event that could worsen, or affect negatively, the perception of a company's reliability, of its services' quality, its management fairness, or, more generally, its trustworthiness. This negative or worsened perception could spread from its own employees and customers, to financial markets, investors, shareholders, counterparties, governments, and/or regulators. Consequently, reputational risk is arguably the worst type of risk a financial institution is exposed to. Nowadays, it could result from financing risky or controversial industries such as nuclear power plant projects, mining in emerging market countries, or the production of weapons, but also from the financial sector's typical exposure, ranging from money laundering and internal fraud (both of these having reputational and operational risk effects) to product distribution with both credit, reputational, and operational risk impacts, or service disruption, again with a dual reputational and operational impact. This shows not only how reputational

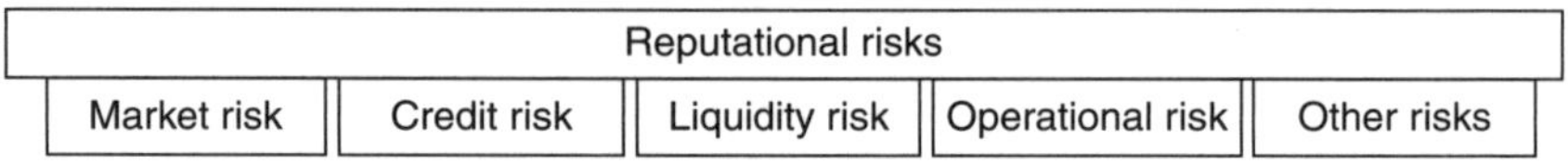

Figure 5.1 Reputational risk model

and operational risks are strictly related, but that credit and market risks are toolinked (boundary risk concept, see Figure 5.1). Some of these events could surely hit the media; management will be under pressure from regulators and markets, and the company's share price could likely be affected. Management will then experience further pressure from shareholders, regulators, and rating agencies.

Measuring reputational risk exposure is not simple; above all, it will prove extremely difficult to separate a purely reputational effect from other risk types. Identifying the specific reputational component, as distinct from the credit, market, or operational risks, will require internal principles for its identification to avoid wanton results or capital overcharges. A second challenge, once rules for identification of what constitutes reputational impact have been correctly set, will be determining acceptable capital at risk figures; we will look at some alternative techniques later.

As per its definition, we stress that reputational risk modeling isn't yet a well-consolidated field, although more articles are being published and research has increased on the subject in recent years.

We think it useful, for completeness, to look briefly at how a company manages reputational risk. In our experience, assessing reputational risk impacts is a key element of the control and of management's decision-making process.

5.2 A FINANCIAL INSTITUTION'S REPUTATIONAL RISK EXPOSURE

Reputational risk is probably the greatest risk a financial institution is exposed to in today's markets, especially for listed companies, as the occurrence of an event with a significant and widespread effect will inevitably have an impact on the stock price, and bring huge pressure to management. In addition, sometimes events happening to other financial institutions might affect the whole sector, as the market may assume the entire industry is exposed to similar risks. We list below possible effects of a reputational risk event.

- A fall in the company's share price. This could last for a short period of time or have a longer, more enduring effect, depending on the company's reputational risk management process (see next paragraph), its ability to communicate with the financial markets and regulatory authorities, and the choices made to reduce or handle these situations. A company must also consider that strength and consistency in managing reputational risk over time will have a long-term effect on its credibility on the investors' and the customers' side, and its long-term sustainability in terms of product and service distribution, regulatory approval, rating agency assessment, and finally its profitability.
- For many reputational events, the most immediate, and often long-term, effect will be the loss of business and revenue, as it will cause clients to opt for alternative service providers and will create difficulties in winning advisory mandates as the markets prefers other financial institutions. In addition, there will be higher costs to regain customers' trust and market confidence.
- There may be a relevant impact on the company's image and branding, requiring a review and campaign to change and/or modify for example the logo, advertising strategy, and/or market communication policy. It might even force the company to exit certain markets, leading to full disposal of the company's assets and losses.
- There could be events affecting employee confidence in the company's strategy or trustworthiness, causing demotivation, high staff turn-over, and difficulties in attracting high-profile resources.
- Increased market scrutiny could also result from certain reputational events, with regulatory authorities and rating agencies requiring greater disclosure and reassurance on quality control and reliance, leading to increased costs for staff and systems dedicated to internal controls.

We are convinced that companies should clearly analyze and assess the financial impact of reputational risks (see Section 5.4 for risk measurement), providing estimates of extreme or critical events to management, so that an adequate reputational risk management strategy may be identified and the processes structured accordingly. In the following paragraphs we will indicate how to structure a reputational risk policy – a foundation of the reputational risk management process.

A bank ought to assess its exposure to reputational risk, identifying the services and business that could most be jeopardized by the occurrence of specific events. We shall first list the potential reputation-damaging events and the business areas where these could lead to a relevant problem. We suggest banks to consider the list below, making sure it is shared with process and business managers:

1. Internal and external fraud and bribery, including cases of senior management involvement.
2. Breaches of law and regulations or antitrust behavior, paying particular attention to the risk of client class actions against the company or possible withdrawal of banking or other business licenses.
3. Key service interruption or failure, such as cash machines, settlement, or internet banking, wrong information reported in clients' statements, or delayed executions.
4. External outsourcing contracts and management – particularly critical as these might affect the services rendered to clients or have an impact on the company's image depending on the criteria and logic applied in driving the outsourcing strategy.
5. Involvement in industries with significant scrutiny by the media and nongovernmental organizations (e.g. nuclear energy financing), affecting credit underwriting.
6. The company's environmental policy, looking at energy and renewable sources, set criteria and investments, also the company's employment policy, verifying antidiscrimination measures are applied in staff recruitment and management.

Special focus, in our experience, must be given to the reputational risk linked to financing some industry sector that encounters high scrutiny from the media due to its impact on the environment or other hotly debated, controversial issues, such as nuclear power plant development, raw material mining including uranium, oil and gas rigging, pipelines and refineries, or manufacturing of weapons for either military or civil use.

5.3 MANAGING REPUTATIONAL RISK: A MATTER OF POLICY

In managing reputational risk, we believe absolute priority should be drafting an internal reputational risk policy, outlining a process for managing reputational risks. This policy should indicate roles and responsibility in the organization, including board of directors and managing board. It should define powers and responsibilities, risk limits and issues requiring the board's approval, and the risk control structure to management and the board. The more detailed the policy, the more likely in our experience, that is requires updating frequently. We recommend a very detailed, structured document where organizational responsibilities are clearly stated. The Board must be directly involved in the control and management of reputational risk.

The policy should identify the internal function responsible for the approval of reputational risk-sensitive financing, projects, products, or investments, handling of critical situation. A dedicated Committee is a viable solution, although we found more effective if few relevant members of the managing board are responsible for decision in such cases. Other possibilities include ad hoc business committees, additional responsibilities of existing control functions such as Risk or ALCO Committees (asset and liability committee), or creating a dedicated reputational risk unit. The policy should list cases requiring the involvement of committees or Board and exceptions.

We mentioned the possibility of an internal dedicated reputational risk unit, responsible for control, similarly to market, credit or operational risk. With Basel 2 coming into force, banks made significant investments reinforcing all existing control processes, building the operational risk management function, and strengthening or simply structuring ex novo the compliance structure. This required great investments in people, information technology systems, and consultancy support. It involved process reengineering, additional training, specific internal communication. We deem for reputational risk control, this may be premature and might even generate confusion with other control functions. Rather, creating a dedicated reputational risk function might prove effective, specifying a reputational risk control policy, addressing roles and interaction with other internal risk control functions – internal audit, risk management, compliance. It will be necessary for an internal coordinating reference unit to monitor the reputational risk exposure. A possible solution would be excluding the responsibilities of existing control functions, including reputational risk. The operational risk management function could be an easy and logical solution, as it already controls events generating reputational risk. Alternatively, the compliance function could also be suitable.

5.4 REPUTATIONAL RISK MEASUREMENT

The measurement of reputational risk presents many similarities with that of operational risk. Frauds, systems interruption, employee discrimination, aggressive product distribution, and other operational event types could all have a reputational impact: applying similar techniques to those proposed for operational risk modeling could be possible: once reputation specific cases have been identified, similar techniques could be used, verifying the reputational risks are selected from the operational risk calculation dataset. We think this isn't necessarily the best way of modeling reputational risk, as the effects are different, causing more than just a loss. Reputational risk has an impact that goes far beyond the profit & loss account. We then tried alternative techniques: these are presented in the following paragraphs, complete with some examples and our indications of possible advantages and weaknesses.

Reputational risk is, linked to the other risk types – market, credit, operational, business – and recognition of what constitutes only reputational Value at Risk is not simple. We present three different methods. A simple approach is to use a model driven by share price volatility, as in the Arbitrage Pricing Theory. We then look at a kind of scenario-based approach, similar to qualitative operational risk modeling. A third one applies scoring cards techniques: risk measurement is obtained from qualitative assessment.

5.4.1 Reputational Risk as a Function of Share Price Volatility

We start reputational risk measuring its impact on the company's share price.

The assumption is that reputational events will directly impact the company's market value, this approach can only be used for listed financial institutions, a limitation to its application. The correlation between a company's reputational risk and its market value implies that a firm's stock price is equal to the present discounted expected value of the cash flow it will generate. If the shareholders are not confident of the company's management and its capability to generate future cash flows, the stock value will decrease.

We then define the econometric capturing the reputational risk embedded in the share price and measure the reputational capital at risk.

Assuming volatility of the market efficiency hypothesis, a company share price will reflect the new information announced, including reputational type events. We estimate the impact of a reputational event applying a multifactorial model based on Arbitrage Pricing Theory (APT).

In its elementary version, APT reputational risk APT model relates the return R_{it} of the generic stock i at time t to the return $R_{(Mkt,t)}$ of a market portfolio; that is

$$R_{it} = \alpha_i + \beta_i R_{(M\ kt,t)} + \epsilon_{it}$$

where

α_i is the part of R_{it} that cannot be explained by $R_{(Mkt,t)}$
β_i measures the sensitivity of R_{it} to variations of $R_{(Mkt,t)}$
ϵ_{it} is the residual term of the stock i at time t

This simple reputational risk model relates the return of the stock only to the whole market and does not allow to separate the reputational risk components from other market share price drivers. In order to identify the reputational risk factor, the variable $R_{Bank,t}$ representing the institution industry sector and the variable $R_{Rep,t}$ mirroring the hypothetical reputational events are then included. $R_{Rep,t}$ is a dicotomic variable one when a reputational event occurs at time t, and equal to zero otherwise. The return R_{it} of the generic share price of i at time t is thus described by the equation

$$R_{it} = \alpha_i + \beta_{i1}\ R_{(Mkt,t)} + \beta_{i2} R_{Bank,t} + \beta_{i3}\ R_{(Rep,t)} + \epsilon_{it} \qquad (5.1)$$

where each element of the vector $\boldsymbol{\beta}_i$ explains the sensitivity of R_{it} to variations in the corresponding factors.

Given the qualitative nature of $R_{Rep,t}$, its probability distribution function can be determined by applying a probit or logit model. Trying a probit model, the probability distribution function F is determined by the formula

$$F(z) = \Phi(z) = \int_{-\infty}^{z} \frac{1}{\sqrt{2\pi}} \exp\left(-\frac{1}{2}t^2\right) \mathrm{d}t \quad z = (\boldsymbol{\beta}' x_i)$$

where

z is a generic dicotomic variable
$\mathrm{x_i}$ is a vector of dependent variables
$\boldsymbol{\beta}'$ is the vector of the unknown coefficient

Applying instead a logit model, the cumulative distribution function is given by:

$$F(z) = \Lambda(z) = \frac{e^z}{1 + e^z}$$

Once the model is defined and statistically verified, we determine the reputational capital at risk (VaR_{Rep}) as follows.

Let's calculate first the market value of the company, the variable Y_{it} resulting from N_{it}, the number of outstanding shares of security i multiplied by their share price X_{it}:

$$Y_{it} = N_{it} \times X_{it}$$

Depending on the time horizon considered, we obtain two different VaR_{Rep} measures. VaR_{Rep} is then calculated as:

$$VaR_{Rep} = \delta \times Y \times \beta_+$$

where

$\delta = \boldsymbol{\beta}' x_i$
$\beta_+ = t_{\frac{\alpha}{2}} \sigma(\hat{\beta} R_{Rep,t})$
σ the standard deviation.

In order to measure the capital at risk, we must calculate the quantity δ, considering R_{Rep} as the dependent variable in the first model. Once the vector $\boldsymbol{\beta}$ is estimated, the quantity δ, representing R_{Rep}, is measured applying the probit or logit model, we estimate VaR_{Rep} as a function of the variations of the returns.

If we consider instead a longer time horizon, the reputational value at risk will be calculated as

$$VaR_{Rep} = Y \times \beta_+ \left(\Phi^{-1}_{1-\alpha} \times \hat{\sigma}_{\text{MKTINDEX}}\right)$$

where

$\hat{\sigma}_{\text{MKTINDEX}}$ is the market volatility estimate.

We will apply the model described to an example. We consider a real reputational event involving Banca Italease, a listed Italian bank, in 2007. Banca Italease SpA's troubles started in May 2007: the Chief Executive Officer was reported to be involved in a fraud perpetrated by a real estate investor, who was arrested in March upon charges of fraudulent bankruptcy and misappropriation of funds. The news resulted in a drop in Banca Italease market share. The company was then hit by another, more damaging reputational event, an estimated €600 million loss on derivatives distributed to clients.

It's interesting to look at the company's share price behaviour: in the days just before May 2007, the share price traded at 45 Euros, while as at 20th August, just before the appointment of Banca Italease SpA's new chairman, hit 13 Euros, a 70% fall in market capitalization.

The events reported here are taken from the Bloomberg's website.[1]

March 2, 2007: Italian real estate investor Danilo Coppola was arrested on charges of criminal association.

May 3, 2007: Massimo Faenza, the Banca Italease SpA Chief Executive Officer, was involved in the inquiry on Danilo Coppola's criminal charges.

June 1, 2007: Banca Italease SpA shares dropped as much as 13% as a consequence of the company's announcement of €400 millions potential losses by its clients.

June 7, 2007: Massimo Mazzega was named Italease Chief Executive Officer.

June 8, 2007: Banca Italease announced 50% higher clients' potential losses in two weeks, increasing from €400 million to €600 million.

June 12, 2007: *La Repubblica*, one of the most representative Italian newspapers reported that Banca Italease was under investigation by Consob, the Italian market regulator, for its derivative distribution.

June 29, 2007: Banca Italease announced the termination of four-fifths of its derivatives position with bank counterparties.

July 24, 2007: Bank of Italy required replacement of the Italease board.

July 25, 2007: Italease announced that, by Bank of Italy estimates, it would lose €500 millions on derivatives contracts it signed with clients.

August 14, 2007: Moody's downgraded Italease from BAA3 to BA1, highest noninvestment grade rating.

August 20, 2007: Radiocor reported the news of the appointment of Lino Benussi as Banca Italease new chairman. Lino Benussi was the former co-CEO of Banca IntesaBci SpA.

August 21, 2007: Lino Benussi appointed Italease new chairman shares rose by 9.6%.

[1] All the dates are reported in the dd/mm/yyyy format.

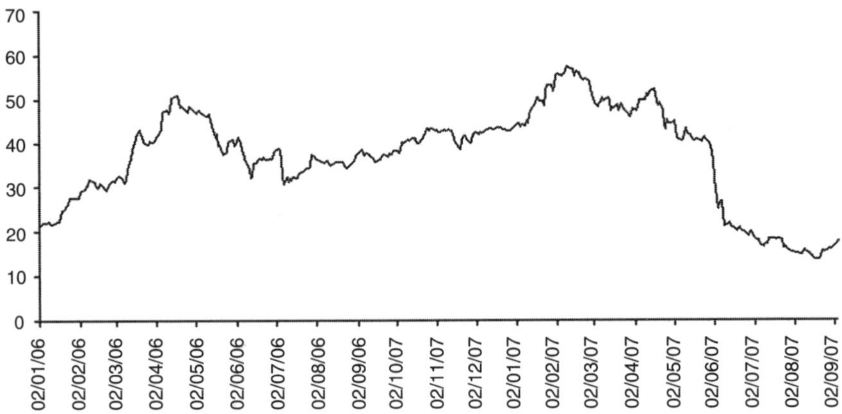

Figure 5.2 Banca Italease SpA share value

We will analyze the plots showing Italease's share price behavior. We considered Italease share prices in the period 01/01/2006–04/09/2007. Figure 5.2, shows the full historical time series, presenting positive trend through 2006 and the first months of 2007. The last part of the graph shows a decline in Italease's share value.

More interesting is Figure 5.3, considering only the period 18/04/2007–03/09/2007. If we look at data ten trading days before first reputational impact events were announced (see history above) and closing ten trading days after 20th August, the 20th August can be set as the trouble's end date.

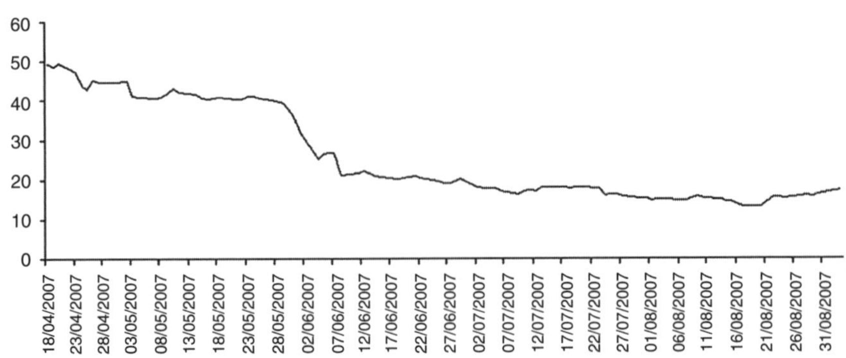

Figure 5.3 Banca Italease SpA share value during the trouble

We also analyzed the company's share price in the period 18/04/2007–03/09/2007.

- In the period 02/05–07/05 there was an 11% decrease in share value, with a 8.5% fall on May 3rd, a consequence of Faenza involvment in the inquiries on Coppola's fraud.
- The period 08/05–24/05 is quite a calm one, with no significant changes in share value.
- 24/05–08/06 is the most critical time. Shares lost 48.6% of their value, while SPMIB, a market index considering the 40 biggest Italian companies reported just a 2.8% decrease. The worst performance's are experienced in 31/05–04/06, where, in just two trading days, dropped from €36.1 to 25.19, on 08/06 alone it went from €26.9 to €21.15. We can easily relate these bad performances to events 3 and 5 in the history description.
- During 12/06–17/08 another significant share price fall, lower but not less extensive than the previous one, characterized by a 39% drop in the share value, from €21.85 to €13.56, with the lowest level on 17th August, when Italease reached its minimum since 2nd January, 2006 meanwhile the SPMIB fell only 7.6%.

We compared Banca Italease with other listed companies. First plot Milan's SPMIB index for the period 01/01/2006–09/04/2007 (Figure 5.4) and then the period 18/04/2007–03/09/2007 (Figure 5.5).

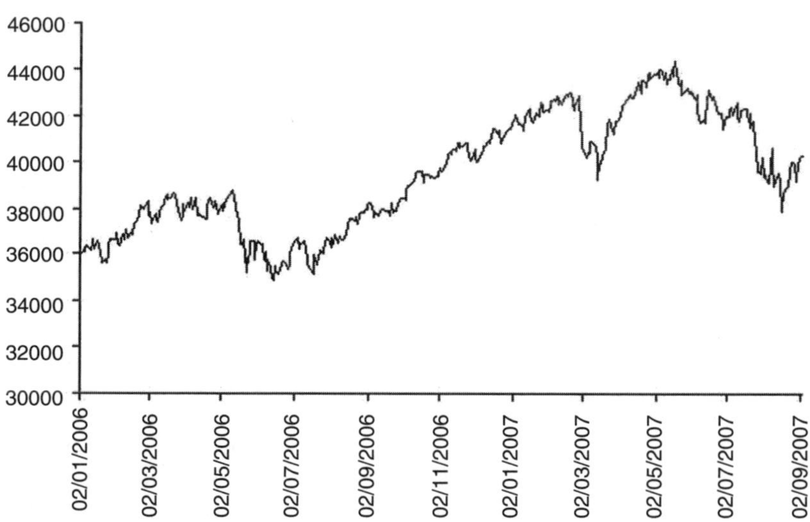

Figure 5.4 SPMIB index

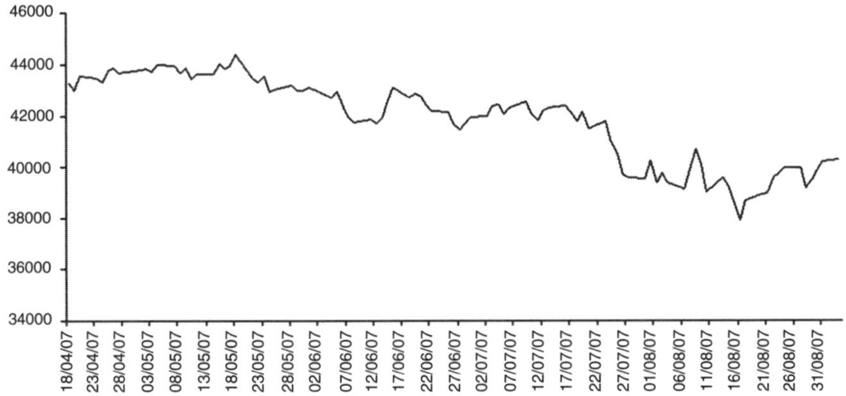

Figure 5.5 SPMIB index during Italease scandal

While Italease shares showed a 65% decrease during 18/04/2007–03/09/2007, the SPMIB index suffered just a 7% decrease. The Italease share value changes are likely due to the reported reputational events.

We carried out a regression analysis considering Italease share market values and the values of the Eurostoxx 50 and Eurostoxx Banks indexes. We considered the European market indexes, instead of a domestic one, to use information related to the whole financial sector. Tables 5.1 and 5.2 show the results.

Eurostoxx 50 is composed of the largest European companies, both financial and nonfinancial. None of the companies with index weight higher than 5%, the smallest being Carrefour SA (0.799%), and the largest BP plc, (4.84%).

Table 5.2 reports the Eurostoxx Banks index components, with 42 Banks.

In order to take into consideration the reputational element, we introduce a dummy variable when a reputational event occurs. We considered three reputational events: 01/06/2007, 08/06/2007 and 12/06/2007. Applying Equation (5.1), $R_{(Mkt,t)}$ is the Eurostoxx 50 index, $R_{Bank,t}$ is the Eurostoxx Banks index. The dummy variable equals one only in the three periods indicated.

The regression analysis did not produce positive results. For the multiple R^2 coefficient we obtained a very small value, 0.014. Then, only 1% of the variability of Banca Italease returns can be explained by such a model. Given poor statistical results, we did not feel worth calculating reputational capital at risk applying this method. The unsatisfactory

Table 5.1 Eurostoxx 50

Name	% Weight in the index
ABN AMRO Holding NV	1.957
Allianz SE	2.076
Anglo American plc	1.825
Assicurazioni Generali SpA	1.072
AstraZeneca plc	1.612
Aviva plc	0.803
AXA SA	1.565
Banco Bilbao Vizcaya Argentaria SA	1.773
Banco Santander SA	2.455
Barclays plc	1.716
BASF AG	1.44
BHP Billiton plc	1.567
BNP Paribas	1.929
BP plc	4.84
BT Group plc	1.17
Carrefour SA	0.799
Credit Suisse Group	1.479
DaimlerChrysler AG	1.937
Deutsche Bank AG	1.422
Deutsche Telekom AG	1.218
Diageo plc	1.261
E.ON AG	2.513
ENI SpA	1.88
Fortis	1.039
France Telecom SA	1.177
GlaxoSmithKline plc	3.561
HBOS plc	1.488
HSBC Holdings plc	4.608
ING Groep NV	1.853
Koninklijke Philips Electronics NV	0.99
Lloyds TSB Group plc	1.322
Nestlé SA	3.758
Nokia OYJ	2.977
Novartis AG	2.915
Rio Tinto plc	1.668
Roche Holding AG	2.727
Royal Bank of Scotland Group plc	2.302
Royal Dutch Shell plc	3.258
SAP AG	1.099
Siemens AG	2.301
Société Générale	1.575
Suez SA	1.345
Telefonaktiebolaget LM Ericsson	1.206
Telefonica SA	2.319
Tesco plc	1.521
Total SA	3.825
UBS AG	2.142
UniCredito Italiano SpA	1.81
Unilever NV	1.153
Vodafone Group plc	3.751

Table 5.2 Eurostoxx Banks

Name	% Weight in the index
ABN AMRO Holding NV	8.232
Allied Irish Banks plc	2.078
Alpha Bank AE	1.216
Anglo Irish Bank Corp plc	1.285
Banca Carige SpA	0.214
Banca Monte dei Paschi di Siena SpA	0.714
Banca Popolare di Milano Scarl	0.532
Banco Bilbao Vizcaya Argentaria SA	7.456
Banco BPI SA	0.258
Banco Comercial Portugues SA	1.411
Banco de Valencia SA	0.299
Banco Espirito Santo SA	0.493
Banco Pastor SA	0.188
Banco Popolare Scarl	1.389
Banco Popular Espanol SA	1.264
Banco Sabadell SA	0.858
Banco Santander SA	10.329
Bank of Greece	0.174
Bank of Ireland	1.624
Bankinter SA	0.332
BNP Paribas	8.106
Capitalia SpA	1.353
Commerzbank AG	2.216
Credit Agricole SA	2.515
Depfa Bank PLC	0.621
Deutsche Bank AG	5.977
Deutsche Postbank AG	0.539
Dexia SA	1.455
EFG Eurobank Ergasias SA	0.956
Erste Bank der Oesterreichischen Sparkas	1.46
Fortis	4.383
Intesa Sanpaolo SpA	6.424
KBC Groep NV	2.009
Mediobanca SpA	0.739
National Bank of Greece SA	2.637
Natixis	0.721
OKO Bank plc	0.255
Piraeus Bank SA	1.033
Raiffeisen International Bank Holding AG	0.561
Société Générale	6.606
UniCredito Italiano SpA	7.622
Unione di Banche Italiane SCPA	1.467

statistical results, seem to reinforce our opinion on reputational risk modeling: we believe that a qualitative approach could produce a better fitting.

This methodology is commonly used because it is based on a possible link with the market value, although results could be misleading. It is a very hard task to identify the reputational component from any very significant element affecting a company just looking at share value, as this might be affected by other risk types and other forces at play.

Considering the nature of reputational events, one could integrate the model with some qualitative components. A useful instrument could be the Reputation Quotient of the Reputation Institute of New York: the quotient considers the opinion of investors, customers, and employees in assessing the company's market valuation.

5.4.2 Measuring Reputational Risk Using Scenarios

Looking at alternative methods to measure reputational risk, we developed a scenario based technique.

A scenario is defined as a hypothetical event that has not yet occurred but could hit the bank. Each scenario assessment should be carried out performing extensive management interviews. The typical steps we follow for a complete scenario analysis:

- individual risks and critical processes identification
- scenario definition;
- scenario evaluation;
- final assessment.

As scenario analysis cannot be performed for all of the processes, a priority: list must be drafted, checking risk exposure and ordering the processes in terms of risk. This will be combined to a review of the market environment and an assessment of how this could affect its financial condition, as certain markets or process types may be highly exposed at particular times. We also considered risk indicators, loss trends, and market conditions, analyzing external events and taking into consideration auditors' and experts' recommendations.

Considering that during the interview we make a quantitative estimation it is of paramount importance. We gather the following information:

- we verify there are controls in place in case the scenario event occurs;
- we try estimating the likelihood that such an event could occur as frequency per year;

- we determine the average loss amount the scenario could entail;
- we estimate the maximum loss amount in the scenario event;
- we check if insurance coverage exists;
- we gather risk mitigation suggestions, alternatives.

This information (e.g. frequency per year, average loss amount, maximum loss amount, and insurance coverage) is then used to calculate the reputational capital at risk of the selected scenario. As for operational risk, we implement an actuarial model, using the information collected during the interview to estimate the severity and frequency distributions.

More in detail:

- we use the average frequency per year to estimate the frequency distribution;
- the average loss amount and maximum loss amount are applied to estimate the severity distribution;
- annual loss distribution is obtained through Monte Carlo simulation;
- the distribution is adjusted for the insurance coverage;
- expected loss is calculated as the mean (or median) of the annual loss distribution;
- the unexpected loss is calculated as the difference between quantiles at a fixed confidence level (e.g. 99.9%) and expected loss.

We then defined the statistical methodology to estimate severity and frequency.

The frequency of annual events is estimated applying a Poisson distribution with parameter λ. The probability mass function is as follows:

$$\Pr(N = n) = p_n = e^{-\lambda}\frac{\lambda^n}{n!} \tag{5.2}$$

The severity can be estimated through a Weibull distribution with the following probability density function:

$$f(x; \theta, \tau) = \frac{\tau(x/\theta)^\tau \exp(-(x/\theta)^\tau)}{x} \tag{5.3}$$

The Weibull distribution is reparameterized with the mean value and 99.9% quantile:

$$f(x; \theta, \tau) = f(x; \mu,\ q_{99.9\%}) \tag{5.4}$$

The parameters of the distribution will be estimated using the empirical mean and the maximum value of loss data:

$$\hat{\bar{X}} = \frac{1}{n} \sum_{i=1}^{n} x_i \tag{5.5}$$

$$\hat{F}_X^{-1}(0.999) = \max(x_1, \ldots, x_n) \tag{5.6}$$

The mean and the maximum value, taken as the 99.9% quantile, obtained from the questionnaire are converted into the shape and scale parameters of the Weibull distribution, using the following equations:

$$\frac{\bar{X}}{F_X^{-1}(0.999)} = \frac{(3 \cdot \ln 10)^{\frac{1}{\theta}}}{\Gamma\left(1 + \frac{1}{\theta}\right)} \tag{5.7}$$

$$\tau = \frac{\overline{X}}{\Gamma\left(1 + \frac{1}{\theta}\right)} \tag{5.8}$$

where:

$$\Gamma(t) = \int_0^{+\infty} x^{t-1} \cdot e^{-x}\, dx \tag{5.9}$$

Combining the severity and frequency, we obtain the annual loss distribution. The loss distribution describes the distribution of the total loss S in the holding time period (one year), given by the aggregation of severities X of the single losses: $S = \sum_{i=1}^{N} X_i$. The model applies Monte Carlo techniques. The following steps are so repeated for J realizations ($J = 1\,000\,000$ at least):

1. The frequency is estimated sampling from the distribution; the realization obtained is the number of loss events in one year.
2. A certain number of independent realizations are drawn from the severity distribution. That is, the number of events simulated in the previous step if it is not zero.
3. The compound loss is the sum of single losses simulated in the previous step.

A sample of simulated annual losses is obtained: $[s_1, \ldots, s_J]$. If an insurance cover is in place, it can be taken into account by applying a multiplicative factor to the simulated annual losses sample. We suppose that a percentage, α, of the annual loss could be recovered ($0\% \leq \alpha \leq 100\%$), then the annual losses sample is adjusted as follows:

$$[S_1^{\text{ins}} = s_1 \cdot (100\% - \alpha), \ \ldots, s_J^{\text{ins}} = s_J \cdot (100\% - \alpha)] \tag{5.10}$$

From the annual loss distribution, the capital at risk is obtained as the quantile at the 99.9% confidence level (Value at Risk). Provided we sort the losses s_j^{ins}, $j = 1, \ldots, J$ in increasing order: $s_{(1)}^{\text{ins}} \leq s_{(2)}^{\text{ins}} \leq \ldots \leq s_{(J)}^{\text{ins}}$, *VaR* is defined as:

$$VaR_{99.9\%} = F_s^{-1}(99.9\%) = \inf\left\{s_{(j)}^{\text{ins}} : \frac{j}{J} \geq 99.9\%\right\} \tag{5.11}$$

The expected loss can be obtained as the mean (or the median) of the sample $\left[s_1^{\text{ins}}, \ldots s_J^{\text{ins}}\right]$, while unexpected loss is calculated as the difference between *VaR* and *EL*:

$$UL_{99.9\%} = VaR_{99.9\%} - EL \tag{5.12}$$

If more than one scenario is performed, one has to aggregate the results to obtain an overall capital at risk. Suppose we have performed *n* scenarios: the overall capital at risk under the hypothesis of perfect dependence is simply the sum of all *VaRs*:

$$VaR_{99.9\%}^{\text{TOT}} = \sum_{i=1}^{I} VaR_{99.9\%}^{i} \tag{5.13}$$

where $VaR_{99.9\%}^{i}$ is the value at risk for the scenario i and $VaR_{99.9\%}^{\text{TOT}}$ is the overall value at risk.

This hypothesis may be too conservative. A more realistic setting is independence among scenarios. In this case, it is sufficient to add, term by term, the simulated annual loss samples, in random order, obtained from each scenario. Hence, the annual loss distribution in case of independence results:

$$\left[s_1^{\text{TOT}} = \sum_{i=1}^{I} s_1^i, \ldots, s_J^{\text{TOT}} = \sum_{i=1}^{I} s_J^i\right] \tag{5.14}$$

where s_j^i is the annual loss simulated for the year $j = 1, \ldots, J$ referred to the scenario $i = 1, \ldots, I$.

It is also possible an intermediate hypothesis of dependence between scenarios (between independence and perfect dependence) using a copula function. This case is more complicated because it is also necessary assessing the correlation among scenarios.

Once the scenario analysis is completed, the results should be shared with the functions involved, presenting potential losses and recommendations for risk mitigation.

We believe that it is possible to perform scenarios assessing credit, market, and operational events and then adjusting the results by a multiplicative factor considering the reputational risk impact. Alternatively, one could perform scenarios assessing all risk types and subtract the components unrelated to reputational risk. To get a multiplicative factor, the simplest way is to prepare a grid representing the reputational risk exposure to the different processes. We tried two factors, one adjusting severity and the correcting frequency. Once the reputational risk-exposed areas are listed, we map them and derive, for example using questionnaires, risk classifications both in terms of frequency and severity. One can estimate operational, market, or credit risk losses, then adjust the results using these reputational multiplicative factors.

However, we need an assessment not only of the direct effects of a catastrophic event, but also of the indirect ones. And we think that for process owners, who are the best possible people to evaluate the direct consequences of such an event affecting their processes, this could be very hard.

5.4.3 Scoring-Card-Based Models for Reputational Risk Assessment

As for other control assessment functions, be these internal audit, operational risk, service level control, or customer satisfaction surveys, we found that questionnaires – or score cards – could also be applied to reputational risk measurement. In fact, in our opinion, weighted lists of questions, to be filled in by managers, process owners, customers, or business specialists, could prove particularly useful and indicate the value of the multidimensional impacts of reputational type events. By multidimensional, we mean that these will affect revenues, relations with clients, internal processes, information technology or staff training, the company's internal perception, share price and rating, media coverage, and regulatory valuation. Score cards, in fact, have some features that may prove well suited to reputational risk assessment:

- score cards are bespoke (and surely there isn't a standard checklist of questions that industry associations or regulators are recommending to use for reputational risk valuation), rendering them extremely flexible and easy to tailor to the business, process, and company's organization;

- they allow one to focus on and expand specific topics or areas of exposure;
- they can be structured in a simple way and are therefore easy to understand, making then relatively straightforward for people to fill in and grasp results;
- areas of weakness and necessary intervention will be identified easily, as these will show up in the questionnaires;
- the structure – or modeling – of questions and weights assigned can be modified very easily.

Probably the greatest challenge for all the qualitative, expert judgment-based models is that the results may be questionable and it might prove difficult to ensure consistency of the assessment:

- different analysts or interviewed staff could determine very different answers and assessments of the probability or impacts of events or the results of a reputational type situation. On one side this complicates the integration and reading of such information, on the other side it renders the development of a questionnaire that ensures consistent results extremely difficult;
- as the results depend on individual views and judgments, these might present problems when comparing results from time to time, sometimes showing an unexpected increase in the risk profile or, by contrast, unvarying, stable behavior;
- without changing the interviewed sample, we experienced that the same people provide the same answers over time, simply confirming their previous valuations;
- the more articulated the questionnaire, the more time it will take to fill in, causing risks of limited focus or difficulties in completing. It is sometimes difficult and time-consuming to repeat the exercise and extend it to a large number of people.

5.5 A RECENT EXAMPLE OF REPUTATIONAL EVENT

The year 2008 not only started with a number of banks under the AMA regime, but on the 24th January, operational risk managers were also under the spotlight for another reason. That morning Société Générale (or SocGen) announced that it had suffered losses of €4.9 bln due to internal fraud, similar to what happened years before to Barings.

An employee brought into deep financial, regulatory, and reputational trouble a bank considered one of Europe's most solid and profitable banks. The incident caused the loss of most of 2007's annual profit leading to a capital increase of €5.5 bln.

From a regulatory point of view, SocGen was AMA compliant from January 2008. The amount of the loss exceeded all previously known banking sector operational losses. This section will try to describe the event and its consequences from an operational, financial, and reputational point of view. We have based our statements on publicly available information like the press releases of SocGen itself and public data sources.

5.5.1 A Description of the Event

To some extent the SocGen case is similar to other events: we recall Barings (£800 mln loss and bankruptcy of the bank), Allied Irish Bank, or National Australia Bank.

5.5.2 Background

The SocGen trader worked for five years in a middle office and had therefore a good knowledge of internal process and control procedures. In 2005 he moved to the arbitrage department, responsible for arbitrage of financial instruments on European stock markets, a proprietary trading operation.

Arbitrage business involves, for example, buying a portfolio of instruments and selling at the same moment a second portfolio of instruments that is very similar, but slightly different in value. This small difference results in a profit or loss from the arbitrage business. As these differences are so small, this business involves a large number of operations with very high nominal values. However, as the portfolios are so similar and offset each other, the market risk involved is normally very small. The risk of these positions is continuously monitored.

The SocGen trader managed to avoid controls or made them ineffective, inserted fictitious deals, the fake transactions were registered in the bank's systems.

5.5.3 How the Fake Trading Occurred

He developed an initial portfolio through real transactions using futures on the changes of the main European stock market indexes. These are, in line with 'normal' business activity, are checked daily and subject to margin calls, regularly checked and settled by or paid to the bank.

A second portfolio that contained the fake transactions apparently offset the positions in the first one; therefore only a small, residual risk was evident. This way, he managed to hide a huge speculative position.

SocGen supplied the following details:

> 'In order to ensure that these fictitious operations were not immediately identified, the trader used his years of experience in processing and controlling market operations to successively circumvent all the controls which allow the bank to check the characteristics of the operations carried out by its traders, and consequently their real existence.
>
> In practice, the trader combined several fraudulent methods to avoid the controls in place:
>
> - firstly, he ensured that the characteristics of the fictitious operations limited the chances of a control: for example, he chose very specific operations with no cash movements or margin calls and which did not require immediate confirmation;
> - he misappropriated the IT access codes belonging to operators in order to cancel certain operations;
> - he falsified documents allowing him to justify the entry of fictitious operations;
> - he ensured that the fictitious operations involved a different financial instrument to the one he had just cancelled, in order to increase his chances of not being controlled.'

5.5.4 The Discovery and First Reactions

Fraudulent operations seemed to start in 2007, producing a gain of around €1.47 bln at the end of that year and were only discovered in January, 2008.

An employee of a brokerage company, a subsidiary of SocGen, who was used to carrying out the trader's transactions and offseting his positions, 'had been informed by the trader some time ago of the large positions he had taken and of the requests for information by Eurex (the derivatives exchange)', according to SocGen. Eurex alerted SocGen twice in November 2007 and both times SocGen replied in reassuring tones to Eurex.

This is the timeline of the event:

Friday 18th January, 2008

After detecting abnormal counterparty risk on a broker, the explanations provided by the trader cause additional controls (some say this was the result of an 'error' in the trader's fraudulent transaction schemes). The trader's superiors are informed and they inform the division's management. In the afternoon, the counterparty for the recorded operations appears to be a major bank, but the email for confirmation is suspicious. A team is now investigating the situation. An adviser to the trader's lawyer stated later that, at that moment, the trader's position had no loss.

Saturday 19th January, 2008

The trader does not give satisfactory explanations, while the transactions are not recognized by the major bank. The trader then starts to admit having committed unauthorized transactions and having created fake operations. The bank starts to get a grab on the real position.

Sunday 20th January, 2008

In the morning all positions are identified and in the early afternoon the total exposure is known, approximately €50 bln. Note that, on Friday night, SocGen's market capitalization was less than €40 bln. SocGen's Chairman, Daniel Bouton, informs the Governor of the Banque de France. In the Audit Committee that was already planned to review the preliminary 2007 financial results, the Chairman discloses the position to the Committee and announces that 'he has decided to close the position as quickly as possible and, in accordance with market regulations, to postpone all communication on this issue and on the estimated (2007) results until said position has been closed.' He then informs the general secretary of the AMF, the French securities regulator. In the already planned board meeting later that day, the Chairman explains that 'it is impossible to communicate on the estimated results for 2007 on account of the discovery of problems in certain market activities, which could result in substantial losses.'

Monday 21st January, 2008

The closing of the position starts. Conditions are very unfavorable and, to defend the bank against accusations that it depressed the markets on these trading days, SocGen underlines more than once that, already on the afternoon of Friday 18th January there had been a sharp downturn in the European markets and that there was a drop in the Asian markets on Monday (before the European markets opened), for example the Hang Seng dropped 5.4%. The unwinding continued over three days to keep volume levels under 10% (in fact, the maximum level was on Monday, with 8.1% on the Eurostoxx futures, while the bank estimated it had an impact on the market of around 0.5%).

Wednesday 23rd January, 2008

The position is completely closed (or hedged) in the evening. A loss results of €4.9 bln. Another board meeting is held and its members are fully informed of the facts.

Thursday 24th January, 2008

Before the markets open, SocGen informs the markets of the fraud and its consequences; the bank asks trading in its shares to be suspended. Internal and Banque de France investigations start as well as an inquiry by the police.

Saturday 26th January, 2008

The regulatory authorities are informed of the fraud methodology and the actions that have been taken by the bank.

5.5.5 Measures Planned and Taken

As a result, SocGen took a number of actions, some of them described in the prospectus for the new equity issue. In no particular order:

- The trader was suspended as well as his direct line managers, awaiting the results of the investigations.
- The arbitrage activity of the equity derivative arm was downsized.
- New control procedures were implemented.
- An IT security improvement program was developed (frequent password changing, access checking). A biometric identity control system was announced.
- New alert indicators were introduced (control and limits of gross nominal amounts, supervision of cancellations, transactions with deferred start, ongoing confirmation with internal counterparties, control of cash flows, more rigorous monitoring of holidays and unusual behavior, alert distribution list).
- Relations between middle and front offices were reorganized. A department responsible for transaction security was created, including a team responsible for seeking out fraudulent transactions. Fraud risk training and control resources were improved.
- A Special Committee was set up, composed of independent directors to ensure the new control measures were effectively taken and that the bank's correctly reported the results of the investigations.

5.5.6 Immediate Consequences for SocGen

The losses that materialized after unwinding the fraudulent positions, together with worse than expected write-downs related to US residential mortgage assets, required immediate financial action. New shares were issued by SocGen: a €5.5 billion rights issue was launched.

Like most banks, SocGen seems to have insurance against fraud perpetrated by employees, however it was most probably not effective. This kind of insurance covers fraud only when the employee has gained a direct profit from his operations. So far, this was not proven. The policy limit of this insurance unlikely to be sufficient for such a large loss.

'Rogue trader coverage' can be bought from insurance carriers, the worldwide capacity is estimated at around US$1 bln.

Within a short time span, a number of investigations and legal filings also appeared. We registered the following, but this does not claim to be a complete list:

The Banking Commission has started an investigation, while the AMF, the French securities regulator, is making an inquiry into the financial information and market for SocGen shares.

The Brooklyn, New York, district attorney together with the SEC and the CFTC investigated the unwinding of the positions.

A shareholder accused SocGen at the Paris Criminal Court of alleged faults that drove down its share price.

A group of employees and former employees, shareholders of SocGen and members of the Assact SG association, filed a complaint citing that SocGen employees had been financially impacted by the incident.

The rating agencies reviewed their ratings as well. Moody's and Fitch downgraded the bank one notch, to AA2 and AA – respectively, while Standard & Poor's put SocGen on a negative outlook (AA).

5.5.7 Reputational Issues and Comments

Much has been written that has damaged the reputation of SocGen.

French public opinion, according to a poll in the immediate aftermath of the affair, broadly supported the trader: only 15% of the interviewed blamed the trader and more than half of the people blamed senior management for the loss.

As so often in these kinds of situations, former employees stood up to worsen the situation from a reputational point of view. A former SocGen

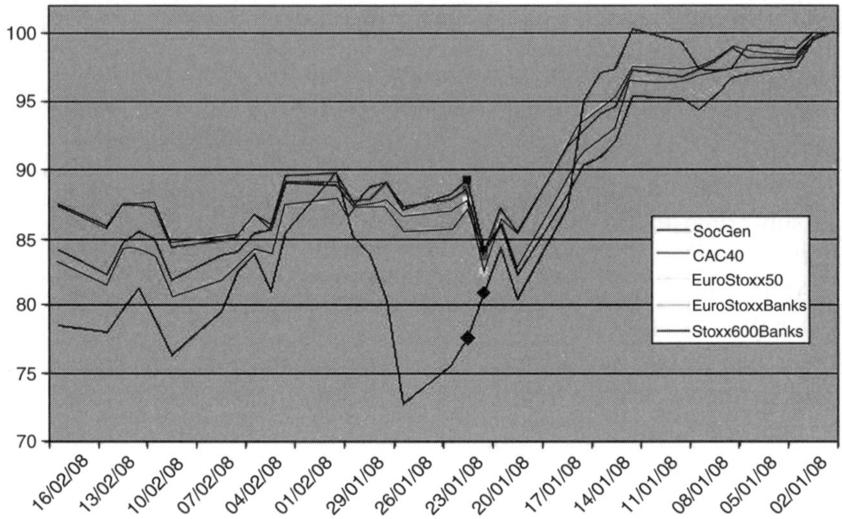

Figure 5.6 Stock market reaction to the SocGen event

internal auditor gave interviews to the press saying that (part of) the cause of the affair was made up of the lack of seniority and experience of its auditing and inspection team. SocGen stated that these comments were defamatory and originated from motives of a personal nature.

Figure 5.6 compares the SocGen share price with a number of stock market indexes, from 2nd January, 2008 (=100) until 18th February, 2008. The closing values have been marked for 23rd January and 24th January, the day of the announcement of the fraud.

On the day of the announcement, the SocGen share price fell 4.1%, the CAC40 index rose 6.0% (and the Eurostoxx 50 6.5%). It is calculated that the reputational damage for SocGen amounted to a 12% drop in the share price, taking into account the positive yield for the rest of the French market (as expressed by the CAC40).

On the following days, when more details were published, the price fell further until 28th January when the lowest price was registered, more than 10% below the share price of 23rd January.

At that point in time, more and more people started to believe in an imminent takeover bid for SocGen, as the price bounced back. On 1st February the price was even 11% above the 23rd January price. Taking over SocGen, however, would not have been easy: any shareholder in SocGen has a maximum of 15% of voting rights, until it acquires more than 50% of the shares, while double voting rights are reserved for 'long-standing shareholders', such as employees and treasury stock (together 20% of voting rights).

From this high, the share price slipped back in the following days and then seemed to follow the ups and downs of the markets in line with the other indexes, influenced now by further announcements on sub-prime losses and the 2007 full-year figures of other financial institutions.

At the end of this period of observation, SocGen stood at around 10% lower than the CAC40 or Eurostoxx 50 and only between 6 and 7% lower than the two banking indexes, Eurostoxx Banks and Eurostoxx600 Banks. Apart from the first few days after the news was made public, the markets seemed therefore, not to penalise SocGen too much. We would like to make some remarks on this:

1. The SocGen stock is present in all of these indexes of comparison, therefore impacting their value. One should calculate the index without the SocGen stock to have a more precise indication.
2. A 'spill-over' effect exists between the announcing bank and all the nonannouncing banks. In other words, an important loss event communicated by one bank has a negative impact on the stock prices of other banks without such a loss event; this effect has been quantified as being up to 37% of the announcing bank's value variation. The prices of other banks and indexes were also influenced negatively by the SocGen announcement, impacting the differential analyses between the SocGen price and the other stock values.

It should also be noted that SocGen was criticized in the first few days for its minimal disclosure. Soon, however, the bank gave more and more detail on the fraud, helping to clarify some points and surely limiting uncertainty and some of the impact on its reputation. In the documentation for the raise in capital, more information was given to the public. The Special Committee published a progress report on 20th February, 2008 (available on the bank's internet site) with much detail on the case. In addition, the findings of PricewaterhouseCoopers, who assist the Special Committee, will be made public.

These efforts have to be seen as an attempt to manage the reputational risk: once the bad thing is known, it is better to be transparent, to give full disclosure, and communicate what you are doing to improve the situation.

For the moment, SocGen seems not to have been penalized very severely by the markets.

A completely different issue concerns the reaction of the banking regulators. Apart from SocGen, how will regulators review the other banks 'after SocGen'? How confident are the regulators of the AMA frameworks of other banks now? Some precise questions are to be expected in regulators' audits in 2008 and 2009. Also, will regulators use Pillar II to increase minimum capital requirements for a 'SocGen risk'?

How this event impacts the calculation of capital requirements of AMA banks? Taken as an external loss data point, this event could raise another bank's capital requirement by as much as €50 million.

5.5.8 The Lessons Learned – What Can We Do to Avoid Being Next?

Although the SocGen case resembles a number of other high losses of the past, for some in the industry this has been a wake-up call. For sure in the last days of January and in the month of February, operational risk, IT, and audit functions were busy making quick reviews in reply to one single question coming from top management and management committees: could this happen to us? And if banks have not done so already, their regulators will ask the same question. UniCredit Group also made a quick review of specific areas exposed.

5.5.9 Psychological, 'Soft' Factors

Sometimes if we review the circumstances that led to a disaster, it seems that this event was just destined to happen. In the SocGen case one might easily think so. Alas, this is only partially true. Some elements are clear only after the damage is done and in particular this is true for some 'soft' factors like a company's culture and individuals' behaviour.

Although not easy to capture for a bank as a whole, direct line managers could have noted some of these 'soft' elements in the trader's behavior. No holidays, discontent and high self-esteem, bonus demands that were out of scope; the overall picture justified an additional control now and then. Control of these softer factors is something banks would probably like to control more and where HR departments could support line management.

5.5.10 Control Instruments

The documents published so far give us a number of suggestions of possible failing controls. Banks, for example, should check whether limits or controls have been set on notional amounts in all products and locations. Other controls should include cash flows, margin calls and payments, guarantee deposits, and counterparty settlements. These can be IT and staff intensive and time consuming but such controls are necessary.

IT security is another critical area; after years of debate, in the SocGen case password protection also played a role, as well as fake emails. The use of a biometric access control for dealing staff is now being considered.

The press has also reported that SocGen is setting up an internal team of 'hackers' to test IT security.

5.5.11 Managing Data and Signals

We would like to make a final remark, possibly the most important one. During the A$360 mln fraud in National Australia Bank in 2004, some traders continued to breach limits because Value at Risk figures used to control the process were ignored, as they were deemed unreliable by their supervisors. Likewise in the SocGen case, apart from the enquiries by Eurex, it seems that 93 alerts in the control process were triggered by the trader's unauthorized transactions (this number was reported in the press; the progress report of the Special Committee of SocGen gives details of 75 such alerts).

We have to dedicate staff and time to control the data.

Finally, that business in derivatives in general has grown very rapidly and many banks struggled to keep up with it, causing confirmation backlogs – regulators warned more than once in 2007 about the dangers this can create. Maybe SocGen's middle and back office were just not growing fast enough to keep up with the successful business growth of its front office.

6

Conclusions

In recent years, financial institutions made major investments in order to comply with the new Basel capital accord requirements. For many banks, this has meant structuring a new function in the company responsible for operational risk management, involved defining its internal rules and responsibilities, relations to functions in charge of other controls and processes, recruiting and training staff, and developing tools and applications supporting the new activities. It took significant time and effort and it still needs further investment, as the gap to other long-established risk control functions remains and the set of regulatory responsibilities is huge, spanning the whole organization and all processes.

Banks ought to remember that great challenges await the operational risk manager in the years to come, with Basel 2 coming into force. Of these challenges, we feel that some deserve greater management attention.

- Current operational risk measurement still requires further research. Whether this be loss distribution approaches such as the one proposed, or scenario-based, or alternative techniques, banks are still at the early stages of operational risk model development. Further work is needed to verify results and approaches are correct; this will take years as backtesting isn't immediate with rare, events-driven risk modelling.
- Increasingly the economic capital is needed at individual business and product level, for correct performance measurement. Current operational risk models, focusing on consolidated capital measurement, shall provide risk figures at such levels.
- Indirect costs must be considered. Information technology costs and all the indirect impacts of inadequate service and inefficiency are not directly translated into losses, and are not necessarily considered in the operational capital at risk, reducing the possibility of measuring risk exposure correctly.
- Controlling operational risk remains extremely difficult and requires regular updates and adjustment to changing processes and business

structures. This represents a managerial challenge if we aim at an efffective operational risk control process.

- Complying with Basel 2 requirements, be these either the basic or advanced requirements, doesn't stop with the accord coming into force. The company should never forget that operational risk encompasses all the processes and represents one of the most difficult types of exposure to monitor and measure.
- Experience tells us that the operational risk management function is new and puny given the tasks and responsibilities assigned by regulators. So far, the operational risk control function hinged on other existing internal control structures, whether internal audit, security, market or credit risk management, or compliance: though the links and relations with these functions remain of fundamental importance, the operational risk management has its own responsibilities that cannot be delegated to other organizational structure. The operational risk responsibilities must be clear to management; must be adequately staffed. The company shouldn't underestimate the commitment given to supervisors (and markets) once applied for Basel 2, in particular for the most advanced models. Regulatory authorities, will expect the companies to approach operational risk control with the utmost attention and continue to dedicate time, investment, and people to strengthening the function.
- Boundary exposure with credit risk represents the next step in regulatory requirement development. In the second accord, financial institutions are simply required to identify credit default files caused by operational events (fraud, execution errors, missing documents, etc., see Chapter 2) and report them in the operational risk management database. Though official statistics are not available on the impact of operational risk on credit defaults, we are convinced this represents a significant part of the total credit risk. The fact that Basel 2 doesn't require a reassessment of their credit risk excluding operation-driven defaults, doesn't mean it should be underestimated: it will likely become compulsory to exclude those files and include them in the operational risk dataset for capital at risk measurement. This will have a non predictable impact on banks' capital at risk valuation, affecting provision levels, capital ratios, and the relevance of an adequate operational risk control process. We believe banks should start the necessary investments *to identify* operational risk in credit underwriting and work out processes: procrastinating will mean greater effort and costs in the future, while addressing it now could ensure a competitive advantage.

- Ensuring effective operational risk control needs relations with other internal control functions. The operational risk function shouldn't rely or delegate its responsibilities to other internal control functions. The operational risk control outlines the interactions between risk management, compliance, security, operational risk control, and internal audit. Banks must make sure that risk control activities aren't duplicated or, remain uncontrolled.

In this book we studied operational and reputational risks, perceiving these as interwoven: a company might find it effective to combine operational and reputational control responsibilities in the operational risk function. As mentioned, reputational risk isn't specifically regulated: this shouldn't leave it uncontrolled, as it represents the greatest of the risks any bank is exposed to. The fact that it isn't necessarily indicated in the list of compulsory regulatory capital elements or that it hasn't yet found a standard measurement and management approach shouldn't lead to underestimation: we think that banks should have a model to measure reputational risk capital, including indirect costs of customers and clients, for a complete and correct capital at risk assessment and performance measurement.

References

1. Banca d'Italia (2006) *Nuove disposizioni di vigilanza prudentaile per le banche – Circolare n. 263 del 27 dicembre 2006.*
2. Basel Committee on Banking Supervision (2004) *International Convergence of Capital Measurement and Capital Standards*, supporting document to the New Basel Capital Accord.
3. Moscadelli, M. (2004) *The Modelling of Operational Risk Experience with the Analysis of the Data Collected by the Basel Committee.* Banca d'Italia, Termini di discussione No. 517.
4. CEBS (2006) *Guidelines on the implementation, validation and assessment of Advanced Measurement (AMA) and Internal Ratings Based (IRB) approaches.*
5. Piacenza, F., Ruspantini, D. and Soprano A. (2006) Operational risk class homogeneity. *The Journal of Operational Risk*, **1**(3), 51–59.
6. Klugman, S., Panjer, H. and Willmot, G. (1998) *Loss Models: From data to decisions*, John Wiley & Sons, Inc., New York.
7. de Fontnouvelle, P., De Jesus-Rueff, V., Jordan, J. and Rosengren, E. (2003) *Using Loss Data to Quantify Operational Risk*, Federal Reserve Bank of Boston.
8. Dutta, K. and Perry, J. (2006) *A Tale of Tails: An empirical analysis of loss distribution models for estimating operational risk capital.* Federal Reserve Bank of Boston, working paper.
9. Gabbi, G., Marsella, M. and Massacesi, M. (2005) *Il rischio operative nelle banche*, Egea.
10. Resti, A. and Sironi, A. (2007) *Risk Management and Shareholders Value in Banking*, John Wiley & Sons, Ltd, Chichester.
11. Tukey, J. (1977) *Exploratory Data Analysis*, Addison-Wesley.
12. Boos, D. D. (1982) Minimum Anderson–Darling estimation, *Communications in Statistics*, **11**(24), 2747–2774.
13. Frachot, A. and Roncalli, T. (2002) *Mixing internal and external data for managing operational risk.* Groupe de Recherche Operationnelle, Credit Lyonnais, France, working paper.
14. Lambrigger, D. D., Shevchenko, P. V. and Wüthrich, M. V. (2007) *The Quantification of Operational Risk using Internal Data, Relevant External Data and Expert Opinions*, working paper.
15. Mignola, G. and Ugoccioni, R. (2006) Effect of a Data Collection Threshold in the Loss Distribution Approach. *Journal of Operational Risk*, **1**(4).

16. Bazzarello, D., Crielaard, B., Piacenza, F. and Soprano A. (2006) Modeling insurance mitigation on operational risk capital. *The Journal of Operational Risk*, **1**(1), 57–65.
17. Neslehová, J., Embrechts, P. and Chavez-Demoulin, V. (2006) Infinite Mean Models and the LDA for Operational Risk. *Journal of Operational Risk*, **1**(1), 3–25.
18. Sklar, A. (1959) *Fonctions de repartition à n dimensions et leurs marges*. Publications de l'Institut de Statistique de l'Université de Paris.
19. McNeal, A. J., Frey, R. and Embrechts, P. (2005) *Quantitative Risk Management*. Ed. Princeton Series in Finance.
20. Gumbel, E. J. (1960) *Distributions des valeurs extremes en plusieurs dimensions*. Publications de FInstitut de Statistique de l'Université de Paris.
21. Hougaard, P. (1986) A Class of Multivariate Failure Time Distributions. *Biometrika*, **73**, 671–678.
22. Aas, K. (2004) *Modeling the dependence structure of financial assets: A survey of four copulas*. Note, Norwegian Computing Centre, December 2004.
23. Romano, C. (2002) *Calibrating and simulating copula functions: An application to the Italian stock market*. Working paper 12, CIDEM.
24. Böcker. K. and Klüppelberg, C. (2005) Operational VAR: A closed-form approximation, *Risk* magazine, December, 90–93.
25. Böcker, K. (2006) Operational Risk: Analytical Results When High Severity Losses Follow a Generalized Pareto Distribution. *Journal of Risk*, **8**(4), 117–120.
26. Böcker, K. and Sprittulla, J. (2006) Operational VAR: Meaningful Means. *Risk* magazine, December.
27. Baud, N., Frachot, A. and Roncalli, T. (2002) *How to avoid overestimating of capital charge*. Groupe de Recherche Operationelle, Credit Lyonnais, France, working paper.
28. Chapelle, A., Crama, Y., Hubner, G. and Peters, J. P. (2004) *Basel II and Operational Risk: Implications for Risk Measurement and Management in the Financial Sector*. National Bank of Belgium, working paper.
29. Mignola, G. and Ugoccioni, R. (2006) Sources of Uncertainty in Modelling Operational Risk Losses. *The Journal of Operational Risk*, **1**(2), 33–50.
30. Aue, F. and Kalkbrener, M. (2007) LDA at Work: Deutsche Bank's Approach to Quantifying Operational Risk. *Journal of Operational Risk*, **1**(4), 49–93.
31. Morone, M., Cornaglia, A. and Mignola, G. (2007) *Economic capital assessment via copulas: aggregation and allocation of different risk types*. Available at http://www.DefaultRisk.com.

Further reading

Artzner, P., Delbaen, F., Eber, J.-M. and Heath, D. (1999) Coherent measures of risk. *Mathematical Finance*, **9**, 203–228.

Azzalini, A. and Vedaldi, R. (1987) *Introduzione all'Inferenza Statistica Parametrica*. Cleup, Padova.

Balkema, A. A. and de Haan, L. (1974) Residual lifetime at great age. *Annals of Probability*, **2**, 792–804.

Barndorff-Nielsen, O. and Lindner, A. (2004) *Some aspects of Lévy copulas*. Preprint. Munich University of Technology. Available at http://www.ma.tum.de/stat/

Basel Committee on Banking Supervision (2003) *The 2002 Loss Data Collection Exercise for Operational Risk: Summary of the Data Collected.*

Basel Committee on Banking Supervision. (2004) *Principles for the Home-Host Recognition of AMA Operational Risk Capital.*

Basel Committee on Banking Supervision. (2005) *The Treatment of Expected Losses by Banks Using the AMA Under the Basel II Framework.*

Basel Committee on Banking Supervision. (2006) *Home-host information sharing for effective Basel II implementation.*

Basel Committee on Banking Supervision. (2007) *Principles for Home-Host Supervisory Cooperation and Allocation Mechanisms in the Context of Advanced Measurement Approaches.*

Basu, A. (2002) Outlier resistant minimum divergence methods in discrete parametric models. *Sankhya: The Indian Journal of Statistics (B)*, **64**, 128–140.

Baud, N., Frachot, A. and Roncalli, T. (2002) How to Avoid Over-Estimating Capital Charge for Operational Risk? *Operational Risk*, February.

Baud, N., Frachot, A. and Roncalli, T. (2002) *Internal data, external data and consortium data for operational risk measurement: How to pool data properly*. Groupe de Recherche Operationnelle, Credit Lyonnais, France, working paper.

Bee, M. (2005) *Copula-based Multivariate Models with Applications to Risk Management and Insurance.*

Bee, M. (2005) *On Maximum Likelihood Estimation of Operational Loss Distributions.*

Bingham, N. H., Goldie, C. M., and Teugels, J. L. (1987) *Regular Variation*. Cambridge University Press, Cambridge.

Bocker, K. and Kluppelberg, C. (2006) *Multivariate Models for Operational Risk.*

Bocker, K. and Kluppelberg, C. (2007) *Multivariate Operational Risk: Dependence Modelling with Levy Copulas.*

Brandts, S. (2004) *Operational Risk and Insurance: Quantitative and Qualitative Aspects*. EFMA 2004 Basel Meetings Paper.

Brown, D. and Wang, J. (2005) Discussion on "Quantitative models for operational risk: extremes, dependence and aggregation". Presentation. *Implementing an AMA to Operational Risk,* Federal Reserve Bank of Boston, May 18–20.

Bühlmann, H., Shevchenko, P. and Wuethrich, M. V. (2007) *A "Toy" Model for Operational Risk Quantification Using Credibility Theory.*

Chanseok, P. and Ayanendranath, B. (2003) The generalized Kullback–Leibler divergence and robust inference. *Journal of Statistical Computation and Simulation,* **73**(5), 311–332.

Chavez-Demoulin, V. and Embrechts, P. (2004) Advanced extremal models for operational risk.

Chavez-Demoulin, V., Embrechts, P. and Neslehova, J. (2006) Quantitative models for operational risk: extremes, dependence and aggregation. *Journal of Banking and Finance*, **30**(10), 2635–2658.

Chernobai, A. and Rachev, S. (2004) *Toward Effective Financial Risk Management: Stable Modeling of Operational Risk.*

Chernobai A. and Rachev S. T. (2004) Stable modelling of operational risk operational risk modelling and analysis, In Cruz M. G. (ed.) *Theory and Practice*, RISK Books, London, pp. 139–169.

Chernobai A. and Rachev S. T. (2006) Applying robust methods to operational risk modelling. *Journal of Operational Risk*, **1**(1), 27–41.

Chernobai A., Burneçki K., Rachev S. T., Trück S. and Weron R. (2006) Modelling catastrophe claims with left-truncated severity distributions. *Computational Statistics*, **21**(3), 537–555.

Chernobai, A., Jorion, P. and Yu, F. (2008) *The Determinants of Operational Losses.* Technical Report, Syracuse University.

Chernobai, A., Menn, C., Trueck, S. and Rachev, S. (2004) *A Note on the Estimation of the Frequency and Severity Distribution of Operational Losses.*

Chernobai, A., Menn, C., Rachev, S. and Trueck, S. (2005) *Estimation of Operational Value-at-Risk in the Presence of Minimum Collection Thresholds.*

Chernobai A., Menn C., Rachev S. T. and Trück S. (2006) A note on the estimation of the frequency and severity of operational losses. *Mathematical Scientist*, **30**(2), 87–97.

Chernobai, A., Menn, C., Rachev, S., Trueck, S. and Moscadelli, M. (2006) Treatment of incomplete data in the field of operational risk: The effects on parameter estimates, EL and UL figures. In Davis, E. (ed.) *The Advanced Measurement Approach to Operational Risk*, RISK Books, London, pp. 145–168.

Chernobai, A., Rachev, S. T. and Fabozzi, F. J. (2007). *Operational Risk: A Guide to Basel II Capital Requirements, Models and Analysis.* John Wiley & Sons, Inc, Hoboken, NJ.

Chernobai, A., Svetlozar, R., and Fabozzi, F. (2005) *Composite goodness-of-fit tests for left-truncated loss samples*, working paper.

Cherubini, U., Luciano, E. and Vecchiato, W. (2004) *Copula Methods in Finance*. John Wiley & Sons, Ltd, Chichester.

Coles, S. (2001) *An Introduction to Statistical Modeling of Extreme Value*, Springer.

Cont, R. and Tankov, P. (2004) *Financial Modelling With Jump Processes*, Chapman & Hall/CRC, Boca Raton.

Cruz, M. G. (2002) *Modeling, Measuring and Hedging Operational Risk*, John Wiley & Sons, Ltd, Chichester.

Cummins, D., Lewis, C. and Wei, R. (2004) *The Market Value Impact of Operational Risk Events For U.S. Banks and Insurers*. Available at: SSRN: http://ssrn.com/abstract=64001.

Da Costa Lewis, N. (2004) *Operational Risk with Excel and VBA: Applied Statistical Methods for Risk Management*. John Wiley & Sons, Ltd, Chichester.

Dalla Valle, L., Fantazzini, D. and Giudici, P. (2006) *Copulae and Operational Risks*.

Daul, S., De Giorgi, E., Lindskog, F. and McNeil, A. J. (2003) Using the grouped t copula. *Risk*, 73–76.

de Fondnouvelle, P. and Jordan, J. (2004) *Implications of Alternative Operational Risk Modeling Techniques*.

de Fondnouvelle, P., DeJesus-Rueff, V., Jordan, J. and Rosengren, E. (2003) *Capital and Risk: New Evidence on Implications of Large Operational Losses*.

Degen, M. and Embrechts, P. (2008) EVT-based estimation of risk capital and convergence of high quantiles. *Advances in Applied Probability* **40**(3), 696–715.

Degen, M., Embrechts, P. and Lambrigger, D. D. (2006) The quantitative modeling of operational risk: between g-and-h and EVT. *ASTIN Bulletin*, **37**(2), 265–291.

Dell'Aquila, R. and Embrechts, P. (2006) Extremes and robustness: a contradiction? *Financial Markets and Portfolio Management*, **20**, 103–118.

Demarta, S. and McNeil, A. J. (2005) The t copula and related copulas. *International Statistical Review*, **73**(1), 111–129.

Dutta, K. and Babbel, F. (2002) *On measuring skewness and kurtosis in short rate distributions: the case of the US dollars London inter bank offer rates*. Wharton – Financial institutions center.

Ebnoether, S., Vanini, P., McNeil, A. J. and Antolinez-Fehr, P. (2003) Operational Risk: A practitioner's view. *Journal of Risk*, **5**(3), 1–15.

El-Gamal, M., Inanoglu, H. and Stengel, M. (2006) *Multivariate Estimation for Operational Risk with Judicious Use of Extreme Value Theory*.

Embrechts, P. (2000) Extreme value theory: Potential and limitations as an integrated risk management tool. *Derivatives Use, Trading & Regulation*, **6**, 449–456.

Embrechts, P. (2000) *Extremes and integrated risk management*. Risk books.

Embrechts, P. (2008) Copulas: A personal view. *Journal of Risk and Insurance*.

Embrechts, P. and Frei, M. (2007) Panjer recursion versus FFT for compound distributions. *Mathematical Methods of Operations Research*.

Embrechts, P. and Höing, A. (2006) Extreme VaR scenarios in higher dimensions. *Extremes*, **9**, 177–192.

Embrechts, P. and Mikosch, T. (2000) *Mathematical Models in Finance*.

Embrechts, P. and Puccetti, G. (2006) Aggregating risk capital, with an application to operational risk. *The Geneva Risk and Insurance Review* **31**(2), 71–90.

Embrechts, P. and Puccetti, G. (2006) Bounds for functions of dependent risks. *Finance and Stochastics*, **10**, 341–352.

Embrechts, P. and Puccetti, G. (2006) Bounds for functions of multivariate risks. *Journal of Multivariate Analysis* **97**(2), 526–547.

Embrechts, P. and Puccetti, G. (2008) Aggregating risk across matrix structured loss data: the case of operational risk. *Journal of Operational Risk*.

Embrechts, P., *et al.* (2001) *An Academic Response to Basel II*, Financial Markets Group, London School of Economics.

Embrechts, P., Furrer, H. and Kaufmann, R. (2003) Quantifying regulatory capital for operational risk. *Derivatives Use, Trading & Regulation*, **9**(3), 217–233.

Embrechts, P., Hoeing, A. and Juri, A. (2003) Using Copulae to bound the Value-at-Risk for functions of dependent risks. *Finance & Stochastics*, **7**(2), 145–167.

Embrechts, P., Kaufmann, R. and Samorodnitsky, G. (2004) Ruin theory revisited: stochastic models for operational risk. In Bernadell, C., *et al.* (eds.) *Risk Management for Central Bank Foreign Reserves*, European Central Bank, Frankfurt A.M., pp. 243–261.

Embrechts, P., Klüppelberg, C. and Mikosch, T. (1997) *Modelling Extremal Events for Insurance and Finance*. Springer.

Embrechts, P., Lambrigger, D. D. Wüthrich, M. V. (2008) Multivariate extremes and the aggregation of dependent risks: examples and counter-examples. *Extremes*.

Embrechts, P., Lindskog, F. and McNeil, A. (2003) Modelling dependence with copulas and applications to risk management. In Rachev, S. (ed.) *Handbook of Heavy Tailed Distributions in Finance*, Elsevier, Chapter 8, pp. 329–384.

Embrechts, P., McNeil, A. and Straumann, D. (2002) Correlation and dependence in risk management: Properties and pitfalls. In Dempster, M. (ed.) *Risk Management: Value at Risk and Beyond*, Cambridge Univesity Press, pp. 176–223.

Embrechts, P., McNeil, A. and Frey, R. (2005) *Quantitative risk management*. Princeton.

Embrechts, P., Resnick, S. and Samorodnitsky, G. (1999) Extreme value theory as a risk management tool. *North American Actuarial Journal* **3**, 30–41.

Federal Reserve System (2005) *Results of the 2004 Loss Data Collection Exercise for Operational Risk*.

Fombrun, C. J. and Van Riel, C. B. M. (2004) *Fame and fortune: how successful companies build winning reputaions*. Financial Times/Prentice Hall.

Frachot, A., Georges, P. and Roncalli, T. (2001) *Loss Distribution Approach for operational risk*. Groupe de Recherche Operationnelle, Credit Lyonnais, France, working paper.

Frachot, A., Moudoulaud, O. and Roncalli, T. (2003) *Loss Distribution Approach in Practice*. Groupe de Recherche Operationnelle, Credit Lyonnais, France, working paper.

Frachot, A., Roncalli, T. and Salomon, E. (2004) The Correlation Problem in Operational Risk.

Frees, E. W. and Valdez, E. A. (1998) Understanding relationships using copulas. *North American Actuarial Journal*, **2**, 1–25.

Genest, C. and Neslehova J. (2008) Analytical proofs of classical inequalities between Kendall's tau and Spearman's rho. *Proceedings of the 8th Tartu Conference on Multivariate Statistics & the 6th Conference on Multivariate Distributions with Fixed Marginals, to appear*.

Genest, C. and Rivest, L. (1993) Statistical inference procedures for bivariate Archimedean copulas. *Journal of the American Statistical Association*, **88**, 1034–1043.

Giacometti, R., Rachev, S. T., Chernobai, A., Bertocchi, M. and Consigli, G. (2007) Heavy-tailed distributional model for operational losses. *Journal of Operational Risk*, **2**(1), 55–90.

Giacometti, R., Rachev, S. T., Chernobai, A. and Bertocchi, M. (2008) Aggregation Issues in Operational Risk. *Journal of Operational Risk*, **3**(3).

Hosking, J. R. M., Wallis, J. R. and Wood, E. F. (1985) Estimation of the generalized extreme-value distribution by the method of probability-weighted moments, *Technometrics*, **27**, 251–261.

Hosking, J. R. M. and Wallis, J. R. (1987) Parameter and quantile estimation for the generalized pareto distribution. *Technometrics*, **29**(3).

Jobst, A. (2007) *Operational Risk - The Sting is Still in the Tail But the Poison Depends on the Dose*.

Jorion, P. (2000) *Value at Risk*. McGraw Hill.

Kallsen, J. and Tankov, P. (2006) Characterization of dependence of multivariate Lévy processes using Lévy copulas. *Journal of Multivariate Analysis*, **97**, 1551–1572.

Kim, J. and Lee, S. (1999) *An iterative algorithm for the Cramer–von Mises distance estimator*.

Klüppelberg, C. and Mikosch, T. (1997) Large deviations of heavy-tailed random sums with applications in insurance and finance. *Journal of Applied Probability*, **34**, 293–308.

Kullback, S. (1959) *Information Theory and Statistics*. Dover Publications, New York.

Kullback, S. and Leibler, R. A. (1951) *On information and sufficiency. Annals of Mathematics and Statistics*, **22**, 79–86.

Lane, M. (2002) *Alternative Risk Strategies*. Risk Books.

Larkin, J. (2002) *Strategic Reputation Risk Management*, Palgrave Macmillan.

Lindskog, F, McNeil, A. J. and Schmock, U. (2003) Kendall's tau for elliptical distributions. In Bol, Nakhaeizadeh, Rachev, Ridder and Vollmer., (eds.) *Credit Risk - Measurement, Evaluation and Management*, Physica-Verlag Heidelberg.

McConnell, P. J. (2006) *A Perfect Storm - Why Are Some Operational Losses Larger than Others?*

McNeil, A. J. (1997) Estimating the tails of loss severity distributions using extreme value theory. *ASTIN Bulletin*, **27**, 117–137.

McNeil, A. J. (1999) *Extreme Value Theory for Risk Managers*.

McNeil, A. J. (2008) Sampling nested Archimedean copulas. *Journal of Statistical Computation and Simulation*, **78**(6), 567–581.

McNeil, A. J. and Frey, R (2000) Estimation of tail-related risk measures for heteroscedastic financial time series: an extreme value approach. *Journal of Empirical Finance*, **7**, 271–300.

McNeil, A. J. and Saladin, T. (1997) The peaks over thresholds method for estimating high quantiles of loss distributions. *Proceedings of 28th International ASTIN Colloquium*.

McNeil, A. J. and Saladin, T. (2000) Developing scenarios for future extreme losses using the POT method. In Embrechts, P. M. E., (ed.) *Extremes and Integrated Risk Management*, RISK books, London.

Medova, E. (2001) *Operational Risk Capital Allocation and Integration of Risks*.

Mignola, G. and Ugoccioni, R. (2005) *Tests of Extreme Value Theory Applied to Operational Risk Data*.

Moscadelli, M., Chernobai, A. and Rachev S. T. (2005) Treatment of missing data in the field of operational risk: The impacts on parameter estimates, EL, VaR, and CVaR figures. *Operational Risk*, **6**(6), pp. 28–34.

Nam, D. (2001) *Value at risk: a quantile-based distribution approach for incorporating skewness and fat-tailedness*. INHA University, PhD thesis.

Nelsen, R. B. (1999) *An Introduction to Copulas*. Lecture Notes in Statistics 139, Springer, N.Y.

Nguyen, M. and Ottmann, M. (2005) Das dicke Ende. *RiskNews*, July.

Pappadà, A. (2003) *I rischi operativi nelle banche. Misurazione e gestione*. edibank.

Perry, J. and de Fontnouvelle, P. (2005). *Measuring Reputational Risk: The market Reaction to Operational Loss Announcements*. Technical Report, Federal Reserve Bank of Boston.

Peters, G., Johansen, A. and Doucet, A. (2007) *Simulation of the Annual Loss Distribution in Operational Risk via Panjer Recursions and Volterra Integral Equations for Value at Risk and Expected Shortfall Estimation*.

Pfeifer, D. and Neslehova, J. (2003) Modeling Dependence in Finance and Insurance: the Copula Approach. *Blätter der deutschen Gesellschaft für Versicherungs- und Finanzmathematik, Bd. XXVI/2*.

Pickands, J. III. (1975) *Statistical inference using extreme order statistics. Annals of Statistics*, **3**, 119–131.

Powosjowski, M. R., Reynolds, D. and Tuenter, J. H. (2002) Dependent events and operational risk. *Algo Research Quarterly*, **5**(2), 65–73.

Rachev, S. T., Chernobai, A. and Menn, C. (2006) Empirical examination of operational loss distributions. In Morlock, M., *et al.* (eds.) *Perspectives on Operational Research*, Deutscher Universitaet-Verlag/GWV Fachverlage GmbH, Wiesbaden, pp. 379–401.

Rayner, G. D. and MacGillivray, H. L. (2002) Numerical maximum likelihood estimation for the g-and-k generalized g-and-h distributions. *Statistics and Computing*, **12**(1), 57–75.

Reshetar, A. (2004) *Operational Risk and the Effect of Diversification on Capital*. Working Paper.

Resnick, S. I. (1987) *Extreme Values, Regular Variation, and Point Processes*, Springer, New York.

Romano, C. and Di Clemente, A. (2003) *A Copula Extreme Value Theory Approach for Modeling Operational Risk*. Working Paper.

Rosenberg, J. V. and Schuermann, T., (2006) A general approach to integrated risk management with skewed, fat-tailed risks. *The Journal of Financial Economics*, **79**(3), 569–614.

Shevchenko, P. and Wuethrich, M. V. (2006) *The Structural Modelling of Operational Risk via Bayesian Inference: Combining Loss Data with Expert Opinions*.

Sklar, A. (1996) Random variables, distribution functions, and copulas – a personal look backward and forward. In *Distributions with Fixed Marginals and Related Topics*, L. Rüschendorff, B. Schweizer and M. Taylor (Eds), Institute of Mathematical Statistics, Hayward, CA, pp. 1–14.

Steinhoff, C. and Baule, R. (2006) *How to Validate Op Risk Distributions*.

Tang, A. and Valdez, E. A. (2006) *Economic Capital and the Aggregation of Risks Using Copulas*.

Venables, W. N. and Ripley, B. D. (2002) *Modern Applied Statistics with S*. Springer.

Wegman, E. J. (1981) Density estimation. In *Encyclopedia of Statistical Sciences*, S. Kotz and N. L. Johnston (Eds), John Wiley & Sons, Inc. New York, **2**, 209–315.

Yasuda, Y. (2003) *Application of Bayesian Inference to Operational Risk Management*.

Index

Note: Page references in *italics* refer to Figures; those in **bold** refer to Tables

Index compiled by Annette Musker